ROOTS OF LANGUAGE

Derek Bickerton

Roots of
Language

1981

KAROMA PUBLISHERS, INC.   ANN ARBOR

ISBN 0-89720-044-6 (Hardcover)

First hardcover printing, November 18th, 1981; Second hardcover printing, March 31st, 1982; Third hardcover printing, January 11th, 1983

First paperback printing, April 1st, 1985: ISBN 0-89720-073-X

To the people of Palmares,
        El Palenque de San Basilio,
        The Cockpit Country,
        and the Saramacca River,
who fought for decency, dignity, and freedom
against the Cartesian savagery of Western colonialists
        and slavemakers;
whose tongues, having survived
to confound pedagogue and philosopher alike,
now, by an ironic stroke of justice,
offer us indispensable keys to the knowledge of
        our species.

ACKNOWLEDGMENTS

The research on which the first two chapters of this volume are based would not have been possible without the support of NSF Grants Nos. GS-39748 and SOC75-14481, for which grateful acknowledgment is hereby made. I am also indebted to the University of Hawaii for granting me an additional leave of absence which, together with my regular sabbatical leave, gave me two years in which to work out the theory presented here.

The ideas contained in this volume have been discussed, in person and in correspondence, with many colleagues; while it is in a sense invidious to pick out names, Paul Chapin, Talmy Givón, Tom Markey, and Dan Slobin have been among the most long-suffering listeners. I am also grateful to Frank Byrne, Chris Corne, Greg Lee, and Dennis Preston for reading parts of the manuscript. Needless to say, I alone remain responsible for whatever errors and omissions may still be present.

ABBREVIATIONS AND ACRONYMS

BC	Belize Creole
CNCD	Causative-Noncausative Distinction
CR	Crioulo
DJ	Djuka
Eng.	English
Fr.	French
GC	Guyanese Creole
GU	Guyanais
HC	Haitian Creole
HCE	Hawaiian Creole English
HPE	Hawaiian Pidgin English
IOC	Indian Ocean Creole(s)
JC	Jamaican Creole
KR	Krio
LAC	Lesser Antillean Creole
LAD	Language Acquisition Device
MC	Mauritian Creole
Pg.	Portuguese
PIC	Propositional Island Constraint
PIC	Providence Island Creole
PK	Papia Kristang
PNPD	Punctual-Nonpunctual Distinction
PP	Papiamentu
PQ	Palenquero
RC	Réunion Creole
SA	Saramaccan
SC	Seychelles Creole
SNSD	Specific-Nonspecific Distinction
SPD	State-Process Distinction
SR	Sranan
SSC	Specified Subject Condition
ST	São Tomense
TP	Tok Pisin

CONTENTS

INTRODUCTION

Of all the fields of study to which human beings have devoted themselves, linguistics could lay claim to being the most conservative. Two thousand five hundred years ago, Panini began it by describing an individual human language, and describing individual languages is what the majority of linguists are still doing. Even during the last couple of decades, in which linguists have begun to be interested in some of the larger issues that language involves, the main thrust toward clarifying those issues has involved making more and more detailed and ingenious descriptions of currently existing natural languages. In consequence, little headway has been made toward answering the really important questions which language raises, such as: how is language acquired by the individual, and how was it acquired by the species?

The importance of these questions is, I think, impossible to exaggerate. Language has made our species what it is, and until we really understand it—that is, understand what is necessary for it to be acquired and transmitted, and how it interacts with the rest of our cognitive apparatus—we cannot hope to understand ourselves. And unless we can understand ourselves, we will continue to watch in helpless frustration while the world we have created slips further and further from our control.

The larger and, in a popular sense, more human issues which language involves lie outside the scope of the present work, and will be dealt with at length in a forthcoming volume, *Language and Species*. First, there is a good deal of academic spadework to be done. In the chapters that follow, I shall try to develop a unified theory which will propose at least a partial answer to three questions, none of which has as yet been satisfactorily resolved:

1) How did creole languages originate?
2) How do children acquire language?
3) How did human language originate?

Traditionally, these three questions, insofar as they have been treated at all, have been treated as wholly unrelated. None of the solutions offered for (1) have had any relevance to (2) or (3); none of the solutions offered for (2) have had any relevance to (1) or (3); and none of the solutions offered for (3) have had any relevance to (1) or (2). It has even been explicitly denied, although without a shred of supporting evidence, that an answer to (1) could possibly be an answer to (3) (Sankoff 1979). Here and there, a few insightful scholars have hinted at possible links between the problems, and such insights will be acknowledged in subsequent pages. However, a single, unified treatment has never even been attempted, and this book, whatever its shortcomings, may therefore claim at least some measure of originality. Doubtless many of its details will need revision or replacement; the explorer is seldom the best cartographer. However, of one thing I am totally convinced: that the three questions are really one question, and that an answer to any one of them which does not at the same time answer the other two will be, ipso facto, a wrong answer.

I shall begin with the origin of creoles. To some, this may appear the least general and least interesting question of the three. However, as I shall show, creoles constitute the indispensable key to the two larger problems, and this should come as no surprise to those familiar with the history of science, in which, repeatedly, the sideshow of one generation has been the central arena of the next. In Chapter 1, I shall examine the relationship between the variety of Creole English spoken in Hawaii and the pidgin which immediately preceded it, and I shall show how several elements of that creole could not have been derived from its antecedent pidgin, or from any of the other languages that were in contact at the time of creole formation, and that therefore these elements must have been, in some sense, "invented." In Chapter 2 I shall discuss some (not all—there would not be space for all) of the features which are shared by a wide range of creole languages and show some striking resemblances between the "inventions" of Hawaii and "inventions" of other regions which must have emerged quite independently; and I shall also try to probe more deeply into certain aspects of creole syntax and semantics which may prove significant when we come to deal with the other two questions. In Chapter 3, which will deal with "normal" language acquisition in noncreole societies, I shall show that some of the things which children seem to acquire effortlessly, as well as some which they get consistently wrong—both equally puzzling to previous accounts of "language learning"—follow naturally from the theory which was developed to account for creole origins: that all members of our species are born with a bioprogram for language which can function even in the absence of adequate input. In Chapter 4, I shall try to show where this bioprogram comes from: partly from the species-specific structure of human perception and cognition, and partly from processes inherent in the expansion of a linear language. At the same time, we will be able to resolve the continuity paradox ("language is too different from animal communication systems to have ever evolved from them"; "language, like any other adaptive mechanism, must have been derived by regular evolutionary processes") which has lain like some huge roadblock across the study of language origins. In the final chapter, I shall briefly summarize and integrate the findings of previous chapters, and suggest answers to some of the criticisms which may be brought against the concept of a genetic program for human language.

Chapter 1
PIDGIN INTO CREOLE

If one wants to account, ultimately, for the origins of human language (as I shall try to do in Chapter 4), it seems reasonable for one to begin by trying to find out how individual human languages came into existence. But, in most cases, such a search would be futile. Modern Italian, for example, would be found to fade back into a maze of dialects deriving ultimately from Latin, which developed out of Indo-European, which sprang, presumably, from some antecedent language now wholly inaccessible to us; and at no point in the continuous transmission of language could we name a date and say, "Here Latin ended," or "Here Italian began."

But there is one class of languages for which we can point, with reasonable accuracy, to the year of birth: we can say that before 1530, there was no São Tomense; before 1650, no Sranan; before 1690, no Haitian Creole; and before 1880, no Hawaiian Creole. And yet two or three decades after those dates, those languages existed. Of course no one would claim that these languages were quite devoid of ancestry; indeed, their relationships with several sets of putative ancestors have been and continue to be a subject of controversy (for a critical summary and bibliography of the relevant literature, see Bickerton 1976).

But even controversy could not exist unless the lines of descent were, at the very least, considerably more obscure than they are for most other languages.

Creole languages arose as a direct result of European colonial expansion. Between 1500 and 1900, there came into existence, on tropical islands and in isolated sections of tropical littorals, small, autocratic, rigidly stratified societies, mostly engaged in monoculture (usually of sugar), which consisted of a ruling minority from some European nation and a large mass of (mainly non-European) laborers, drawn in most cases from many different language groups. The early linguistic history of these enclaves is virtually unknown; it is generally assumed (but see Alleyne 1971, 1979) that speakers of different languages at first evolved some form of auxiliary contact-language, native to none of them (known as a *pidgin*), and that this language, suitably expanded, eventually became the native (or *creole*) language of the community which exists today. These creoles were in most cases different enough from any of the languages of the original contact situation to be considered "new" languages. Superficially, their closest resemblance was to their European parent, but this was mainly because the bulk of the vocabulary items were drawn from that source, and even here, there were extensive phonological and semantic shifts. In the area of syntax, features were much less easily traceable.

In general, the term *creole* is used to refer to any language which was once a pidgin and which subsequently became a native language; some scholars have extended the term to any language, ex-pidgin or not, that has undergone massive structural change due to language contact (one who shall be nameless confessed to me that he did this solely to obtain access to a conference which, like most creole conferences, was held in an exotic tropical setting!). In fact, I think that even the traditional definition is too wide, since it covers a range of situations which may differ in kind rather than in degree.

Since my aim here is not to account for the origins of all languages known as creoles (which would be an absurd aim anyway since they do not constitute a proper set) but rather to search for certain fundamental properties of human language in general, my interests lie, not in creoles per se, but in situations where the normal continuity of language transmission is most severely disrupted. While it is true that the circumstances under which pidginization and creolization take place represent "a catastrophic break in linguistic tradition that is unparalleled" (Sankoff 1979:24), there are still a number of areas where the severity of that break was mitigated by other factors. Let us consider two quite different cases of such mitigation: Réunion Creole and Tok Pisin (a.k.a. Neo-Melanesian, New Guinea Pidgin, etc.).

One factor that would limit the extent of language disruption would be the presence of any large homogeneous linguistic group in the community—more especially if that group happened to consist of speakers of the dominant language. According to Chaudenson (1974), in Réunion during the first few decades of settlement nearly half the population consisted of native speakers of French; in consequence, although the resultant language bears the creole label, the distance between that language and French is much less than the distance between most creoles and their superstrates, while (more important still from the present viewpoint) the language differs in many respects from creoles formed where access to the superstrate was more restricted.

In New Guinea, the percentage of superstrate speakers was low, but the pidgin existed for several generations alongside the indigenous language before it began to acquire native speakers. Thus Tok Pisin was able to expand gradually, through normal use, rather than very rapidly, under the communicative pressure of a generation that had, for practical purposes, no other option available as a first language. The bilingual speakers of Tok Pisin had ongoing lives in their own languages and, perhaps more importantly still, in their own traditional communities; whereas in the classic creole situation, people had been torn from their traditional communities and forced into wholly novel communities in which the value of traditional languages was low or nil. The two situations are not commensurate, and we would expect to find, as we do, that while Tok Pisin differs from English much more than Réunion Creole does from French, it lacks, again, a number of the features found in the classic creole languages, and possesses a number of features which those creoles, in turn, do not share.

Accordingly, in the text that follows, I shall use the word *creole* to refer to languages which:

1) Arose out of a prior pidgin which had not existed for more than a generation.
2) Arose in a population where not more than 20 percent were native speakers of the dominant language and where the remaining 80 percent was composed of diverse language groups.

The first condition rules out Tok Pisin and perhaps other (e.g., Australian Aboriginal) creoles; the second rules out Réunion Creole and perhaps other creoles also (the varieties of Portuguese creoles that evolved in Asian trading enclaves such as Goa or Macao are possible candidates for exclusion under this condition). Given the above, I shall continue to refer to certain languages or groups of languages as "English creoles," "French creoles," etc.; this usage implies no conclusions as to the affiliations of these languages and is merely for convenience.

By limiting our research area in this way, it becomes possible to concentrate on those situations in which the human linguistic capacity is stretched to the uttermost. As I have said, we know little or nothing of the early linguistic history of most creoles, but what evidence we do have (e.g., Rens 1953, for Sranan) suggests that they emerged from the pidgin stage fairly rapidly, within twenty or thirty years after first settlement of the areas concerned. Such a time span gives space for the first locally-born generation to come to maturity, but it hardly gives space for a stable, systematic, and referentially adequate pidgin to be evolved in a community which might initially speak dozens of mutually unintelligible languages; certainly, in the one case of which we have direct knowledge (Hawaii), no stable, systematic, or referentially adequate pidgin had developed within that time frame, and there are no real grounds for supposing that the Hawaiian situation was any less favorable to the development of such a pidgin than were the situations in other creole-forming regions. We can assume, therefore, that in each of these regions, immediately prior to creolization, there existed, just as there existed in Hawaii, a highly variable, extremely rudimentary language state such as has been sometimes described as a "jargon" or "pre-pidgin continuum" rather than a developed pidgin language. Since none of the available vernaculars would permit access to more than a tiny proportion of the community, and since the cultures and communities with which those vernaculars were associated were now receding rapidly into the past, the child born of pidgin-speaking parents would seldom have had any other option than to learn that rudimentary language, however inadequate for human purposes it might be.

We should pause here to consider the position of such children, for no one else has done so, even in the vast literature on language acquisition. That position differs crucially from the position of children in more normal communities. The latter have a ready-made, custom-validated, referentially adequate language to learn, and mothers, elder siblings, etc., ready to help them learn it. The former have, instead, something which may be adequate for emergency use, but which is quite unfit to serve as anyone's primary tongue; which, by reason of its variability, does not present even the little it offers in a form that would permit anyone to learn it; and which the parent, with the best will in the world, cannot teach, since that parent knows no more of the language than the child (and will pretty soon know less). Everywhere else in the world it goes without saying that the parent knows more language than the child; here, if the child is to have an adequate language, he must speedily outstrip the knowledge of the parent. Yet every study of first-language acquisition that I know of assumes without question that the more general situation is universal; *every existing theory of acquisition is based on the presupposition that there is always and everywhere an adequate language to be acquired.*

It is true that the situation I am describing is extremely rare and can indeed occur only once even for a creole language. However, the rarity or frequency of a phenomenon contains no clues as to its scientific importance.

The act of "expanding" the antecedent pidgin, which each first creole generation has to undertake, involves, among other things, acquiring new rules of syntax. In the conventional wisdom, children are supposed to derive rules by processing input (with or without the help of some specific language-learning device); in this way, they arrive at a rule system similar to, if not identical with, that of their elders. If this were all children could do, then they would simply learn the pidgin, and there would be no significant gap between the generations. In Hawaii, at least, we have empirical proof that this did not happen—that the first creole generation produced rules for which there was no evidence in the previous generation's speech.

How can a child produce a rule for which he has no evidence? No one has answered this question; most people haven't even asked it; and yet, until it is answered, we cannot really claim to know anything about how languages in general are acquired. For it violates both parsimony and common sense to suppose that children use one set of acquisition strategies for "normal" acquisition situations, and then switch to another set when they find themselves in a pidgin-speaking community: parsimony because two explanations would be required where one should be adequate, and common sense because there is no way in which a child could tell what kind of community he had been born into, and therefore no way he could decide which set of strategies to use.

I shall return to the topic of acquisition in Chapter 3; in the present chapter, I shall simply describe what happened in Hawaii when pidgin turned into creole.

For a century after the first European contact, the population of Hawaii consisted mainly of native Hawaiians, with a small but growing minority of native English speakers. A small but growing minority of Hawaiians spoke English with varying degrees of proficiency; the lower end of this spectrum acquired the name *hapa-haole* 'half-white'. *Hapa-haole* was not a true pidgin, or even a true pre-pidgin, in the sense discussed above; rather it was a continuum of "foreigner's English," similar to Whinnom's (1971) description of *cocoliche*. It was, apparently, limited to the towns, still hardly heard in country areas even in the 1870s. There was a small sugar industry, but the labor force was almost entirely Hawaiian, and, as far as one can discover, the plantation work-language was Hawaiian.

In 1876, a revision of U.S. tariff laws allowing the free importation of Hawaiian sugar caused the industry to increase its productivity by several hundred percent. The native Hawaiian population had so declined in numbers that workers had to be imported, first from China, and then from Portugal, Japan, Korea, the Philippines, Puerto Rico, etc. In a few years there came into existence a multilingual community that greatly outnumbered the former population, Hawaiian and *haole* alike.

A pidgin English was probably not the first, and certainly not the only, contact language used on the Hawaiian plantations after 1876. A pidgin based on Hawaiian and known as *olelo pa'i'ai* 'taro-language'—so called because it allegedly originated with the Chinese, who largely took over taro growing from the native Hawaiians—was widely used in the last two decades of the 19th century (Bickerton 1977:307-8) and perhaps for some years afterward, since one speaker, a Filipino, was still alive in the mid-1970s. So far, it has proved impossible to determine whether pidgin English grew up alongside pidgin Hawaiian or whether the former grew out of the latter by a gradual relexification process. The two processes may not be mutually exclusive, especially when we consider that population balances and other demographic factors differed widely from island to island. But one certain consequence of the existence of *olelo pa'i'ai* is that it delayed the development of any form of pidgin English, especially on the outer islands, where the Hawaiian language was strongest.

In 1973 and 1974, I and my team of assistants made recordings of several hundred hours of speech from both immigrant speakers of Hawaiian Pidgin English (HPE) and locally-born speakers of Hawaiian Creole English (HCE); this work is described in detail in Bickerton and Odo (1976), Bickerton and Givón (1976), and Bickerton (1977). The earliest immigrant arrival in the group we recorded was 1907, a time which, if our theory about the delayed development of HPE is correct, may have been only a few years after the beginning of HPE. The latest arrival was 1930. In other words, a period of from forty-three to sixty-six years had elapsed between our subjects' dates of arrival and our recordings. Can recordings made after such a long period give us an adequate idea of what HPE was like in the period 1907-1930?

Although it is widely held that an individual's speech changes little after maturity has been reached, this may not necessarily be true of second languages or contact languages. Pidginization is a process, not a state, and it is therefore possible that at least some of our subjects may now speak differently from the way they spoke when they first arrived in Hawaii, even though the vast majority were already adults at that time. However, one thing is certain. If their version of HPE has changed in those intervening years, then it must be more complex in structure and less subject to idiosyncratic or ethnic-group variation than it was in the years that immediately followed their arrival. It is unthinkable that after several decades of life in a community that was steadily becoming more integrated their version of HPE should have grown less complex or more idiosyncratic. We must therefore assume that either their HPE now adequately represents the HPE of the early pidginization period, or that the latter was even more primitive and more unstable than the versions they use today.

But even if modern HPE represents early HPE quite accurately, it does not follow that all HPE speakers are equally good guides to the state of HPE as it was when creolization took place. On the basis of evidence discussed at length in Bickerton (1977), we can place the time of creolization somewhere around 1910, and certainly no later than 1920. There are considerable differences between the HPE spoken by the earliest arrivals among our subjects and that spoken by those who arrived in the 1920s. The former is considerably more rudimentary in its structure; the complications that developed after 1920 could have been due to internal developments in HPE, but were more probably caused by feedback from the newly-developed HCE, whose earliest speakers would have come to maturity by 1920 if not before (this issue, too, is explicitly dealt with in Bickerton [1977:Chapter 4]). We shall therefore make the reasonable assumption that at the time of creolization HPE was either adequately represented by our recordings of earlier (pre-1920) immigrants, or it was at a still more primitive level of development.

At first glance, the second possibility might seem hard to credit. The HPE of the older surviving speakers is both highly restricted and highly variable. The main source of instability is first-language influence. Labov (1971) claimed that these transference-governed versions of HPE were the idiosyncratic inventions of social isolates; our much more widely-based research indicates that instead they represent one of the earliest stages in the pidginization process in which the more isolated the speakers, the more likely they are to become fossilized. However, speakers who produced such versions were by no means all socially isolated, and in particular, we noted that speakers of more evolved versions of HPE would sometimes relapse into this mode when they became excited or when they had to deal with complex or unfamiliar topics (the speaker who produced /12/ below also produced, in the middle of a long and exciting narrative, /2/).

Typical of very early HPE as produced by speakers born in Japan are the following:

/1/ mista karsan-*no tokoro* tu eika sel *shite*
Mr. Carson-POSS place two acre sell do
'I sold two acres to Mr. Carson's place'
/2/ *sore kara* kech *shite kara* pul ap
and then catch do then pull up
'When he had caught it, he pulled it up'

In these examples, the italicized lexical items are Japanese, and anaphora is maintained by zero forms rather than by pronouns. In /1/ the structure (with both direct and indirect objects preceding the verb and the auxiliary following the main verb) represents direct transference from Japanese syntax. Example /2/ can hardly be said to have anything recognizable as structure; lexical items from the English and Japanese lexicons are simply strung together. But what is striking about these two sentences is that six out of the seven Japanese morphemes are grammatical, not lexical, items; it is as if the speakers felt the need for some kind of grammatical glue with which to stick their sentences together, and perforce used the only brand available to them.

Speakers who immigrated into areas where there was a large native-Hawaiian population show a rather different tendency; here, it is Hawaiian rather than native-language vocabulary that is mixed with English items:

/3/   ifu laik meiki, mo beta *make* taim, mani no kaen *hapai*
      if like make, more better die time, money no can carry
      'If you wanted to build (a temple), you should do it just before
      you die—you can't take it with you!'
/4/   *Luna*, hu *hapai? Hapai* awl, *hemo* awl
      Foreman, who carry? Carry all, cut all
      'Who'll carry it, boss? Everyone'll cut it and everyone'll carry it'

Example /3/ was uttered by a Japanese speaker, /4/ by a Filipino speaker; note that the predominantly OV syntax of the former is replaced by a predominantly VS syntax in the latter, reflecting the speaker's native Visayan. Here, however, all the Hawaiian items carry lexical meaning, in contrast with the Japanese items in /1/ and /2/; this lends support to the claim that even as late as the 1910s, in some areas, either *olelo pa'i'ai* was still dominant, or its relexification by English was still far from complete.

Certainly examples /1/-/4/ suggest an extreme instability in the language model that would confront the first locally-born generation.

That the macaronic elements in these examples may represent a deliberate strategy on the part of speakers is suggested by the following perceptive comment from an old Hawaiian woman:

/5/   So we use the Hawaiian and Chinese together in one sentence, see? And they ask me if that's a Hawaiian word, I said no, maybe that's a Japanese word we put it in, to make a sentence with a Hawaiian word. And the Chinese the same way too, in order to make a sentence for them to understand you.

In other words, in the original linguistic melting pot from which HPE eventually issued, the more skilled speakers acquired a core vocabulary in which the commonest items, both lexical and grammatical, might be represented by forms drawn from three or four languages. Small wonder that a Japanese woman, asked if she spoke English, answered: "No, *hapa-hapa* [Hawaiian 'half-half'] *shite* [Japanese 'do'] "—i.e., 'I speak a mixture'—and added (in Japanese), "I never know whether I'm speaking one thing or the other."

Even at a subsequent stage of pidginization, represented by speakers whose vocabulary is drawn predominantly from English, syntactic features characteristic of their native languages will still distinguish, for example, Japanese from Filipino speakers. The former continue to produce sentences such as /6/ and /7/, with final verbs:

/6/   tumach mani mi tink kechi do
      plenty money I think catch though
      'I think he earns a lot of money, though'
/7/   da pua pipl awl poteito it
      'The poor people ate only potatoes'

Filipinos, however, often produce sentences in which verbs or predicate adjectives precede their subjects:

/8/   wok had dis pipl
      'These people work hard'

/9/   mo plaeni da ilokano en da tagalog
        'Ilocanos were more numerous than Tagalogs'

The patterns of /6/-/9/ were probably never categorical for any speaker; all the speakers in our sample showed some SVO syntax. Variation, however, was fairly unpredictable; Japanese speakers varied between 30 percent and 60 percent of SOV sentences, although the figures for particular sentence types might range between 10 percent and 90 percent (see Bickerton and Givón [1976] for full details), while among Filipinos, percentages of VS structures ranged between 15 percent and 50 percent in sentences where S was a full noun rather than a pronoun. On the other hand, VS sentences from Japanese speakers and OV sentences from Filipino speakers, while extremely rare, did occur from time to time. Since the Japanese and the Filipinos constituted the two largest immigrant groups, a child in Hawaii who sought to learn basic word order by inductive processes alone would have ended up in a state of total bewilderment.

Other features besides word order distinguish Japanese from Filipino speakers. Among Japanese, *when*-clauses were frequently expressed by compound nominals such as:

/10/   as-bihoa-stei-taim
        us-before-stay-time
        'when we used to live here'

Filipinos never used such expressions, except for *smaw-taim* 'when I was young', which became a universal HPE idiom. Filipino speakers inserted pronouns between most full-noun subjects and their verbs, for example:

/11/   josafin brada hi laik *hapai* mi
        'Josephine's brother wants to take me (with him)'

Japanese speakers seldom if ever used this structure. With regard to articles, Japanese speakers rarely used either definite or indefinite; Filipino speakers, on the other hand, often over-generalized the definite article, as in /9/ above. While both groups relied on zero anaphora more than English does, pronouns were far more frequent among Filipino speakers. In short, anyone (in particular a child) trying to learn HPE would have encountered formidable obstacles to even figuring out what the rules of HPE were supposed to be.

But its variability was by no means the only obstacle to child acquisition of HPE. The presence of two conflicting models, A and B, still leaves the learner three theoretical choices: learn A, learn B, or learn some mixture of A and B. But when neither of the models, nor the two together, constitutes an adequate variety of human language, the problem is of a different order altogether.

Let us be quite clear as to what the deficiencies of HPE were, for it has been claimed (e.g., Samarin 1971) that anything at all can be said in a pidgin. There is a sense in which this is probably correct, even of an immature pidgin like HPE, provided we do not count the cost of saying it. Take the following remarkable speech:

/12/ samtaim gud rod get, samtaim, olsem ben get, enguru ['angle'] get, no? enikain seim. olsem hyuman laif, olsem. gud rodu get, enguru get, mauntin get—no? awl, enikain, stawmu get, nais dei get—olsem. enibadi, mi olsem, smawl taim.

'Sometimes there's a good road, sometimes there's, like, bends, corners, right? Everything's like that. Human life's just like that. There's good roads, there's sharp corners, there's mountains—right? All sorts of things, there's storms, nice days—it's like that for everybody, it was for me, too, when I was young'

This philosophic statement would be a striking piece of rhetoric in any language. But it is an achievement against the grain of the language, so to speak; the speaker, a retired bus driver (which probably accounts for his choice of imagery), triumphs by sheer force of imagination over the minimal vocabulary and narrow range of structural options within which he is obliged to work.

Similarly, HPE does not prevent speakers from finding ingenious ways of replacing lexical items which they lack or are unsure of; here is one subject who cannot recall *library:*

/13/   rai . . . rai . . . *ano* buk eniting boro *dekiru tokoro*
       li . . . li . . . that book anything borrow can place
       'Li . . . Li . . . That place where you can borrow any of the
       books'

It is not absolutely necessary, for communicative purposes, that a language have either an extensive vocabulary or a variety of syntactic structures; but the goals of language, whether social communication or mental computation, seem to be better served if a language has these things. HPE lacks, wholly or partially, many of the building blocks which all native languages possess. Among HPE speakers who arrived prior to 1920, the following features are largely or completely missing: consistent marking of tense, aspect, and modality; relative clauses; movement rules, embedded complements, in particular infinitival constructions; articles, especially indefinite. On the rare occasion when such features do appear, they often do so in forms modeled directly on the speaker's native language—for example, the relative clauses that precede, rather than follow, their head-nouns that are sometimes produced by Japanese speakers:

/14/   aen luk laik pankin kain get
       and look like pumpkin kind get
       'And there were some that looked like pumpkins'

For the most part, however, sentences would consist of short strings of nouns and verbs paratactically linked. Often even verbs would be omitted, as in the following two examples:

/15/ aena tu macha churen, samawl churen, haus mani pei
and too much children, small children, house money pay
'And I HAD too many children, small children, I HAD to pay
the rent' (Korean speaker)
/16/ bihoa mil no moa hilipino no nating
before mill no more Filipino no nothing
'Before the mill WAS BUILT, THERE WERE no Filipinos here
at all' (Japanese speaker)

If it were the case that children simply induced rules from input,
one might suppose that when children were born to HPE speakers they
learned the grammars of their parents. If their parents were Filipinos,
they would learn the rules characteristic of Filipino speakers; if their
parents were Japanese, they would learn the rules characteristic of
Japanese speakers, and so on. One might argue that when Japanese and
Filipino children went to school they met one another and ironed out
their differences; but if this, or something like it, did take place, it must
have had more to do with their being children than with their being
in contact with one another. Fifty years of contact were not enough to
erase language-group differences from the speech of adults. And while
similar phenomena have been observed among children of immigrant
groups on the U.S. mainland, it must be remembered that the latter
had a ready-made target, while the first creole generation in Hawaii
did not.

Whatever processes were involved, the erasure of group differences in that generation was complete. Even other locally-born persons
cannot determine the ethnic background of an HCE speaker by his
speech alone, although the same persons can readily identify that of
an HPE speaker by listening to him for a few seconds.

Now it is true that we could construct an argument similar to
that already constructed for HPE speakers. The reader will recall the
claim that while the contemporary speech of old HPE speakers may be
the same as, or more developed than, their speech shortly after time of

arrival, it could hardly be less developed. Similarly, one might claim that older HCE speakers do not necessarily speak now as they spoke in their childhood or early maturity; that, again, it would be absurd to suggest that they then spoke a variety more developed than they speak now; and that, therefore, their speech may have changed and become considerably more complex since they reached adulthood. Indeed, on this showing, they might have spoken, as children, varieties as rudimentary and as ethnic-tongue-influenced as their parents did; subsequently, and very gradually, they could have developed the more stable, yet more complex, variety of language that they use today. If this were true, the apparently sudden break between HPE and HCE would be a misleading artifact of the analysis, produced by back-projection from synchronic data.

Since we lack direct evidence from the period in question, this argument cannot be conclusively disproved. However, it is an implausible one, and for the following reason. If the argument is correct, then the homogeneity of modern HCE must have come about by a gradual leveling process in which group differences were gradually removed through intergroup contacts. What were the critical differences between the immigrant and first locally-born generations? Not, apparently, bilingualism versus monolingualism, since all the older, locally-born subjects we interviewed spoke at least one other language besides HCE when they were children. The only significant difference between the two generations is that the first encountered HPE as adults, while the second encountered it as small children.

Similar arguments can be mounted with regard to the greater complexity of HCE. Again, we cannot prove empirically that this complexity did not result from gradual increment. If we assume that it did, however, we have to explain why HPE did not also become more complex; and we can only conclude, again, that such an explanation must lie in the difference between language-learning by adults and language-learning by children.

Finally, as we will see in Chapter 2, the forms and structures arrived at by HCE resemble far beyond the scope of chance the forms and structures arrived at by a variety of other creole languages, often with substrata very different from Hawaii's (and from one another's too). It defies belief that a language formed by the leveling of several substratum-influenced versions of a pidgin should exhibit the degree of identity that will be illustrated with languages so diverse in their origins, all of which must have evolved in a similar manner; the odds against this happening, unless some set of external guiding principles was conditioning the result, must be fantastic. It seems reasonable, therefore, to assume that the gap between HPE and HCE that is reflected in our data is a genuine phenomenon, accounted for by extremely abrupt changes which took place while the first creole generation was growing to maturity.

I shall now examine some of the substantive differences between HPE and HCE in the following five areas:

a) movement rules
b) articles
c) verbal auxiliaries
d) *for-to* complementization
e) relativization and pronoun-copying

I claimed above that HPE had no movement rules. In fact, HPE could not have had any movement rules if we use the term in a rather restricted sense to cover processes such as those which convert sentences like /17/ and /19/ into sentences like /18/ and /20/:

/17/ I spoke to John.
/18/ It was John that I spoke to.
/19/ Mary loaned us a book.
/20/ The one who loaned us a book was Mary.

Rules of this kind are generally associated with certain functions, e.g., that of focusing one particular constituent of a sentence, and they perform this function in some English cases by adding structure but always by changing the basic, unmarked word order of the sentence.

We saw that in HPE there were several possible sentence orders: SVO, for all speakers sometimes; SOV, very often for Japanese speakers; and VS, quite often for Filipino speakers. However, since Japanese speakers hardly ever produced VS sentences, and Filipino speakers hardly ever produced SOV sentences, the use of the non-SVO structures could hardly indicate focus or any similar emphatic device; they served merely as (probably unintentional) signals of ethnicity. Even within a group—say, the Japanese—it could hardly be the case that SVO (or SOV) represented an unmarked order, while SOV (or SVO) represented a marked order. For instance, if SOV were the basic order, and SVO a marked order, those speakers who produced only 30 percent SOV would be using their marked order more than twice as often as their basic order. But if the relationship were reversed, the result would be just as unlikely for those speakers who produced 60 percent SOV. If there were two groups, one with basic SOV and marked SVO, and the other with basic SVO and marked SOV, then it would become impossible for the listener to be sure whether contrastive emphasis was or was not intended, and the whole purpose of movement rules would be lost. We can therefore assume that differences in word order among HPE speakers are not the result of movement rules but are due to a gradual transition from VS or SOV orders, unmarked in the speakers' native languages, to the equally unmarked SVO which characterizes almost all contact languages.

In HCE, the situation is quite different. HCE is homogeneous (except to the extent that it has been increasingly influenced by English in recent years) both across and within all groups irrespective of the parents' language background. For all speakers, without question, the basic, unmarked word order is SVO. All speakers, however, have rules that will move either objects—/21/, /22/—or predicates—/23/, /24/—to the beginning of the sentence:

/21/ *eni kain lanwij* ai no kaen spik gud
'I can't speak any kind of language well'

/22/ o, *daet wan* ai si
'Oh, I saw that one'

/23/ *es wan ting baed* dakain go futbawl
'That football stuff is a bad thing'

/24/ *daes leitli* dis pain chri
'These pine trees are recent'

Object-fronting occurs only when the speaker wishes to contrast one NP with another, or to contradict some inference that has been or might be drawn from a previous utterance. This can be shown if we look at some context for /22/, for instance:

/25/ Interviewer: You ever saw any ghost?
MJ75M: no—ai no si.
Interviewer: What about, you know, dakine fireball?
MJ75M: *o, daet wan ai si.*

The interviewer is referring to *akualele*, supernatural fireballs, allegedly controlled by members of the *kahuna* or Hawaiian priestly caste. MJ75M (the letters and numbers indicate: sex, masculine; ethnicity, Japanese; age, 75; and island of residence, Maui, respectively) has just denied knowledge of supernatural entities and uses object-fronting to mark the exception to this denial, as soon as it is brought to his attention.

Predicate-fronting occurs when a predicate that contains new information is introduced in conjunction with a subject which has been explicitly stated or implied in the immediately preceding discourse. This can be shown by extended context for /24/:

/26/ bifoa don haev mach *chriz* hia. in daet hil dea no moa *chriz*.
daes leitli *dis pain chri.*
'There weren't many trees here before. There were no trees

at all on that hill over there. These pine trees (that you now see there) were planted recently'

Here, the speaker realizes that what he said in the first two sentences may seem plainly false in light of what the interviewer can see before him. Since *trees,* although their presence has been denied, have been established as a topic, he can emphasize the recency of the presently visible trees' appearance by fronting the predicate.

This congruence between movement rule and discourse feature is, of course, peculiar to HCE; one cannot find any similar congruence between discourse and variant ordering in HPE. In fact, the result of the HCE rules is a series of orderings which differs markedly from the possible orderings of HPE, both in that it contains orders which HPE does not permit, and in that it does not contain orders which HPE does permit. The situation is shown in Table 1.1:

Order	HPE	HCE
SVO	yes	yes
SOV	yes	no
VS	yes	yes
VOS	no	yes
OSV	no	yes
OVS	no	yes

Table 1.1: Word order in HPE and HCE

The SOV order which is the commonest among older Japanese HPE speakers does not exist in HCE. While VS may occur in both HPE and HCE, its source is different in each case: in HPE, it stems from the retention of verb-first ordering; in HCE, from the operation of a regular rule. That rule, if it applies to transitive sentences, yields VOS order in HCE since objects and other constituents of the verb-phrase move with the verb:

/27/ no laik plei futbawl, dis gaiz
'These guys don't want to play football'

But although VOS is a possible order in Philippine languages, it does not emerge in HPE, possibly because of the absence of either case-marking or consistent intonation to distinguish the roles of the two NPs.

As for the two remaining orders, OSV and OVS, which are present in HCE but not in HPE, the first arises through object-fronting, while the second can occur when both object- and predicate-fronting apply to the same sentences. The result, though infrequent, is occasionally found and is judged grammatical by native speakers:

/28/ difren bilifs dei get, sam gaiz
'Some guys have different beliefs'

There is no way in which the sentence orders that are produced, or the rules which produce them, could have been acquired by the first creole generation from their pidgin-speaking parents. Moreover, even if we assume extensive bilingualism in that generation, those rules could not have been derived from either the substrate languages, or from English. Three substrate languages (Chinese, Portuguese, Spanish), as well as English, have underlying SVO order, but Chinese and English do not permit verb-first or predicate-first sentences, except for one or two highly marked structures like English left-dislocated pseudo-clefts (*Told the landlord, that's what he did*). Portuguese and Spanish are freer in their ordering, tolerating certain types of verb-first sentences, but the equivalents of VOS sentences like /27/ and OVS sentences like /28/ would be ungrammatical in these languages. Conversely, the common Iberian VSX, as exemplified by Portuguese, would be ungrammatical in HCE:

/29/ Chegaram os generais do exercito anoite no Rio
arrived the generals of-the army last-night in-the Rio
'The army generals arrived in Rio last night'

Of course, one might always say something like, "All the structures of HCE are found in at least one of the languages in contact [it would be bizarre if they weren't!], and therefore HCE merely represents a random mix of the structures available to children of various groups, through either the pidgin or their own ethnic tongues." If anyone seriously believed that a language could be built by random mixture, this answer might be satisfactory. But it would not explain why one of the commonest (SOV) orders should be excluded—still less why the particular mixture illustrated in Table 1.1 should have been chosen, rather than one of the many other possible combinations. However, it can hardly be accidental if that particular distribution turns out to be exactly what is generated if one assumes basic SVO order (which is virtually mandatory when you have no other means of marking the two major cases) plus a rule which moves either of the two major constituents, NP and VP, to sentence-initial position.[1] We may therefore claim that the rules which move NPs and VPs cannot have been acquired inductively by the original HCE speakers, but must, in some sense of the term, have been "invented" by them ab ovo.

Next, let us look at articles. These appear sporadically and unpredictably in HPE; typical of early (mainly Japanese) speakers is the 92-year-old 1907 arrival who produced only three indefinite articles (out of 32 that would have been required by English rules of reference, i.e., 9.4 percent) and seven definite articles (out of a total of 40 that English rules would have required, i.e., 17.5 percent). Filipino speakers, on the other hand, generalized the definite articles to many environments in which English does not require them, for example: with generic NPs, as in /9/ above; where there is only one possible referent, as in /30/ or /31/; where there is a clearly nonspecific referent, as in /32/; or where noncount nouns are involved, as in /33/:

/30/   hi get *da* hawaian waif
       'He has a Hawaiian wife'

/31/ istawri pram *da* gad
   'God's story'
/32/ no kaen du nating abaut *da* eniting insai da haus
   'They can't do anything about anything inside the house'
/33/ oni tek tu slais *da* bred
   'I only take two slices of bread'

HCE speakers, however, follow neither the under-generalization of the Japanese speaker nor the over-generalization of the Filipino speaker. The definite article *da* is used for all and only specific-reference NPs that can be assumed known to the listener:

/34/ aefta da boi, da wan wen jink daet milk, awl da maut soa
   'Afterward, the mouth of the boy who had drunk that milk was all sore'

The indefinite article *wan* is used for all and only specific-reference NPs that can be assumed unknown to the listener (typically, first-mention use):

/35/ hi get wan blaek buk. daet buk no du eni gud
   'He has a black book. That book doesn't do any good'

All other NPs have no article and no marker of plurality. This category includes generic NPs, NPs within the scope of negation—i.e., clearly nonspecific NPs—and cases where, while a specific referent may exist, the exact identity of that referent is either unknown to the speaker or irrelevant to the point at issue. Examples include:

/36/ *dag* smat
   'The dog is smart' (in answer to the question, "Which is smarter, *the horse* or *the dog*?")
/37/ *yang fela* dei no du daet
   'Young fellows don't do that'

/38/   poho ai neva bai *big wan*
       'It's a pity I didn't buy a big one'
/39/   bat nobadi gon get *jab*
       'But nobody will get a job'
/40/   hu go daun frs iz *luza*
       'The one who goes down first is the loser'
/41/   *kaenejan waif*, ae, get
       'He has a Canadian wife'
/42/   mi ai get *raesh*
       'As for me, I get a rash'
/43/   as tu bin get had taim reizing *dag*
       'The two of us used to have a hard time raising dogs'

These zero-marked forms would be marked three different
ways in English: with *the* in /36/, /40/; with *a* in /38/, /39/, /41/,
/42/; with zero, but followed by plural -*s*, in /37/, /43/. But note
that the absence of plural marking in the last two cases certainly does
not stem from any more general absence of pluralization in HCE;
specific NPs with plural reference are always appropriately marked in
HCE (although not in HPE), except where numerals or other clear
signs of plurality are already present.

The fact that HCE unites in a single category what English
treats as discrete categories has led to some curious analyses, such as
that of Perlman (1973:99) who writes: "Øs that mark generic singular
NP should be distinguished from those that mark indefinite singular
ones. The distinction may be quite difficult to make. In such cases
as *they go beer parlor, Ewa was never using crane that date, that is
hundred-pound bag, those days they get icebox,* and *olden days we
gotta ride train,* it may actually be neutralized; however, I have distinguished generic from indefinite where possible and discarded uncertain cases like the preceding."

In reality, all Perlman's cases and those cited above have in
common the fact that no specific reference is intended, or, in most
cases, even possible; and the semantic feature *nonspecific* happens to be

shared by both generics and what Perlman calls "indefinite singular." That he uses the word "singular" at all in this context is enough to show that he is looking at his data through English spectacles. English has an obligatory number distinction; every NP has to be either singular or plural. HCE does not have an obligatory number distinction, or rather it has three numbers—singular, plural, and nonspecific (numberless). Thus, while to the English speaker *raesh* in /42/ is clearly singular, while *dag* in /43/ is clearly plural, HCE speakers treat both cases as unmarked for number, because both are nonspecific: the rash, because no particular rash is being referred to—simply the usual consequence when the speaker uses a certain brand of soap; the dogs, because it was not one particular dog or group of dogs that gave the speaker trouble, but rather the business of dog-raising in general.

We shall come back to nonspecificity in each of the next three chapters; for the present, we only need to ask where the specific-nonspecific, marked-unmarked, distinction that is incorporated in the HCE grammar came from. Based on the evidence already shown, it could not have come from HPE. If HCE speakers had followed the Japanese version, they would have marked far fewer NPs than they do, and zero marking would have been assigned to at least some specifics. If they had followed the Filipino model, they would have had far fewer zeros, and some definite articles would have been assigned to non-specific NPs; compare, for instance, /30/ with /41/. A mixing strategy—"Use more articles than Japanese HPE speakers, fewer than Filipino speakers"—would have achieved roughly the right numerical proportions but, if used alone, would hardly have arrived at the rigorous semantic distinction that all HCE speakers in fact make.

As for the influence of the original languages in contact, the glosses for /36/-/43/ show that English can hardly have been a model. Of the substrate languages, many do not have articles at all. Of those that do, none show the same distribution of zero forms; Portuguese and Hawaiian allow, to a varying extent, zero-marked, number-neutral NPs in object position, but demand articles for subject generics like that in /36/. Indeed, those who believe in the strength of substrate influence might note that the speaker who produced /36/, even after a generic with a definite article had been presented to him by his interviewer, was a 79-year-old pure-blooded Hawaiian who had spoken Hawaiian as a child.[2] We must conclude, as with word order, that the zero marking of nonspecifics was an HCE "invention," and one firmly rooted enough to override counterevidence from other languages known to its speakers.

Next, let us examine verbal auxiliaries. HCE has an auxiliary which marks tense, *bin* (which sometimes takes the form *wen*, derived from it by regular phonological rules); an auxiliary which marks modality, *go* (sometimes *gon*); and an auxiliary which marks aspect, *stei*. I shall not discuss the first two here as we will return to a fuller discussion of creole tense-modality-aspect (henceforth TMA) systems in Chapter 2. The aspect marker *stei* will give us a clearer view of how creole creativity works.

Bin and *go* (at least as surface forms, though not with their HCE meanings) occur sporadically and unpredictably in HPE, but *stei* does not—at least not as an auxiliary. It does, however, occur as a main verb, taking locative complements:

/44/   mi iste nalehu tu yia
       'I was in Nalehu for two years'

In all our recordings of pre-1920 immigrants (the only ones who could possibly have provided input to the creolization process) there were only seven sentences in which *stei* preceded another verb. When a feature that occurs so frequently in HCE occurs with such vanishing rarity in HPE, there clearly exists the possibility that it was invented by HCE speakers and was only afterward adopted by some HPE speakers—who, as was suggested earlier, are hardly likely to have lived through a half-century without *any* addition to their grammars. But let us assume the contrary and ask, first, whether the occurrences of *stei* represent a true auxiliary, or whether the sentences contain mere sequences of two main verbs; and second, whether uses such as these could have provided evidence for the HCE speaker to develop a true auxiliary with nonpunctual (progressive plus habitual) meaning. The seven sentences are:

/45/ haus, haus ai stei go in, jaepan taim.
/46/ ai stei kuk.
/47/ mi papa stei help.
/48/ aen istei kam—i kam draib in i ka.
/49/ mai brada hi stei *make* hia.
/50/ oni tu yia mi ai stei wrk had.
/51/ samtaim wan dei stei gat twentipai baeg.

I have not provided glosses since everything turns on what the sentences mean, and what they mean is far from transparent. If /45/ were an HCE utterance, *stei go in* would mean something like 'kept entering', which is improbable here; the most likely meaning, in context, is that the speaker, when she was a girl in Japan, seldom used to leave the house. In the latter case, *stei* would be the main verb with the meaning 'stay', while *go in* would probably have been learned as an undifferentiated chunk meaning something like 'inside'. In /46/, too, the second "verb" may not really be a verb either; *kuk* could represent the noun *cook*, in which case the sentence would mean simply 'I was a cook'. Sentence /47/ could represent verb serialization as easily as auxiliary-plus-verb; 'I stayed *and* helped my father' or 'I stayed *to* help my father' are as plausible as glosses, in context, as 'I was helping my father'. Sentences /48/ and /49/ could contain auxiliaries—the reformulation of /48/ makes it impossible to tell what was intended—but in both cases, punctual events are referred to; the most probable glosses are 'He drove up in his car' and 'My brother died here', respectively. But /49/ is puzzling since the Hawaiian verb *make* alone would mean 'died', while *stei make* would mean literally 'is (or was) dead', which in conjunction with *here* makes little sense.

The only sentences that could have any kind of nonpunctual meaning are /50/ and /51/. Sentence /50/ is most like an HCE sentence with its suggestion of durative activity. Sentence /51/ is more problematic—it could be a past habitual with a zero impersonal subject ('Sometimes they *used to collect* twenty-five bags a day') or some kind of premature attempt at a passive with the quasi-copular *stei* ('Sometimes twenty-five bags *were collected* in a day').

If the input to the first creole generation was as chaotic as this—and, as we saw, it could hardly have been *less* chaotic although it may well have been *more* chaotic—it is impossible to see how children of that generation could have distilled any kind of regular rule out of it, still less the particular rule that they did in fact derive. But if, as is highly possible, sentences such as /45/-/51/ would not have been produced by any HPE speaker prior to 1920, and in fact represent a case of partial imperfect learning of HCE rules by those speakers (a possibility that I shall document in another area later in this chapter), then the achievement of the first creole generation becomes still more mysterious, since it must have been completely ex nihilo.

For if we look at the *stei + V* sentences of HCE speakers, we find no ambiguous cases and no reference to single punctual events. All their uses of *stei* as auxiliary fall into what an English speaker would probably describe as four categories—present continuous, past continuous, present habitual, and past habitual—but these four categories, as I have demonstrated elsewhere (Bickerton 1975:Chapter 2), really constitute a single nonpunctual category, semantically opposed to a punctual category expressing single nondurative actions or events:

/52/ Present continuous:
      ai no kea hu stei hant insai dea, ai gon hunt
      'I don't care who's hunting in there, I'm going to hunt'
/53/ Past continuous:
      wail wi stei paedl, jaen stei put wata insai da kanu—hei, da san av
      a gan haed sink!
      'While we were paddling, John was letting water into the canoe—
      hey, the son-of-a-gun had sunk it!'

/54/ Present habitual:
yu no waet dei stei kawl mi, dakain—kawl mi gad
'You know what they call me, that bunch? They call me God'
/55/ Past habitual:
da meksikan no tel mi nau, da gai laik daunpeimen—i stei tel mi,
o, neks wik, hi kamin, kamin
'Now the Mexican didn't tell me that the guy wanted a down-
payment—he kept telling me, oh, next week it's coming,
it's coming'

A further difference between the HPE examples cited above and
the many hundreds of *stei* sentences we recorded from HCE speakers
is that out of the seven examples, two conjoined *stei* with predicates—
gat and *make*—with which it is never conjoined in HCE. This is because
both are perceived as stative verbs, and in HCE, nonpunctual aspect
cannot be applied to statives: *shi stei no da ansa* is as ungrammatical
as its English equivalent, *she is knowing the answer.* It is true that on
one of our glosses of /51/ *gat* is not stative; but then it would not be
used to express *collect* by an HCE speaker, for whom *gat* is limited
to an alternative form for *get* 'have'.

How could HCE speakers have invented the *stei + V* form? *Stei*
is common as a locative in modern HPE, but there is some doubt
whether it was so common at the time of creole formation. Examples
in Nagara (1972), drawn from data collected from very old speakers
a decade earlier, contain only *stap* as a locative, and the oldest speaker
in our own survey, who arrived prior to 1910, also has only *stap.*
Thus it is conceivable that even the locative use of *stei* was acquired
by HPE speakers from HCE speakers. However, I would think it more
likely that *stei* was a low-frequency variant around 1910 and that HCE
speakers selected it over *stap* because, semantically, *stei* was a more
appropriate expression for durativity.

Locative expressions are a common source of nonpunctual
markers: for instance, forms such as *I am working* derived originally
from *I am AT working*—main verb *be* plus locative preposition plus

gerund—which gave rise first to the form *I'm a-working* (still found in some conservative areas, e.g., West Virginia) and then, via phonological reduction and syntactic reanalysis, to the modern *Aux + V + ing*. These processes in English took several centuries to produce a result which HCE must have produced almost instantly.

Again, we will look in vain for any substratum language which unites all the ingredients which make up HCE nonpunctual: preverbal free morpheme, semantic range inclusive of both progressive and habitual, indifference to the past-nonpast distinction. Many substratum languages express aspect via bound morphemes, or by reduplication (e.g., Philippine languages—it is surely surprising, in view of the frequency with which "reduplication" is hailed as a universal creole characteristic, that HCE speakers did not avail themselves of this particular resource!). Hawaiian uses free morphemes, but these are placed both before and after the verb; Chinese uses preverbal free morphemes, but semantically there is hardly any point of resemblance between the HCE and Chinese TMA systems. Perhaps the closest form to *stei*, semantically, is Japanese *-te iru/-te ita;* these forms cover (very roughly) the same semantic range as *stei*. However, it is the discontinuous segment *-te i-* which carries nonpunctual meaning; *-ru* and *-ta* signify nonpast and past, respectively, and nonpunctuality cannot be marked without marking one or the other of them. Thus, the Japanese form satisfies neither the first nor the third characteristic of *stei*. To assume Japanese influence on *stei* would be to assume that a TMA system can be put together like a jigsaw puzzle;[3] indeed, the implicit supposition that all languages are like erector sets which can be dismantled, cannibalized, and put together again in new combinations lies at the heart of all substratum arguments.

Our fourth area involves a particular type of sentential complementation. It has already been mentioned that sentence embedding of any kind is virtually nonexistent in HPE. Certainly there are no examples of anything resembling English *for-to* complementation, whether *for* is obligatorily present /56/, optionally present /57/, or obligatorily deleted /58/:

/56/   Mary bought this for you to read.
/57/   Mary prefers (for) Bill to go.
/58/   Mary prefers (*for) to go.

HCE does have sentential complements, but these are marked not by *to* but by *fo* (presumably derived from English *for*) and *go;* the precise distribution of these will be discussed shortly.

   First, we must see what, if anything, HCE speakers could have learned from HPE. *Fo* is found in HPE only as a preposition, and it is rare even as a preposition in speakers who arrived prior to the late 1920s. *Go,* however, occurs frequently, and in three contexts: as a main verb, as a marker of imperatives, and as a preverbal modifier of extremely indeterminate meaning and wildly fluctuating distribution (some HPE speakers use it before every third or fourth verb; others don't use it at all). The nearest antecedent to a complementizer *go* derives from its imperative use. One can have paratactic strings of imperative structures, as in /59/:

/59/   go tek tu fala go *hapai* dis wan
       go take two men go carry this one
       'Take two men and take this away'

From their intonation contour, pauses, etc., these are clearly two independent sentences, but production of such sequences in the more rapid tempo of HCE could conceivably serve as a source of true complementation. Such a result might be even more likely in the case of reported imperatives, such as /60/:

/60/   ai no tel yu palas, go join pentikosta
       'I'm not telling you guys, "Join the Pentecostal Church" '

This could, presumably, be reanalyzed as ... *telling you guys TO join* ...; at least with the benefit of the native English speaker's 20/20 hindsight.

Apart from these two constructions—imperative strings and reported imperatives—there is nothing that looks remotely like a *go*-complementizer construction in HPE, and even these two are quite rare. There is thus no precedent for sentences such as the following, which occur with considerable frequency in HCE:

/61/   dei wen go ap dea erli in da mawning go plaen
       'They went up there early in the morning TO plant'
/62/   so ai go daun kiapu go push
       'So I went down to Kiapu TO push (clear land with a bulldozer)'
/63/   ai gata go haia wan kapinta go fiks da fom
       'I had TO hire a carpenter TO fix the form'

However, *fo* often replaces *go* in environments which might appear at first glance to be identical:

/64/   aen dei figa, get sambadi fo push dem
       'And they figured there'd be someone TO encourage them'
/65/   mo beta a bin go hanalulu fo bai maiself
       'It would have been better if I'd gone to Honolulu TO buy it
       myself'
/66/   hau yu ekspek a gai fo mek *pau* hiz haus
       'How do you expect a guy TO finish his house?'

In fact, the two sets of environments differ in an interesting way. The actions described in /61/-/63/ all actually occurred, while those described in /64/-/66/ were all hypothetical: there wasn't anyone to encourage the basketball team referred to in /64/; the speaker of /65/ hadn't gone to Honolulu; and the hypothetical *guy* in /66/ couldn't complete his hypothetical house because the very real bank manager who was being addressed wouldn't issue a loan for that purpose. In other words, HCE marks grammatically the semantic distinction between sentential complements which refer to realized events and those which refer to unrealized events.

The distinction is blurred a little by some sentences which contain both *fo* and *go:*

/67/ pipl no laik tek om fo go wok
 'People don't want TO employ him'
/68/ tumach trabl, ae, fo go fiks om op
 'It's a lot of trouble, you see, TO fix it up'

But again, these complements express hypothetical or even nonoccurring events; thus, these examples confirm the claim that *fo* only occurs with unrealized events, and does not affect the claim that *go,* ALONE, occurs only with realized events.

In this area, then, HCE has made two distinct innovations, one semantic, one syntactic. The syntactic innovation consisted of taking *fo* and *go,* a preposition and an imperative marker, respectively, and using them to introduce embedded sentences, which were themselves an innovation. Even with the possible stimulus supplied by HPE sentences such as /59/ and /60/, this represents a massive change. However, the semantic innovation—distinguishing realized from unrealized complements—was completely without precedent in HPE, in English, or in any of the substrate languages. We should bear this in mind when we encounter widely separated creoles with identical distinctions in Chapter 2.[4]

The fifth and final example of HCE innovation which we will examine here is rather more complex than the previous examples, involving, as it does, the interaction of two rules: a rule of relativization and a rule of subject-copying. Each of these rules itself involves innovation, but I shall say little about these since it is their interaction that shows most dramatically the working of creole creativity.

Insertion of a pronoun between subject and predicate was noted above as a feature of Filipino HPE; this feature is discussed at length in Bickerton and Odo (1976:3.6.1). There is no clear evidence that it is used as anything but a marker of verbal (as distinct from adjectival, nominal, or locative) predicates by any but a small minority of very late (post-1926) arrivals. However, HCE speakers use the same feature for all full-NP subjects on first mention and for all full-NP contrastive subjects; it follows from this that all full-NP subjects of indefinite reference are thus marked (since indefinite reference marks first mention only, and the *some guys* who *do* X turn into the *they* or *those guys* who *do* Y). Thus, in HCE, sentences such as /69/ and /71/ are common, whereas /70/ and /72/ would be ungrammatical:

/69/ sam gaiz samtaimz dei kam
     'Sometimes some guys come'
/70/ *sam gaiz samtaimz kam
/71/ jaepan gaiz dei no giv a haeng, do
     'Guys from Japan don't give a hang, though'
/72/ *jaepan gaiz no giv a haeng, do

The function of pronoun-copying in HCE is clearly linked with that of the movement rules discussed above. All deal with constituents selected for special focus; movement rules move those constituents to the left, but subject NPs are already leftmost constituents and can thus only be "symbolically" moved by inserting something between them and the rest of the sentence.

Relative clauses, among pre-1920 immigrants, are rare, and when they do occur, often they do so in forms influenced by the speaker's native language, cf. /14/ above. Among HCE speakers, relative clauses are common. However, they differ from English relative clauses in that they contain no surface marker of relativization even where English demands one, i.e., in sentences where the noun relativized on is subject of the clause, and either subject /73/ or object /74/ of the main sentence:

/73/ da gai gon lei da vainil fo mi bin kwot mi prais
  'The guy WHO is going to lay the vinyl for me had quoted me a
  price'
/74/ yu si di ailan get koknat
  'You see the island THAT has coconut palms on it?'

We will consider how such sentences may be generated in Chapter 2.

  The interaction of those two rules comes about when full NPs of
indefinite reference and other NPs which must be copied occur as
head nouns of relative clauses and subjects of those clauses. In nonrelative sentences, such as /69/ or /71/, the copy either immediately
follows the NP, as in /71/, or, if an adverb is present, as in /69/,
immediately precedes the verb. In relative-clause sentences, however,
the copy must follow the entire relative clause:

/75/ sam filipinoz wok ova hia dei wen kapl yiaz in filipin ailaenz
  'Some Filipinos WHO worked over here went to the Philippines
    for a couple of years'
/76/ *sam filipinoz dei wok ova hia wen kapl yiaz . . .
/77/ *sam filipinoz dei wok ova hia dei wen kapl yiaz . . .
/78/ *sam filipinoz wok ova hia wen kapl yiaz . . .
/79/ sambadi goin ova dea dei gon hia nau
  'Anybody WHO's going over there will hear it now'
/80/ *sambadi dei goin ova dea gon hia it nau
/81/ *sambadi dei goin ova dea dei gon hia it nau
/82/ *sambadi goin ova dea gon hia it nau

  It cannot be claimed that in /75/ or /79/ the copy represents
some "resumptive" device whose presence is due to the distance between subject and main verb; if this were the case, the subject of /73/,
which is even further from its verb, would be similarly copied. Moreover, a "resumptive" argument does not explain why /77/ and /81/
are ungrammatical, and cannot account for the presence of copies in
/69/ and /71/.

The real problem is explaining the different placement of the copy in, e.g., /71/ and /79/. We can see what is happening if we look at what is probably the underlying structure of /79/ (I shall defend the rule that rewrites NP as S, rather than N S, in the next chapter):

/83/

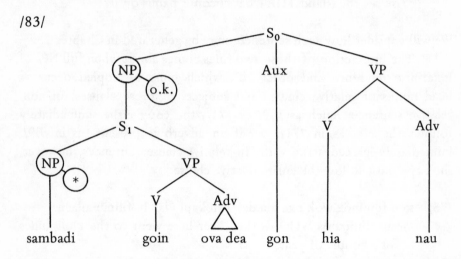

If S_1 constituted an independent sentence, then the rule of subject-copying would place the appropriate pronoun immediately to the right of the NP marked with an asterisk to yield *sambadi dei goin ova dea.* However, when S_1 is embedded in S_0, the higher-circled NP node must have the pronoun adjoined to it in order to yield /79/, rather than the ungrammatical /80/.

Chomsky (1964) proposed a universal principle termed the "A-over-A principle," which states that if a major category, such as NP, is directly dominated by the same major category, then any rule that would normally apply to the lower category node could apply only to the higher node. Although the principle as there formulated has not been widely accepted (cf. Ross 1967), similar phenomena have been observed in a number of languages, and something resembling such a principle must still be regarded as a likely formal universal. Formal universals must be regarded as part of the innate equipment of the species, and HCE speakers, however they may have arrived at the

A-over-A principle, cannot have done so as a result of experience.

In the first place, no sentences involving both relativization and subject-copying are found in pre-1920 arrivals, and therefore the varying distribution of copies in relative and nonrelative sentences cannot have been acquired from HPE speakers. The differences from English are obvious: sentences like /75/ and /79/ would be ungrammatical even in those so-called "substandard" dialects of English which permit subject-copying and/or deletion of relative pronouns in subject position. No substrate language combines similar modes of relativization and focusing; therefore, none of them could have provided relevant evidence. Moreover, in this case we have much clearer proof than before that the current of innovation ran from HCE back into HPE, rather than vice versa.

Among later immigrants, there was just one (arrival date 1930) who attempted complex sentences such as /79/. Although he sometimes got them right, he would, with equal frequency, produce sentences with two copies, as in /81/, or no copies, as in /82/:

/84/ awl diz bigshat pipl dei gat plenti mani dei no kea
'All these big shots who have plenty of money don't care'
/85/ sam kam autsaid kam mo wos
'Some who come out (of jail) become worse'

These sentences are of course ungrammatical in HCE, and no locally-born speaker would have produced them. But they are just the kind of vague approximations that are made by foreign-language learners when they try to apply a new and imperfectly-acquired rule. Indeed, HCE, once established, was just that—a new foreign language—and joined earlier versions of HPE as a part of the input to immigrant speakers who arrived in Hawaii after 1920.

We have now surveyed five quite distinct aspects of HCE grammar and found in each of them clear innovations by the earliest HCE speakers; developments in the grammar which can have owed little or nothing to HPE, to English, or to any of the substrate languages involved. We may briefly review those developments by presenting a more formal summary in terms of the grammatical rules involved, showing first the HPE rules—if HPE can be said to have rules or a grammar of its own; I think that HPE would really have to have an analysis like that proposed by Silverstein (1972) for Chinook Jargon, in which the pidgin forms would be produced by extensions and modifications of the HPE speakers' original native languages—and then the HCE rules for each of the five areas.

With regard to basic sentence-structure and movement rules, HPE would have the following phrase-structure (PS) rules:

/86/ $S \rightarrow \begin{Bmatrix} NP \ V \ (NP) \\ NP \ (NP) \ V \\ V \ NP \end{Bmatrix}$

HPE would have no movement rules. HCE, on the other hand, would have the following PS rules:

/87/ $S \rightarrow NP \ Aux \ VP$
/88/ $VP \rightarrow V \ (NP) \ (PP)$

and in addition the following movement rules:

/89/ SD: NP VP
           1 2 $\rightarrow$
    SC: 2 1
/90/ SD: X V NP
          1 2 3 $\rightarrow$
    SC: 3 1 2

For the second area, involving articles, HPE, if it had any rule at all, would have something like /91/:

/91/ NP → { (da) } N
         { (wan) }

There would be no rule that would determine the circumstances under which *da, wan,* or Ø would be generated. HCE, on the other hand, would have the following rule (I will ignore determiners other than articles):

/92/ NP → Art   N
/93/ Art → { Definite }
           { Nondefinite }
           { Nonspecific }
/94/ Definite → *da*
/95/ Nondefinite → *wan*
/96/ Nonspecific → Ø

For the third area, involving *stei* and other auxiliaries, it is not clear what rules, if any, HPE would have—possibly a rule such as /97/, which would also account for the fact that some auxiliaries, such as *kaen,* may function as main verbs, as in *no kaen* '(You) can't (do it)'/ 'It's impossible':

/97/ V → (V) V

HCE, however, would have /87/, plus the following PS rules:

/98/ Aux → (Tense) (Modal) (Aspect)
/99/ Tense → Anterior
/100/ Modal → ... Irrealis ...
/101/ Aspect → Nonpunctual
/102/ Anterior → *bin*
/103/ Irrealis → *go*
/104/ Nonpunctual → *stei*

For the fourth area, involving *fo, go,* and sentential complements, HPE would have no rules. HCE would possibly have something
like the following PS rule (but see Chapter 2 on the status of complementizers in creoles generally):

/105/ NP → (COMP) S
/106/ COMP → $\left\{ \begin{array}{l} \text{Realized} \\ \text{Unrealized} \end{array} \right\}$
/107/ Realized → *go*
/108/ Unrealized → *fo*

In addition, HCE would require something analogous to (but probably
not identical with) the English rule of equi-deletion.

Finally, for the fifth area, involving relativization, subject-
copying, and their interaction, we might need a rule for Filipino speakers which would modify /97/ to something like /109/:

/109/ V → $\left\{ \begin{array}{ll} (V) & V \\ (i) & V \\ \text{Pred} \end{array} \right\}$

(All but the later HCE-influenced HPE speakers realize the copy, if
indeed for them it is a copy—it is more likely a marker of a particular
predicate type—as an invariant *i,* i.e., in contradistinction to the HCE
rule, subject features such as *plural* or *feminine* are not copied onto
it.) A few speakers might have, in addition, a rule for relativization
that would simply replace NP by S. HCE speakers would have a well-
established rule:

/110/ NP → S

In addition, they would have the following transformational rule:

/111/ SD: NP   VP
$$\begin{bmatrix} \alpha \ \text{number} \\ \beta \ \text{gender} \end{bmatrix}$$
              1   2   →
     SC: 1 + pro   2
$$\begin{bmatrix} \alpha \ \text{number} \\ \beta \ \text{gender} \end{bmatrix}$$

The A-over-A principle, or whatever general constraint governs the subject-copying rule in relativized sentences, would not need to be separately stated in the HCE grammar since it would presumably be a universal.

All that remains for us is to ask how these quite substantial innovations could have been produced. There would seem to be only two logically possible alternatives. They could have been produced by some kind of general problem-solving device such as might be applied in any field of human behavior where the required human institutions were lacking—much as survivors of a shipwreck or an atomic holocaust might reconstruct government, laws, and other social institutions. Or they might have been produced by the operation of innate faculties genetically programmed to provide at least the basis for an adequate human language.

If Hawaii were the only place where people had been faced with the problem of reconstructing human language, it would be impossible to decide between these alternatives. However, Hawaii is far from unique. There are a number of creole languages in other parts of the globe, but produced under very similar circumstances, several of which have been described well enough to make comparison possible. It is true that in these cases we do not have the antecedent pidgin for comparative purposes,[5] but we shall see that there are still some oblique indications of antecedent structure. In any case, it is difficult to see, given the rapidity with which creoles arose, how those antecedent pidgins could have developed any further than Hawaii's did.

Now, of the two alternatives stated above, each would seem to make different predictions about the general nature of creoles. If some general problem-solving device were at work, we would not expect that in every different circumstance it would reach the same set of conclusions. There are any number of possible solutions to the structural and communicative problems that language poses, as the very diversity of the world's languages shows, and we would expect to find that, given the differences in geographical region, culture, contributing languages, and so on, each group faced with the task of reconstructing language would arrive at quite different solutions. Indeed, unless I am mistaken, orthodox generativists, even while believing in an innate language faculty, might predict the same result since their theory assigns to that faculty nothing more than those formal and substantive universals which are reflected in all languages. Thus, they could predict no more of a creole than that it should not violate any universal constraint.

However, if all creoles could be shown to exhibit an identity far beyond the scope of chance, this would constitute strong evidence that some genetic program common to all members of the species was decisively shaping the result.

Chapter 2
CREOLE

Although similarities among creoles have been known to exist at least since the pioneering work of Schuchardt and others in the latter half of the 19th century, it was not until the middle of the present century that articles by Taylor (1960, 1963, etc.), Thompson (1961), Whinnom (1956, 1965), and others began to spell out these similarities in any detail. Curiously, their pioneering efforts were not systematically developed; in general, creolists continued to describe individual creoles, or (much more rarely) groups of creoles with a common superstratum (e.g., Goodman 1964, Hancock 1970, Alleyne 1980), or else simply used already existing data in long-drawn-out and essentially fruitless debates on issues such as monogenesis versus poly-genesis, or substrate versus superstrate influence (Bickerton [1976] provides a brief summary of these).

While the profession badly needs a volume that would systema-tically compare all the well-known creoles, such a task lies beyond the scope of the present volume. Instead, I shall look at general creole patterns in the five areas covered in the last chapter, plus some other areas, to give a rough general picture which should enable us to deter-mine how far they, and HCE, resemble one another; and I shall then explore in greater depth two areas—verb-phrase complementation and the syntax and semantics of TMA systems—which have already been treated by various writers more extensively than other areas. We should then be in a position to answer the questions posed at the end of the previous chapter.

Before embarking on this task, however, it is necessary to say a few words about some of the peculiar problems it involves. One set of problems arises from the limitations of many existing descriptions of creoles. No creole language has yet been provided the kind of comprehensive and detailed reference grammar that is taken for granted in most areal fields. With too few exceptions, creole grammars tend to stop where the syntax gets interesting, e.g., "complex sentences" are often dismissed with a page or two of unanalyzed examples. For many creoles, only outline sketches are available. Moreover, some descriptions may be based on incorrect data or contain incorrect analyses. As for the two creoles that I know best—Guyanese Creole and Hawaiian Creole English—I must regretfully state that I find all previous descriptions deficient or misleading in a number of respects.

It might be argued here that it is premature to begin any general or theoretical work, especially one of a novel or controversial nature, until these lacunae have been filled and these errors amended. For instance, Corne (1977:2) states: "Questions about the 'genesis' of the creole languages, their genetic relations with each other and with their source language(s), the processes of creolisation (and pidginisation), cannot be approached seriously unless we know something about the object being talked about, and that we shall not know (in sufficient detail) until a lot more of the unglamourous drudgery of careful descriptive work has been completed." This statement shows a profound misunderstanding of the ways in which science is developed and knowledge increases. Empirical knowledge is no guarantee of certitude, and its absence no barrier to insight; I would oppose, to Corne, the following statement by Dingwall (1979:3): "Relying on logical argument alone, Leucippus was able to develop the atomic theory, while Aristotle, able to rely on the results of numerous dissections, failed to discover the correct function of the brain, imagining it to be the cooling system of the body."

The view that theorists are mere grandstanding prima donnas, while the real work of the trade is done by the modest empirical plodder, is a widespread misconception in creole studies that merely underlines the immaturity of the field. In the real world, unglamorous drudges never arrive at that moment of revelation which is always, like the rainbow, just beyond the next bend. For them, it's always "a little too early to judge"; the data are "not yet all in." They bequeath to their successors no more than mountains of fact, which may or may not contain the nuggets that would genuinely enrich us; more often, I suspect, the latter, since the facts one can gather about any language are infinite in number, and by no means all of equal value. What is needed is not dogged fact-gathering (with or without moral sermons) but the capacity to distinguish between the trivial and the nontrivial. The task of the theorist is to tell the field worker where to look and what to look for, and if the latter chooses to reject such aid, he has about as much brain as the man who throws away his metal detector and proceeds to dig by hand the three-acre field where he thinks treasure lies buried.

Another problem in creole studies is the question of how to interpret differences among creoles, where they genuinely exist. Are we to assume that any and every difference must be given equal weight? Such an assumption would be naive, as I shall try to show.

Creoles are the nearest thing one can find to ab ovo creations of language, but they are not and cannot be purely ab ovo creations. At the very least, pidgins provide some input to them, and this, even if deficient, even if sometimes rejected, as we saw, is still input. Since pidgins show clear substratum differences, and since the composition of substrata differs from place to place, that input must also be a variable, which must somehow be factored out if we are to determine the extent to which creoles are genuinely creative.

But there is another variable in pidgins that may have more far-reaching consequences than differences in the pidgin substrata: that is, the extent of superstrate influence on the pidgin. This in turn will depend on ratios of superstrate to nonsuperstrate speakers; if the former are numerous, there will be more superstrate features available to the first creole generation. We have already noted the case of Réunion. But there are some areas in which population ratios during the pidginization stage are unknown; hence, even if we exclude known cases like Réunion, this variable cannot be entirely eliminated. Moreover, factors other than demographic may influence it. Population ratios in Hawaii differed little from those in the Caribbean, but the (relative) freedom of an indentured as opposed to a slave society must have had some effects on the quantity and quality of linguistic interaction, and may well explain why we find more English features in both HPE and HCE than we do in a creole like Sranan, or even in the basilectal varieties of Guyanese or Jamaican Creole.

Other problems arise from the operation of linguistic change processes, be those processes internal or contact produced.

Internal changes affect languages regardless of their ancestry, and one would imagine that creoles, by the very recency of their emergence from rudimentary pre-pidgins, would be more, rather than less, subject to such changes than more developed languages. The oldest creoles have a time depth approaching five hundred years, which is certainly adequate for a number of significant changes to have taken place; but in most cases the absence of written records from earlier periods, and the unreliability of such records where they do exist— not necessarily the fault of the witnesses, since these were Europeans, and code-switching presumably existed in the 17th century as it does today—makes it difficult indeed to estimate the extent and nature of such changes.[1]

However, in addition to internal change there is the contact-stimulated type of change known as decreolization. This can affect any creole which has remained in contact with its superstrate, as most have. Decreolization is well documented for some English creoles

(DeCamp 1971, Bickerton 1973a, 1975), but has been largely ignored in studies of other creoles. Valdman (1973) suggests that it is equally widespread among French varieties, and its presence in Cabo Verdiense and some other Portuguese creoles is quite apparent. The result of decreolization is to create a continuum of intermediate varieties between creole and superstrate. If this process is sufficiently long and intense, the continuum may be progressively eroded at its creole end. The result may be a synchronic state in which the most conservative variety recoverable is already considerably different from (and considerably closer to the superstrate than) the original creole; this is obvious in some cases, e.g., Trinidad, but may be less so elsewhere.

Again, in some cases where truly conservative varieties are recoverable, researchers may have failed to unearth them (the observations of Bailey [1971] on the texts in Le Page and DeCamp [1960] are very relevant here). To compare a partially decreolized creole with a nondecreolized one can only produce an appearance of difference which might not have existed had it been possible to compare the two languages in their pristine condition. Yet, given present uncertainties as to which creoles have decreolized, and how much, this trap is one into which the most careful scholar might inadvertently fall.

A field so fraught with possible sources of error might seem to provide the comparativist with an inexhaustible source of alibis. Faced with any apparent difference, he could say: "Well, this must be due to one or another of these interfering factors, so let's just forget it!" Any such procedure would turn the inquiry into a farce, and yet, in light of the foregoing paragraphs, it would be equally irresponsible to take every difference at its face value and accord equal weight to each. If, as indicated in Chapter 1, there is some unique, creative force at work in the formation of creoles, we must try to distinguish this from other forces that might interact with it and serve to mask it. But unless we can show precisely *which* factor is involved, *why* it should have taken effect, and *how* it could have worked to provide the observed results, our efforts will be valueless.

A final problem concerns the weighing of evidence and the criteria for making judgments. This is of particular importance when we come to deal with apparent cases of substratum influence.

Claims of substratum influence still persist strongly in creole studies and are made in such recent works as Jansen, Koopman and Muysken (1978), Alleyne (1979, 1980), etc. However, substrato-maniacs, if I may give them their convenient and traditional name, seem to be satisfied with selecting particular structures in one or more creole languages and showing that superficially similar structures can be found in one or more West African languages (at least one careful study, Huttar [1975], has shown that such structures are not always as similar as they might appear at first glance). This may be just as well; if they pursued their inquiries any further, they would find that not only would they have to confront some rather serious diffi-culties, but that even if they overcame these, they would, perforce, wind up in a position which is only a step away from that which is proposed here.

Let us suppose that a very common structure in Caribbean creoles is also attested for Yoruba and perhaps one or two other rela-tively minor languages (this case is not hypothetical; we shall meet with it in the very next section). To most substratomaniacs, the mere existence of such similarities constitutes self-evident proof of the connection. They seldom even consider the problem of transmission. How does a rule get from Yoruba into a creole?

Theoretically, there are several possibilities. One at least—some kind of monogenetic ancestor which would have taken structure from Yoruba and other languages and passed it on to a wide range of descen-dents—has been proposed many times, but no body of evidence (save for just those creole similarities it purports to explain!) has ever been presented for such a language, and until one is, we can safely ignore it. Consequently, we must assume that our rule, and perhaps others, passed from Yoruba into the antecedent pidgins of a number of creoles, and thence into those creoles. For this to have happened, a substantial number of Yoruba speakers must have been present during the pidgin

phase in each area, or at least no later than the earliest phase of creolization. If not, if a substantial number did not arrive in a given area
until after the creole had been formed, then previous speakers would
hardly abandon the rules they themselves had arrived at and replace
them with new rules, unless the number of Yoruba was so great as to
constitute an absolute majority—and that, to the best of present knowledge, was never true at any time for any Caribbean territory.[2]

Now, while it would be difficult, if not impossible, to prove that
there were *no* Yorubas in any given area at the time of creolization,
there are a number of areas where their presence must have been
heavily outweighed by members of other groups. If we take Saramaccan, for instance, generally regarded as the most African-like of
creoles, we find very few lexical survivals even from the whole Kwa
group (of which Yoruba is a member) but very many from Bantu languages, in particular Kikongo (Daeleman 1972). One would think that
the first task in constructing any substratum theory would be to show
that the necessary groups were in the necessary places at the necessary
times. But this has simply not been done.

There are linguistic as well as historical problems to be faced by
any serious substratum theory. As things stand, we are asked to believe
that different African languages contributed different rules and features
to particular creoles. To accept that this is possible is to accept what
Dillard (1970), in a slightly different context, aptly termed the "Cafeteria Principle." Dillard was arguing against the once widespread belief
that creoles were mixtures of rules and features from various regional
dialects of the British Isles. But if it is absurd to suppose that a creole
could mix fragments of Irish, Wessex, Norfolk, and Yorkshire dialects,
it is at least as absurd to suppose that a creole could mix fragments of
Yoruba, Akan, Igbo, Mandinka, and Wolof—to mention some of the
African languages which substratomaniacs most frequently invoke.

Let us suppose, however, that such miracles were possible, and
that Yoruba speakers were indeed distributed in such a way that the

requisite input could be provided. Nobody can deny that, in every case, there were many other African languages involved in each area, and nobody who knows anything about African languages can deny that, even within the Kwa group—and a fortiori outside it—there are wide differences in rules and rule systems. What could be so special about a particular Yoruba rule (such as the one for verb-focusing which we will shortly discuss) that would cause it to be accepted over all competitors in a number of different and quite separate groups?

This question has been raised with respect to one feature which is by no means limited to Yoruba: verb-serialization. In their analysis of this phenomenon, Jansen, Koopman and Muysken (1978), while accepting the standard substratum explanation, wonder why it is that creoles, with their clear preference for features that are unmarked in the Jakobsonian sense, should have selected one which is quite rare among the world's languages, and highly unstable (subject to rapid change) even in those that have it. They are unable to provide an answer, although I shall suggest one in the latter part of this chapter.

In a general sense, we can claim that the only possible factor that could lead a group to accept a particular rule out of a set of alternatives must have to do with the emerging system of the language which that group is engaged in developing. It could only be that, at any given stage in that development, the language could only incorporate rules of a certain type, and would have to reject others. Although we still know far too little about dynamic processes in language to be able to say what such constraints on development might be like, we can be reasonably certain that they exist. Languages, even creoles, are systems, systems have structure, and things incompatible with that structure cannot be borrowed; SVO languages cannot borrow a set of postpositions, to take an extreme and obvious case. If a marked structure is incorporated (and if verb-serialization is highly marked, then verb-focusing is super-highly marked), it can only be because the language, at that particular stage of its development, has to have some such rule.

That a creole language has to have certain types of rules is exactly what the present study is designed to prove. If such rules happen to be present in the input in certain cases, that is in no way counter to the theory expressed here; the creole will acquire such rules, not because they are in the input, for many conflicting rules must be there also, but because such a rule is required by the structure of the emerging language. Indeed, presence in the input may not even be a necessary, let alone a sufficient, condition since the first creole generation could well have devised such a rule for itself; we saw in the first chapter that that generation can and does invent rules without benefit of experience. But even if we accept the entire substratum case, the situation is not substantively changed; the first creole generation has merely acquired the kind of rule that it was programmed to acquire, and saved itself the trouble, so to speak, of having to invent something equivalent. Thus, when taken to their logical conclusions, substratum arguments only bring us back to the question this book will try to solve: why do creole speakers acquire some types of rule, but not others?

With these points clarified, we can now survey some key areas of grammar and see something of the range and extent of the similarities which any creole theory must somehow account for.

Movement Rules

HCE, as we have seen, moved focused constituents to sentence-initial position. The same procedure, with some modifications which I shall discuss in a moment, is followed by all other creoles.

It is sometimes suggested that there is nothing very remarkable about this fact, since many languages have similar processes. But it is also true that many languages have also, or instead, other methods of marking focus, such as changes in stress or tone patterns, or the use of focusing particles. The fact that creoles have adopted none of these alternative strategies cannot be without significance.

However, there are certain differences between HCE and the Caribbean creoles in the ways in which this general strategy is implemented. I shall illustrate the Caribbean strategy from Guyanese Creole (GC), since this language seems to be typical in all respects.

Let us start with a simple declarative sentence such as /1/:

/1/   Jan bin sii wan uman
       'John had seen a woman'

The subject can be focused by adjoining the equative copula *a* to the first NP:

/2/   a Jan bin sii wan uman
       'It was John who had seen a woman'

The object can be focused by moving the NP to sentence-initial position and again adjoining *a:*

/3/   a wan uman Jan bin sii
       'It was a woman that John had seen'

Other VP constituents such as oblique-case NPs and adverbials can be focused in an identical manner. However, the verb can also be focused by a rather different procedure; it is again preposed and *a* is adjoined to it, but a copy is obligatorily left at the extraction site:

/4/   a sii Jan bin sii wan uman

There is no exact equivalent to /4/ in English; it is roughly equivalent to 'John had *seen* a woman' or 'John had *really* seen a woman' or 'Seen a woman, that's what John had done'. In English, it is impossible to apply a movement rule to V alone; English movement rules apply to major categories, and major categories in English are NP and VP.

This fact must immediately raise doubts about the status of

VP in GC, for while NP and V can be moved freely, VP cannot:

/5/ *a sii wan uman Jan bin
/6/ *a bin sii wan uman Jan
/7/ *a sii wan uman Jan bin sii
/8/ *a bin sii wan uman Jan bin sii

Note that /6/ without *a* and with appropriate lexical and phonological changes would be grammatical in HCE:

/9/ (i) bin si wan wahini, Jan.

One difference between GC and HCE could then be due to the fact that the latter has the category VP while the former does not. VP has always been a problem for generative grammar; many scholars have been unwilling to accept it as a universal category since (among other things) it is hard to posit for VSO languages where it would be a discontinuous constituent in deep structure. I know of no rule in GC for which VP has to be specified in the structural description (GC does not have the equivalent of English VP deletion, for example).

However, this seems like a pretty massive difference to begin our list of similarities with. If creoles are constrained by a genetic program, how could things like this possibly come about?

If, as will be claimed in Chapter 4, the original building blocks of language are just NPs and Vs, then VP is not a primitive constituent, but V is; thus, in the earliest stages of a creole, I would predict that V, but not VP, would be a category. However, either as a result of decreolization, involving contact with a language which already has VP as a category, or of internal change, a creole can develop VP.

Previously, we established that superstrate influence was one of the factors which would disrupt natural creole development, whether that influence came during pidginization or, much later, through decreolization. That the results of influence at these two points can be virtually identical and impossible to disentangle is testified by the eloquent bafflement of Corne's comments on the status of Réunion Creole (Corne 1977:223-24).[3] For instance, as mesolectal varieties of GC come under English influence, they develop VP. Now, it seems plausible to suppose that HCE, which, as we have seen, was influenced by English more strongly than most other English creoles, acquired VP at birth, rather than two or three hundred years later (though I would agree that for the moment there is no obvious way to prove this). If this is so, then HCE would not be typical of the most natural creole development; but the overall theory would be unaffected, since Washabaugh's (1979) claim that any genetically-programmed feature should appear universally in creoles, irrespective of other conflicting factors, is a blatant straw man.

However, we still have to show why GC copies the verb. Here, the hypothetical case of the Yoruba rule discussed in the preceding section becomes real, for Yoruba does indeed have a rule that yields sentences very similar to, although not identical with /4/. At first sight this rule looks so weird that one thinks (I myself thought for several years) that direct borrowing must be the only possible source. However, consider for a moment what would happen if GC had a rule which said, "Move all major categories" (probably true of any human language), plus a condition which specified that major categories were NP and V (which is highly probable based on the evidence), but this movement did NOT leave a copy of V at the extraction site.

Such a rule would separate verbs from their auxiliaries, and this would immediately cause severe processing problems for speakers of creoles. It is a condition on transformations generally that meaning be recoverable, but since a number of auxiliaries (e.g., GC *go*) are homophonous with full verbs or can modify zero copulas, and since many full verbs are homophonous with the nouns derived from them, sentences in which only V is fronted could wind up with meanings completely different from those they originally had. Take the following examples:

/10/ Jan bin go wok a haspital
    'John would have worked at the hospital'
/11/ *a wok *Jan bin go a haspital*

The italicized main clause in /11/ constitutes a complete sentence with the meaning 'John had gone to the hospital'. Since *wok* can be noun or verb, and since nouns are fronted without copying, as in /2/ and /3/, /11/ could be, and almost certainly would be, interpreted as 'It was work that John had gone to the hospital for'. Again, if V-fronting minus copying were applied to /1/ above, it would yield:

/12/ *a sii Jan bin wan uman

This could only be interpreted as a (slightly ungrammatical) version of 'He (or I) saw that John was a woman!' Thus, if a copy is not left, meaning is irrecoverable. It would seem, therefore, that any language with movement rules that involve V only, rather than VP, MUST develop a copying rule (or if, as has often been suggested in the literature, movement rules normally consist of two parts, one which Chomsky-adjoins a copy of the constituent to S and one which deletes the original constituent, it must then merely suppress the second half of the process). No borrowing from any other language would be required. Moreover, a claim that GC borrowed the rule from Yoruba sets up an infinite regress: where did Yoruba borrow it from? It is much more plausible to suppose that languages independently invent rules when these are demanded by the structure of the language plus functional requirements.

The other difference between GC and HCE rules involves the use of an equative copula. HCE could not use such a copula because it never developed one. Absence of an equative copula seems to be characteristic of those languages (e.g., HCE, Crioulo, the Indian Ocean creoles [IOC]) which show heavier superstrate influence, but as there is no plausible mechanism here to show WHY that influence should have this effect (positive influence is one thing, negative influence quite another), we must note this as a potentially significant difference. In the absence of such a focus-marking device, some other morpheme must be recruited, and creoles seem to have no specific program for either source or position: Crioulo *ki* is drawn from a superstrate relativizer (Pg. *que*) and postposed to the extracted constituent; Seychelles Creoles *sa* is drawn from its own definite article, in turn derived from Fr. *ça,* and optionally preposed; while HCE uses (for subject NP) the quasi-obligatory verb-predicate marker fortuitously present in Filipino versions of HPE, postposing it and adding number and gender. This diversity is in sharp contrast to the generality of left movement, and suggests (we will later provide abundant evidence, not just from creoles but from child language acquisition) that the genetic program which produces language in the species highly specifies some areas of language and leaves others undetermined; this is only to be expected, as a genetic blueprint which leaves no room for variation and development would freeze a species at a single developmental level.

Articles

There seems, in contrast, to be hardly any variation at all in the way that creoles handle articles. Virtually all creoles have a system identical to that of HCE: a definite article for presupposed-specific NP; an indefinite article for asserted-specific NP; and zero for nonspecific NP. GC provides the following examples:

/13/ Jan bai di buk
      'John bought the book (that you already know about)'
/14/ Jan bai wan buk
      'John bought a (particular) book'
/15/ Jan bai buk
      'John bought a book or books'
/16/ buk dia fi tru
      'Books are really expensive!'

Papiamentu (PP) provides the following examples:

/17/ mi tin e buki
'I have the book'
/18/ mi tin e bukinan
'I have the books'
/19/ mi tin un buki
'I have a book'
/20/ mi tin buki
'I have books'
/21/ buki ta caru
'Books are expensive'

Seychelles Creole (SC) provides the following examples:

/22/ mô pe aste sa banan
'I am buying the banana'
/23/ mô pe aste ban banan
'I am buying the bananas'
/24/ mô pe aste ê banan
'I am buying a banana'

Corne (1977:13) follows the same Anglocentric route as Perlman (1973) did for HCE when dealing with nonspecifics; he cites the following two examples, /25/ and /26/, as "zero form . . . in NP of the VP" and "Ind + plural," respectively:

/25/ fakter i n amen let isi?
postman PM COMP bring letter here
'Did the postman bring a letter (here)?'[4]
/26/ nu pu al pret zuti
we IRR go borrow tool
'We shall go and borrow some tools'

Corne does not mention subject generics, but we can assume that these too are treated as nonspecifics.

Similar illustrations could be produced for almost any creole. This area of grammar seems to be highly specified in creoles; the distinction between specific and nonspecific is particularly clear and consistent, and when we look at language acquisition in Chapter 3, we will find confirmatory evidence that it is probably innate.

Tense-Modality-Aspect (TMA) Systems

A majority of creoles, like HCE, express tense, modality, and aspect by means of three preverbal free morphemes, placed (if they co-occur) in that order. I have already discussed the typical creole system elsewhere (Bickerton 1974; 1975:Chapter 2), so here I shall give only a brief outline, returning later in the chapter to go much more deeply into some apparent counterexamples which have been mentioned in the literature.

In the typical system—which HCE shares with GC, Sranan (SR), Saramaccan (SA), Haitian Creole (HC), and a number of other creoles—ranges of meaning of the particles are identical: the tense particle expresses [+Anterior] (very roughly, past-before-past for action verbs and past for stative verbs);[5] the modality particle expresses [+Irrealis] (which includes futures and conditionals); while the aspect particle expresses [+Nonpunctual] (progressive-durative plus habitual-iterative). The stem form in isolation expresses the unmarked term in these three oppositions, i.e., present statives and past nonstatives. In addition, there exist combined forms, some of which in some languages have been eroded (in GC by phonological rules, in HCE by decreolization), but of which the full set is attested for HC (Hall 1953) and SR (Voorhoeve 1957). Again, wherever combined forms are present, their meaning is the same: anterior plus irrealis, counterfactual conditions; anterior plus nonpunctual, past-before-past durative or habitual actions; irrealis plus nonpunctual, habitual or durative unrealized actions; anterior plus irrealis plus nonpunctual, counterfactuals which express duration or habituality.

Surface forms, of course, take a number of different shapes: anterior, GC *bin*, SA *bi*, SR *ben*, HC and Lesser Antillean Creole (LAC) *te;* irrealis, GC *sa/go*, SA *o*, SR *sa*, HC *ava*, LAC *ke;* nonpunctual, GC *a*, SA *ta*, SR *e*, HC *ape*, LAC *ka.*

HCE, with *bin, go,* and *stei,* shares even two of the GC surface forms, although the two languages are several thousand miles apart and their speakers have never been in contact. Combined forms have almost disappeared through decreolization, but are retained by a few speakers (Bickerton 1974), and/or are attested for earlier periods (Reinecke 1969, Tsuzaki 1971), although nowadays those who remember them are so unsure of what they once meant that one investigator (Perlman 1973) accused his consultants of making them up! (See discussion in Bickerton 1977:183ff.) Thus, we can again claim a highly programmed area, and many details of the ways in which children acquire quite different kinds of TMA systems (see Chapter 3, below) will serve to confirm this claim.

Realized and Unrealized Complements

What work has so far been done on creole complementation has focused largely on verb serialization, so data on this topic are extremely scarce. However, all the languages for which I have been able to find good data attest an identical structure to that of HCE, i.e., complementizers which are selected by the semantics of the embedded S.

Roberts (1975) reports the following contrast from Jamaican Creole (JC):

/27/ im gaan fi bied, bot im duon bied
'He went to wash, but he didn't wash'
/28/ *im gaan go bied, bot im duon bied

Here, *go* as complementizer cannot co-occur with a negative conjunct because its meaning expresses a realized action. However, *fi* is fully compatible with negative conjuncts since the actions it introduces are not (or, perhaps, are not necessarily) realized.

Jansen, Koopman and Muysken (1978) report an identical contrast in Sranan:

/29/   a teki a nefi foe koti a brede, ma no koti en
       'He took the knife to cut the bread, but did not cut it'
/30/   *a teki a nefi koti a brede, ma no koti en

Here, the contrast is between *foe* and $\emptyset$ as complementizers, but the semantic distinction is identical.[6]

The examples so far have all been from English creoles although it is obvious that the distinction cannot have been derived from a language which does not make it:

/31/   *I managed to stop* (entails "I stopped").
/32/   *I failed to stop* (entails "I did not stop").
/33/   *I went to see Mary and we talked about old times.*
/34/   *I went to see Mary but she wasn't home.*

Fortunately for those who might still hypothesize some occult English influence, the same contrast is found in Mauritian Creole (MC). In one of the texts in Baker (1972), we find /35/:

/35/   li desid al met posoh ladah
       she decide go put fish in-it
       'She decided to put a fish in (the pool)'

A line or so later, /36/ follows:

/36/   li don posoh-la en ti noh-gate
       she give fish-the one small nickname
       'She gave the fish a little nickname'

In other words, she had indeed done what she decided to do, i.e., put a fish in the pool. The *al*-complement, therefore, indicates a realized action. However, in another text we find /37/:

/37/ li ti pe ale aswar pu al bril lakaz sa garsoh-la
     he TNS MOD go evening for go burn house that boy-the
     me lor sime ban dayin fin atake li
     but on path PL witch COMP attack him
     'He would have gone that evening to burn the boy's house, but
       on the way he was attacked by witches'

Here, the subject of the sentence was prevented from carrying out his intention by the witches; accordingly, the complement is marked with *pu al*. Since Baker does not discuss this construction, we have no way of knowing if, as I suspect, /38/ would be ungrammatical in that particular context:

/38/ li ti pe ale aswar al bril lakaz . . .

However, all realized complements in Baker's texts are marked with *al* or Ø, and all unrealized complements are marked with *pu* or *pu al*.
    These similarities, not previously pointed out in any published work, are particularly striking in that the structure looks like a highly marked one, being attested in few if any noncreole languages; and yet the identity is not merely semantic and syntactic; it extends even to the choice of lexical items—for *pu* derives from Fr. *pour* 'for', and Eng. *for* is the source for HCE *fo*, JC *fi*, SR *foe*,[7] while MC *al* 'go' and MC Ø parallel HCE *go*, JC *go*, and SR Ø. While it is conceivable that JC and SR might have some kind of genetic connection (although no historical or systematic linguistic evidence has been advanced), there is no possibility that either could have any connection with HCE, and it is, if that is possible, even less likely that there was ever any connection between these three and MC, which has a different superstrate *and* different substratum language. It is impossible to imagine any other

explanation than one based on the possession, by speakers in all four areas, of some quite specific program for language-building.

Relativization and Subject-Copying

In these areas there exist certain differences. Most creoles have relative pronouns, at least when the head-noun is also subject of the relative clause, but HCE does not. However, the time that most creoles have had to gain relative pronouns is little less than the time it took English to gain them in this position (Bever and Langendoen 1971). If creoles were indeed born without surface relativizers, then the same processing problems that Bever and Langendoen discuss would have applied to them, and there would have been a similar pressure to borrow or adapt some feature that would serve to avoid such problems.

However, any such speculation would be pure conjecture, if it were not for the fact that in a number of creoles there still exist conservative dialects or restricted sentence types in which relative pronouns are deletable in subject position—or rather, more probably, were never inserted. In GC, for instance, this can happen when the head-noun of the relative clause is the object of the higher sentence and when the main verb of that sentence is an equivalent of *have* or *be* (the regular GC relative pronoun is *we*):

/39/   wan a dem a di man bin get di bam
       'One of them was the man who had the bomb'
/40/   shi get wan grandaata bina main
       'She had a grand-daughter who was being looked after (by her)'

Corne (1977:38) gives some examples of relative clauses in SC where, also, the head-noun is object of the main clause, and where no relativizer is present on the surface:

/41/   i ana Bom Lulu i dâse deor
       PM there-is good-guy wolf PM dance outside
       'There is Old Wolf who is dancing outside'

/42/   zot truv sa pov drayver i âkor pe atâ mem
       they see the poor driver PM still ASP wait same
       'They see the poor driver who is *still* waiting'

Again, although in general the Portuguese creoles of the Bight of
Benin have relative pronouns, Valkoff (1966:97) reports a conservative dialect of Annobones which lacks them:

/43/   me mu gogo na-mina sa gavi
       mother my like PL-child be good
       'My mother likes the children who are good'

Thus, although there is no proof that creoles started without
relative pronouns, the possibility cannot be ruled out. Moreover, as we
shall see later, a rather indirect argument based on grammatical sim-
plicity points in the same direction.

From what we have already seen of movement rules, we would
not expect to find much similarity in the area of subject-copying. This,
at least initially, is some kind of focusing device, and we saw that other
creoles have means for focusing which employ other features. However,
there are at least two creoles, Crioulo (CR) and SC, which have a form *i*
that characteristically occurs between subject and predicate, but is also
the third person singular subject pronoun in both cases. Clearly, whatever function this form may originally have had, it has now become
obligatory in certain contexts; for instance, it serves to mark present
tense nonverbal predicates, i.e., it functions as a kind of copula:

/44/   CR: elis i amiigu
            they PM friend
            'They are friends'
/45/   CR: i amiigu
            he friend
            'He is a friend'

/46/   SC: lerua i bet
            king PM stupid
            'The king is stupid'
/47/   SC: i bet
            he stupid
            'He is stupid'

I shall not explore the meanings and functions of this particle since
Wilson (1962), practically the only source for CR, does not provide
adequate data, while at the other extreme, Corne (1974-75) and (1977)
presents masses of data on the SC form and shows that its complexities
will not yield easily to analysis. In any case, the principal point that
was made with regard to HCE was not specifically to do with either
relativization or subject-copying.

   We saw in Chapter 1 that when the subject of the higher clause
is also subject of the relative clause, the subject-copy pronoun follows
the relative clause rather than the subject noun, although elsewhere
it directly follows the subject noun—as *i* does in /46/, for example.
Now, in both CR and SC, in other words in the only two creoles in
which we could look for an analogue of the HCE structure (since they
are the only ones with anything like a subject copy), we find that in
subject-subject relative-clause sentences, *i* follows the relative clause
and not the noun subject, i.e., it also obeys the A-over-A principle
or its equivalent (examples from Wilson 1962:30; Corne 1977:53):

/48/   CR: ɔɔmi kə bay awɔnti i riba
            man who go yesterday PM return
            'The man who went yesterday has returned'
/49/   SC: sel abitâ ki mô kapab al trôp li i zis sa vie tôtô
            only farmer that I can go fool him PM just that old man
            'The only farmer that I can go and fool is just that old man'

   Moreover, these are not the only cases where the A-over-A
principle applies to creoles: the placement of HC articles in relative-

clause sentences is also affected. Normally, the HC definite article *la* immediately follows the noun: *chwal-la* 'the horse', *kaptên-na* 'the captain'. However, if the noun is head-noun of a relative clause, the definite article follows that clause, i.e., it is adjoined to the higher rather than the lower NP:

/50/ kaptên ki té-arété-l-la t-ap-mété-l nâ-bétiz
     captain who TNS-arrest-him-the TNS-ASP-put-him in-ridicule
     'The captain who had arrested him was making fun of him'
/51/ li voyé chwal yo pou-râplasé sila ki mouri-a
     he send horse PL for-replace that which die-the
     'He was sending the horses to replace the one which had died'

We have now surveyed the five areas which were discussed in Chapter 1 and found that in three of them (articles, TMA markers, and realized/unrealized complements) the "innovations" made by the original speakers of HCE were identical with the equivalent forms and meanings in all or most creoles, while in the remaining two there were broad, general similarities along with some differences in detail. It is worth noting that the similarities are most striking where a combination of semantic and syntactic factors interact; where purely syntactic rules are involved, as with movement rules and relativization, there is a lesser degree of identity. Why this should be so will be explained in Chapter 4, fn. 15.

I shall now, much more briefly, indicate some other areas in which strong creole resemblances can be found, before proceeding to a more thorough analysis of TMA systems and VP complementation.

Negation

In creoles generally, nondefinite subjects as well as nondefinite VP constituents must be negated, as well as the verb, in negative sentences. Examples are from GC and Papia Kristang (PK):

/52/ non dag na bait non kyat
  'No dog bit any cat'
/53/ ngka ng'koza nte mersimentu
  not no-thing not-have value
  'Nothing has any value'

Sentences of this kind do occur occasionally in HCE, e.g.:

/54/ nowan no kaen bit diz gaiz
  'No one can beat these guys'

However, while negated VP constituents are common, negated subjects with negative verb are rare, perhaps because of persecution in the schools.

Existential and Possessive

Over a wide range of creoles, the same lexical item is used to express existentials ("there is") and possessives ("have"), even though this is not true of any of the superstrates (it may be true of some substandard Portuguese dialects of Brazil, but these may well be de-creolized remains of an earlier creole). Examples are from GC, HC, PP, and São Tomense (ST), respectively:

/55/ dem *get* wan uman we *get* gyal-pikni
  'There is a woman who has a daughter'
/56/ *gê* you fâm ki *gê* you pitit-fi
  have one woman who have one child-daughter
  'There is a woman who has a daughter'
/57/ *tin* un muhe cu *tin* un yiu-muhe
  have a woman who have a child-woman
  'There is a woman who has a daughter'
/58/ *te* ua mwala ku *te* ua mina-mosa
  have a woman who have a child-girl
  'There is a woman who has a daughter'

HCE follows an identical pattern:

/59/ *get* wan wahini shi *get* wan data
      'There is a woman who has a daughter'

We will refer to this area again in Chapter 4.

Copula
      Practically all creoles show some similarities in this area. Adjectives are surface verbs in creoles (see next section) and therefore require no copula. Locatives are introduced by verbs which normally are limited to that role, i.e., do not extend to existential or prenominal environments. A split occurs over treatment of nominal complements: the more heavily superstrate-influenced creoles (HCE, the Indian Ocean creoles, some Asian Portuguese creoles) tend to have zero copulas here also, although in some (SC, CR) the *i* form appears here as a predicate marker; the less heavily superstrate-influenced creoles of the Caribbean generally have a distinct verb in these environments.
      There are minor exceptions to these generalizations. GC locative *de* can express existentials, which HCE *stei*, for example, cannot:

/60/ wok na de
      'There isn't any work'
/61/ *wok no stei
/62/ nomo wok
      'There isn't any work'

HCE and SC have negative existentials—*nomo* and *napa*—a feature found in few if any other creoles which, in the HCE case at least, represents an inheritance from the antecedent pidgin. The locative *ye* in HC appears only sentence-finally, i.e., where it is stressed, which, together with its phonetic shape, suggests that it disappeared from medial position through phonological reduction processes.

Although some of these differences may arise from pidgin retentions or post-creolization changes, it would seem that the copula area is only moderately specified. There is a general tendency toward semantic transparency, i.e., having separate forms for each semantically distinct copula function (attribution, with adjectives; equation or class membership, with predicate nominals; locative, with adverbials of place). However, since these semantic distinctions are unambiguously marked by predicate type, to mark them a second time with distinctive copulas may seem redundant, and perhaps this accounts for copula variability within individual creoles as well as across the class.

Adjectives as Verbs

In a number of creoles (e.g., JC, Bailey 1966; GC, Bickerton 1973) the adjective has been analyzed as forming a subcategory of stative verbs. Evidence from GC is the identical behavior of verbs and adjectives under a number of rules:

/63/ i wok
'He worked'
/64/ i wiiri
'He is tired'
/65/ i a wok
'He is working'
/66/ i a wiiri
'He is getting tired'
/67/ au i wok!
'How he works!'
/68/ au i wiiri!
'How tired he is!'
/69/ a wok i wok
'Work, that's what he did'
/70/ a wiiri i wiiri
'Tired, that's what he is'

Note that though syntactic rules apply identically, semantic interpretation is often different in the two cases.[8]

Originally, all writers on the Indian Ocean creoles who dealt with this area (Baker 1972; Corne 1973, 1977; Papen 1975, 1978; Bollée 1977; etc.) treated verbs and adjectives as distinct classes and posited an underlying copula before predicate adjectives, which was subsequently deleted. However, in an insightful article, Corne (1981) renounces his former analysis and sets up a class of "Verbals," which would contain predicate adjectives as well as verbs and which would not require a copula in underlying structure; these "verbals" would then undergo at least some (Corne seems hesitant to push his argument too hard) of the processes which verbs undergo. It is worth noting that some of the evidence Corne surveys bears a striking resemblance to that found in GC, in particular the "inchoative" meaning of the nonpunctual marker *pe* when applied to adjectives, as compared to the meaning of the GC nonpunctual marker *a* when similarly acquired; compare the following with /66/:

/71/ li pe malad
     he ASP sick
     'He is getting sick'
/72/ li pe â-koler
     'He is getting angry'
/73/ mô pe lafê
     'I am getting hungry'

This resemblance between creoles so widely separated in location and origin is quite striking. Moreover, I know of no creole where an alternative analysis of adjectives would be required. HCE, not surprisingly, has a similar "inchoative" sense when nonpunctual and adjective are conjoined:

/74/ ho, ai stei wail wid da meksikan gai
     'Wow, I was getting mad at the Mexican guy'

Questions

No creole shows any difference in syntactic structure between questions and statements. Question-particles, where they occur, are sentence-final and optional:

/75/ GC: i bai di eg-dem
         'He bought the eggs'
/76/ GC: i bai di eg-dem?
         'Did he buy the eggs?'
/77/ HC: yo pa-t-a-vlé mênê-m lakay-li
         they not-TNS-MOD-want take-me house-his
         'They wouldn't have wanted to take me to his house'
/78/ HC: yo pa-t-a-vlé mênê-m lakay-li?
         'Wouldn't they have wanted to take me to his house?'

Question Words

In WH-questions, the question-word is directly preposed to the declarative form of the sentence. The question-words themselves, if not clearly adapted from their superstrate equivalents, are always composed in the following manner: they are bimorphemic; the first morpheme is derived from a superstrate question-word—English creole *we, wi,* or *wa* from Eng. *which* or *what,* French creole *ki* from Fr. *qui* 'who' or *que* 'what', Portuguese creole *ke* from Pg. *que* 'what':

/79/ GC: wisaid yu bin de?
         which side you TNS be-LOC
         'Where have you been?'
/80/ HC: ki koté ou wè pwasô-a?
         what side you see fish-the
         'Where did you see the fish?'
/81/ ST: ke situ e pe mi n-e-e?
         what place he put maize in-it-QP
         'Where did he put the maize?'

Other forms in English creoles include Cameroons Creole *wetin*, lit., 'what thing', 'what'; GC *wa mek*, lit., 'what makes', 'why'.

Very often a creole has doublets, a superstrate adaptation and a bimorphemic creole form. Papen (1978:509) gives the following sets for SC and RC:

/82/ where = (i) *(a)kot(e)* (Fr. *à côté de* 'at')
               (ii) *ki ladrua* (Fr. **qui l'endroit*), 'Which place?'
                    ki bor (Fr. **qui bord*), 'Which edge?'
/83/ how   = (i) *koma* (Fr. *comment* 'how')
               (ii) *ki maner* (Fr. **qui maniere*), 'What way?'
/84/ why   = (i) *(l)akoz ki* (Fr. *la cause que* 'the reason that')
               (ii) *ki fer* (Fr. **qui faire*), 'What makes?'
/85/ when   = (i) *ka* (Fr. *quand* 'when')
               (ii) *ki ler* (Fr. **qui l'heure*), 'What hour?'

Papen does not state whether, in his estimation, one set is older or more creole than the other (failure to make any serious attempt to sort variants is a grave weakness in the otherwise thorough work done recently on Indian Ocean creoles), but we can be reasonably certain that the periphrastic forms represent the original creole; if the quasi-French forms existed already, why should others have been invented?

Since HPE speakers acquired the full set of English question-words except for *why* (HPE *wasamata*, lit., 'What's the matter?', which seems not to have been passed on to HCE), HCE was never required to develop a bimorphemic set. However, the similarities above are so close that we can predict that any creole which did not borrow directly from its superstrate would develop a set of forms along these lines.

Passive Equivalents

Passive constructions in creoles are extremely rare, and those that exist (the *wordu* and *ser* passives in PP, cf. Markey and Fodale 1980; the *gay* passive in MC and SC, cf. Corne 1977; and the *get* passive in

GC) are either marginal to the language or relatively recent superstrate borrowings, or both. The general pattern of creoles is described
by Markey and Fodale (1980) as "rampant lexical diathesis"; for any
V-transitive, N V N will be interpreted as "actor-action-patient," while
any N V will be interpreted as "patient-action":

/86/   GC: dem a ponish abi
            'They are making us suffer'
/87/   GC: abi a ponish
            'We are suffering/being made to suffer'
/88/   JC: dem plaan di tri
            'They planted the tree'
/89/   JC: di tri plaan
            'The tree was planted'
/90/   HCE: dei wen teik foa boad
              'They took four boards'
/91/   HCE: foa boad wen teik
              'Four boards were taken'

We shall return to structures of this type in Chapter 3.

    We have now surveyed seven areas of the grammar in addition to
the five already examined in greater depth. Of those seven, HCE shows
substantial identity with all other creoles in four (existential/possessive,
adjective as verb, questions, and passive equivalents); substantial identity with a number of other creoles in one (copula); and little similarity in two (negation, question-words). Thus, out of the twelve areas,
HCE is identical with all or with a large percentage of creoles in eight,
shows a fair degree of similarity in two, and differs sharply in two,
one of which (negation) may well have followed the regular creole
pattern before decreolization set in.

    This degree of identity is quite remarkable when we consider
that HCE shares none of the substratum languages of the other creoles—

except that a superstrate language for some creoles was a substrate language in HCE, i.e., Portuguese! However, there is nothing in the grammar of HCE except perhaps *stei* as locative that one can point to as having stemmed from Portuguese influence. The only thing HCE seems to have in common with other creoles (apart from the similar social conditions that gave birth to them) is that all have European superstrates, a fact which has been used to caution creolists against premature universalist claims (Reinecke 1977).[9] However, since practically all the common features of creoles are not only not shared by, but run dead counter to the structural tendencies of, Western European languages (the latter have well-established single copulas, well-established passives, use subject-verb or subject-auxiliary inversion in questions, etc.), no one could invoke this shared ancestry to explain creole similarities unless he were to propose that creoles, like naughty children, do everything the opposite of what their parents tell them to do!

However, an earlier work of mine (Bickerton 1974) that was limited to a discussion of TMA systems has been the subject of a number of criticisms, several to the effect that there were a number of exceptions to the generalizations made therein. I shall therefore deal with the issues raised in the most cogent and extensive of these criticisms, namely, Muysken (1981a), before going on to show that all the genuine divergences from the classic TMA pattern can be accounted for by the impingement on that pattern of three factors. Two of these factors are quite extraneous and have already been discussed: influence of the antecedent pidgin and language change. A third will have to wait until Chapter 4 for a full explanation; for the time being, let us call it "indeterminacy in semantic space."

Muysken challenges my analysis of creole TMA systems by evidence drawn from six languages: Papiamentu, Negerhollands, Senegal Kriol, Seychellois, Tok Pisin, and São Tomense. Data from two of these are quite irrelevant to the issues involved. Tok Pisin has already been ruled as having arisen under circumstances so vastly different from those of the classic creoles that the fact that it is now some people's native language—hence, nominally a creole—has no bearing on the present discussion. Senegal Kriol is described by Muysken himself as an "inter-tribal lingua franca which may have had native speakers in the past and which has some recent ones now in urban areas"; since he himself is forced to admit that this checkered history may have "given it a very marked, deviant character," one wonders why he should have bothered to present data from it.

Negerhollands is, or rather was, a genuine creole in the terms of this study, but there are at least two reasons why evidence drawn from it cannot stand up against evidence from languages which are still vital. First, the language is dead; one has to rely entirely on printed sources. This may not present a genuine obstacle to the writing of grammars of classical languages, but the case of creoles is quite different. If one takes the text of a Hittite law or a Sanskrit prayer, one can be reasonably certain that it was written by a native speaker; if one takes any text of Negerhollands, one can be certain that it was not written by a native speaker. As with virtually all other creoles, texts—whether they take the form of fact or fiction, catechism or simulated dialogue—were written by Europeans, with all the biases of their time and without any special linguistic skills or training. Many of the texts were written by missionaries, who are notorious for producing Europeanized varieties of pidgins and creoles wherever they go (Voorhoeve 1971). This is not to say that a European, even a European missionary, could not on occasion accurately represent a creole. The problem is knowing when a creole *is* being accurately represented.

For example, there is one excellent literary source for GC: Quow (1877). It is too excellent, if anything, because it gives several stylistic levels without the facts that might enable one to sort them out. There are also a number of other sources, of widely varying quality. If I had had to write a GC grammar from written sources only, there is no way that I could have learned to prefer Quow whenever he is in conflict with other evidence; that knowledge came from having four years of unrestricted access to native speakers.[10] Consequently, my work would have seriously misrepresented the language.

The second reason against using Negerhollands as evidence for any general creole tendency is that although languages, like people, die, they do not, like some people, drop dead. On the contrary, like Charles II, they are an unconscionable time a-dying, and since we know that in language death languages become severely distorted, but do not know at what time the process started, there is no way in which we can be certain what any text represents—whether the full flush of the language, the early onset of decrepitude, or the final phases of decay, in which key forms are lost or, worse, replaced by forms from competing languages and dialects. For these reasons, we can dismiss the third of Muysken's six languages.

This leaves PP, SC, and ST. Muysken does not state where he acquired the data from São Tomense. To the best of my knowledge, there are only two recent descriptions of the ST TMA system—Valkoff 1966 and Ferraz 1979—although perhaps one should say that there are three, since Valkoff gives two different ones in the same chapter. His account is a somewhat tortuous one, and the exact status of these two descriptions is far from clear; he seems to suggest that the first is in some sense hypothetical, though whether intended as a reconstruction of some earlier phase of ST, or of proto-Bight-of-Benin, is far from clear. Be that as it may, one of the two forms he specifically stars as hypothetical turns up as real in Muysken's account, while four forms that appear in his second description do not appear in the first. Ferraz mentions Valkoff's work but does not discuss it; nor does he explain why, or even note, that his own account differs substantively from either of Valkoff's. Finally, Muysken's account bears scant resemblance to any of the previous three.

In Table 2.1 on the following page, the various auxiliaries and combinations of auxiliaries claimed to occur in ST are arranged along the horizontal axis, and the four accounts (V_1 and V_2, Valkoff 1966; F, Ferraz 1979; M, Muysken 1981a) along the vertical. Pluses and minuses have the same values as in distinctive feature tables.

	ka	tava	ta	ska	kia	te	sa	bi	za
V_1	+	−	+	+	−	−	+	−	−
V_2	+	+	−	+	+	−	−	−	+
F	+	+	−	+	+	−	−	−	−
M	+	+	−	−	−	+	+	+	−

	tava ka	ta ka	sa ka	te di	ka bi	ka te
V_1	−	+	−	+	+	−
V_2	+	−	−	+	+	−
F	+	−	−	−	−	−
M	+	−	+	−	+	+

Table 2.1: Four accounts of the ST TMA system

In addition, Muysken's account suggests four more forms (*tava ka te, tava ka bi, sa ka te,* and *sa ka bi*) which are not attested anywhere else, although to do him justice this impression may merely result from a faulty formalism. Even making allowances for this, he attests four forms that the other sources do not attest, and he fails to attest two that both the other writers attest, as Table 2.1 shows.

If this picture seems confused, the reader had better not even attempt to follow the names which the various tenses, modes, and aspects are given by these three authors. I shall give a single example. The names of the *ka* + *V* form are given, respectively, as: incompletive aorist, Valkoff$_1$; habitual, Valkoff$_2$; aorist, Ferraz; incompletive, Muysken. This pattern is followed throughout. If a tense, mode, or aspect is mentioned in two accounts, it has two names; if in three, three names; if in four, four names. Sometimes the differences in name merely disguise the semantic similarities of the accounts; sometimes they mark real conflicts; sometimes it is impossible to tell. In one case where there is a clear similarity between Valkoff's and Ferraz's accounts, Muysken is clearly wrong. Valkoff calls *tava* + *V* "completive in the past," Ferraz calls it "pluperfect," but it is obvious from their example sentences that whatever it is (and it looks like the anterior of the present analysis), it is not a simple past—which is what Muysken says it is. Here, of course, the evidence of Ferraz and Valkoff supports the position that Muysken is attacking.

Muysken's analysis is supported by two example sentences. The original form of the analysis he is attempting to undermine, in Bickerton (1975:Chapter 2), is supported by ninety-eight example sentences. Further comment should be superfluous. Until someone is prepared to devote to the analysis of the ST system at least a fraction of the amount of careful work that went into the analysis of the GC system, we can dismiss the fourth of Muysken's six counterexemplary systems.

The two remaining systems, those of PP and SC, have TMA systems too widely known to undergo much distortion, although even here Muysken's account is unsatisfactory in several respects. However, since the features of these and other systems which differ from my predictions have been mentioned by other writers (see Hill 1979), I shall not comment further on Muysken's particular analysis, although I shall return to some broader aspects of his paper in Chapter 4.

The major and, if we were to eliminate sloppy scholarship, perhaps the only deviations from the regular creole TMA system are the following:

A) The presence in Crioulo of an anterior marker, *ba,* that follows rather than precedes the main verb.
B) The presence in Papiamentu of an irrealis marker, *lo,* that may occur before rather than after the subject.
C) The presence in certain creoles (e.g., Papiamentu, Palenquero, Papia Kristang, and Negerhollands) of tense markers that look more like +past than +anterior.
D) The presence in Indian Ocean creoles of two markers, *ti* and *(fi)n,* which compete for some kind of pastness, and two markers, *pu* and *a(va),* which compete for some kind of irrealis.

E) The merging of iteratives/habituals with either punctuals or
   irrealis, claimed to occur in a number of creoles (cf. Taylor
   1971), thus reducing the nonpunctual category to no more
   than a progressive/durative.

The first two deviations involve only syntactic aspects of TMA
systems, while the other three involve semantic aspects. It will be
convenient if we take (A) and (B) together since both arise from the
nature of antecedent pidgins.

Alleyne (1979), in arguing against the existence of a pidgin-creole
cycle, claims that no vestiges of pidgins can be found in creoles. This,
if true, would be unsurprising—as unsurprising as the fact that we find
no trace of the caterpillar in the butterfly, and for similar reasons. In
fact, the data now to be surveyed show some exceptions to the general
irrecoverability of pre-creole pidgins.

As is widely known (but see Labov [1971] for explicit discussion), pidgins express temporal relations by means of sentence adverbs,
in clause-external position, which indicate the temporal sequence of
events. HPE has two, *baimbai* 'then, later, afterward', and *pau* 'done,
already, finished':

/92/   bambai mi waif hapai, bambai wan lil boi kam
       'Then my wife got pregnant, and later a little boy was born'
/93/   pau wrk fraidei, go daun kauai
       'After work on Friday, we went down to Kauai'

Both *baimbai* and *pau* can occur clause-finally, although this is much
more frequently the case with *pau;* another speaker might well have
begun /93/ with *fraidei, hanahana pau* . . . 'On Friday, when work was
over . . .'.

If creoles were, as they are popularly supposed to be, no more
than "expansions" of pidgins, one would expect them to take markers
of this kind, transmute them into obligatory markers of tense, modality, or aspect (the "later" sequence-marker into a future or irrealis, the

"earlier" sequence-marker into a past, anterior, or completive), and incorporate them into an Aux category. But this development is the creole exception rather than the creole rule.

When HCE developed out of HPE, neither *pau* nor *baimbai* underwent any change of meaning, nor were they incorporated into Aux. Two quite different forms, *bin* and *go*, were selected to express anterior and irrealis, respectively. *Pau* and *baimbai* are retained as optional, clause-external adverbs, but their frequency in HCE drops dramatically compared with their frequency in HPE (in the set of recordings which most accurately reflect basilectal HCE, *bin* and *go* occur a total of 433 times, while *pau* and *baimbai* occur a total of 38 times; Bickerton 1977:Tables 3.1, 3.6, 3.9).

Good data on pidgins are even harder to come by than good data on creoles, and data of any kind on the antecedent pidgins of any creole but HCE are simply nonexistent; however, I still think that reconstruction is possible if we make the simple and reasonable assumption that other pidgins resembled HPE in taking their "later" marker from some temporal adverb and their "earlier" marker from some verb with the general meaning of *finish* (the meaning of *pau* in Hawaiian). We can then go on to show that while a majority of creoles decisively rejected "later" markers, most, if not all, accepted "earlier" markers with a marginal status, while some, at a later stage, allowed them, more or less grudgingly, to occupy positions within Aux. This is understandable since, if we are right, "earlier" markers have a verbal source, while "later" ones have a nonverbal source.

Most creole irrealis markers are derived from verbs or auxiliaries. English creole *go* is an obvious case; SR *sa* is usually (I am not sure if correctly) attributed to Eng. *shall*, JC *wi* to Eng. *will*. The form that underlies most French creole irrealis markers is Fr. *va* '(3rd pers. sing.) go', yielding *ava*, reduced to *a*. LAC *ke* and ST *ka* remain mysterious; for the latter, Ferraz (1979) suggests two possible sources—Bini *ya*, an irrealis marker, and Twi *ka* 'to be usual'—while another possible source is Pg. *ficar* 'remain'. Only a few Portuguese creoles show a different tendency, e.g., PK *logo*, derived from the adverbial Pg. *logo* 'next, soon' and reducible to *lo*. And *lo*, as we have seen, is the Papiamentu form which deviates from the regular model.

We will return to *lo* in a moment. First, let us look at the provenance of *ba*. Most creoles have an "earlier" form which is derived from a verb with the meaning 'finish'; in addition to *pau*, we find IOC *(fi)n* from Fr. *fini* 'finished (p. part.)', English creole *don* from another past participle, Eng. *done*, and Portuguese creole *(ka)ba* from Pg. *acabar* 'finish' (*kaba* is found in SR also). Looking over the range of creoles, it would seem that such markers can have three distinct distributions.

First, they may remain as marginal particles, occurring optionally in clause-final position. This state is exemplified by SR, in which *kaba* can only occur clause-finally and is never incorporated into Aux. The same is true of PP *caba*. In basilectal GC, *don* often occurs clause-finally (cf. Bickerton 1975:Examples 2.65-67).

Second, they may be incorporated into Aux but without its being possible to combine them with other Aux constituents. This state is exemplified by mesolectal GC *don* and possibly also JC and other Caribbean *don* and by HC *fin*.

Third, they may be incorporated into Aux where they may combine with other Aux constituents quite freely. This state is exemplified by Krio (KR) *don*, and IOC *(fi)n*, among others.

If we were working with a static-synchronic model, we would have to stop with this statement. However, since we have to work with a dynamic model in order to account for creole development, we can next propose that these three "states" in fact constitute stages in a diachronic development and exemplify a gradual process of incorporation which is well advanced in some creoles and has not begun in others. In order to prove that states in different languages show different stages of the same process, it is desirable to be able to point to languages in which two stages co-exist synchronically. Basilectal GC has both postclausal and preverbal *don*, the latter becoming obligatory in the mesolectal varieties; thus GC represents the transition between states one and two. Evidence for IOC is conflicting, but by at least some accounts, stages intermediate between noncombinability and free combinability (states two and three) are to be found there.

Crioulo *ba* clearly derives from *kaba,* which in accordance with its Portuguese etymon is stressed on the final syllable. Papiamentu *lo* equally clearly derives from Pg. *logo.* We can assume that in Portuguese pre-creole pidgins generally *logo* and *kaba* were, respectively, the "later" and "earlier" forms that corresponded to HPE *baimbai* and *pau.* Papiamentu retained both; Crioulo (as far as we can tell with present, inadequate data) retained only the second; and both PP *lo* and CR *ba* were incorporated *semantically* into the TMA system (i.e., were allotted the expected meanings of irrealis and anterior) while remaining *syntactically* outside it (i.e., retained clause-external position, obligatory in the case of *ba,* co-varying with subject type in the case of *lo*).

It is one thing to show that deviations (A) and (B) (p. 77) could have arisen from pidgin features; it is quite another to explain why in these two cases, but not in others, pidgin characteristics should have been able to override creole ones. However, we can make what is at least a very plausible conjecture.

The only other member of the pidgin-creole family in which pidgin sequence-markers have graduated to creole auxiliaries is Tok Pisin (TP). Here, "later"-marker *baimbai* reduced to *bai,* acquired irrealis meaning, and is in the process of being incorporated into the auxiliary by native speakers (Sankoff and Laberge 1974); "earlier"-marker *pinis* (from Eng. *finish*) has followed a similar course, except that it continues to occur only postverbally. I have consistently claimed that differences between TP and classic creoles would result from differences in their histories, in particular the period of several genera-tions which TP passed as a pidgin prior to creolization. Such a period would allow time for the original sequence-markers to become firmly established in the language and to take on more tense-like and modal-like meanings through the operations of natural change. By the time TP creolized, therefore, it had already developed a complex auxiliary system, without any of the catastrophic suddenness which, as we saw in Chapter 1, characterizes true creoles. The first creole generation in TP was therefore presented with a fait accompli; all it could do was accept the markers bequeathed to it and carry out some minor cosmetic operations on *baimbai,* phonologically reducing it and shifting it to a more "appropriate" position.

The gap between TP and true creoles is not, of course, an absolute one. Some of the features that distinguish TP (prolonged growth period, sustained bilingualism, etc.) could be shared to a lesser extent with some of the true creoles. In the case of Crioulo, evidence is flatly contradictory: "Crioulo . . . has no native speakers" (Alleyne 1979); "Crioulo . . . [is] the first language of many who are born and bred in the main towns" (Wilson 1962:vii). A plausible compromise would seem to be late creolization followed by the persistence of a small native-speaker core within a wide lingua-franca penumbra. Under such circumstances, a more gradual transition from pidgin to creole, with concomitant retention of more pidgin features, is certainly a possibility.

Curaçao, home of Papiamentu, might at first sight look very different from the Guinea of Crioulo—a Caribbean island where sustained bilingualism would have been impossible. However, Curaçao differs from most Caribbean islands in that it is extremely dry and infertile. For over a century, before the Dutch seized it, and indeed to some extent thereafter, it served as a staging post in the slave trade, a place where slaves were held and seasoned while awaiting transportation to other points in the Caribbean or Latin America. With a constant turnover in the population, and transients always heavily outnumbering the minority who remained, it may well be that a pidgin stage persisted here much longer than it did elsewhere in the Caribbean, or at least long enough for more pidgin features to establish themselves. Clearly, in both cases, more historical study is needed, but the hypothesis of somewhat delayed creolization would both explain the phenomena involved and accord with our present knowledge of social history.

Let us turn now to Deviation C (p. 77), the past versus anterior issue. In the first place, it must be made clear that GC, SR, and HC were generally claimed to have past-tense markers, prior to my reanalysis of their TMA systems (see, e.g., Hall [1953] for HC, Voorhoeve [1957] for SR, etc.). However, that reanalysis has not been seriously challenged.[11] It seems reasonable, therefore, to suppose that in a number of other creoles which I did not specifically examine, markers are still being described as "past" which in reality are +anterior.

Let us examine a language, Seychelles Creole, of which this claim is frequently made. According to Corne (1977:102), "the marker *ti* defines the past, both simple and habitual"; according to Bollée (1977:55), "*ti* expresses the past, definite or indefinite; it is comparable to the past tense in English." However, these confident and sweeping statements are immediately modified by both parties. Corne observes that "once past time has been established in a given situation, *ti* is frequently omitted," especially in narratives "where, after an initial use (or uses) of *ti*, much of the remainder of the story may be told with verb forms unmarked for Past (i.e., as a sort of 'historical present')." This "historical present" also crops up in Bollée's second thoughts. While, according to her, the zero or stem form of the verb "has the value of the French present tense"—the reader will note the Eurocentrism that unites these accounts—it also expresses the "historical present" which is "above all others the narrative tense . . . . After a brief introduction in the past, the rest of the story is told in the present." However, she immediately adds a second second thought: "The above is not quite correct; the past often reappears at the opening of a new paragraph."

Accounts of this nature inevitably arouse one's suspicions, especially as the First Law of Creole Studies states: "Every creolist's analysis can be directly contradicted by that creolist's own texts and citations." To demonstrate this law, I will analyze the middle portion of the second paragraph of the story *Sabotaz ai de ser* (Bollée 1977: 166):

/94/   *Biro leformasjo i* resevwar *e let sorta lafras,*
Bureau information PM receive a letter leaving France
avoje par e garso nome Msje Lezen ki ti ana *trat-a,*
sent by a fellow name M. Lezen who TNS have thirty years
ki ti ule *gaj portre e fij seselwas . . .*
who TNS want get portrait a girl Seychellois
Me kom sa zofisje ti kon *bje Msje ek Madam Lamur . . .*
but as the agent TNS know well M. and Mme. Lamur
alor i gaj *e konsiderasjo . . .*
then he take into consideration

'The Bureau of Information received a letter from France, sent
by someone called Mr. Lezen, who was thirty years old, and who
wanted to obtain a portrait of a Seychellois girl . . . . But as the
agent knew Mr. and Mrs. Lamur well . . . he took into consideration . . .'

Here, as in many other places in Bollée's texts, the narrative
switches from "historical present" into "past" and back again, right
in mid-paragraph. Even Bollée's final disclaimer, therefore, will not
work here. What is the explanation?

The alert reader will perhaps have noticed that the "historical
present" verbs that immediately precede and follow the switch into
"past" are both nonstatives—*resevwar* 'receive', *gaj(e)* 'obtain, take'—
while the three verbs marked with *ti* are all statives—*ana* 'have', *ule*
'want', and *kone* 'know'. If we refer back to the story openings that
both Corne and Bollée mention, we find that the verbs marked there by
ti are also statives. Folktales almost invariably begin with one or several
of these: "Once upon a time there *was* a girl . . . she *was called* such and
such . . . she *had* two sisters . . ." It is this simple coincidence that
has given rise to the hard-dying creole myth about "narrative tenses"
and "historical presents."

In fact, in systems which have the feature anterior, past-reference
nonstatives are unmarked, while past-reference statives receive anterior

marking (see Bickerton [1975:Chapter 2] for an explanation of why this is so). Thus, the distribution of *ti* and zero in SC texts follows exactly the same rule of anterior marking that affects stative and nonstative pasts in GC, HC, SR, etc.

Bollée and Corne cannot be blamed too heavily for this faulty analysis since SC is not a pure anterior system but one which underwent certain changes when the completive *(fi)n* was incorporated into Aux and permitted to combine with other markers. We shall see the consequences of this when we return to SC in the discussion of Deviation D.

However, there are creoles in which the presence of the category past cannot be attributed to faulty analyses. Papiamentu is perhaps the best attested of these so, pending adequate data on the few creoles that seem to resemble it, we may take the PP model as typical. I propose to claim that wherever this deviance is attested, it is the result of either heavy superstrate influence on the pidgin stage, or (more probable in the majority of cases) subsequent decreolization.

In the first place, in both HCE and GC, where decreolization phenomena are clear and well understood, the shift from anterior marking to past marking represents one of the earliest superstrate-influenced changes (Bickerton 1975, 1977). Even in Sranan, no longer in contact with its superstrate, a similar change is taking place at least among literate Sranan-Dutch bilinguals as can be seen if we compare the most recent texts with earlier ones in, e.g., Voorhoeve and Lichtveld (1976).

However, a problem arises in the case of languages for which, unlike GC or SR, no prior anterior stage is attested. Can we reconstruct such a stage from synchronic evidence?

There is a good likelihood that we can. In Bickerton (1980) I showed that we could differentiate between decreolization stages and natural changes: the former changed forms first and functions later; while the latter preserved old forms and gave them new functions. If the changes in PP are due to decreolization, and if there was an original anterior marker, then it follows that whatever is the past marker now could not have been the anterior marker then; in decreolization, instead of the original marker changing its function, a new marker is first adopted alongside of it, originally with an identical meaning (*did* alongside GC *bin*, *wen* alongside HCE *bin*), and then gradually changes its meaning to +past while the original anterior marker disappears or, if we are lucky, remains fossilized in some social or grammatical corner of the language. So, if we are both correct and lucky, we should be able to find in PP both a synchronic past marker and some vestige of the original anterior marker it displaced.

The PP past marker is *a*, presumably cognate with PQ *a*, PK *ya*— all of which most probably derive from Pg. *ja* 'already'. Adverbs, as we have seen, are not a good source for creole TMA markers. Anterior markers are most often recruited from a past copula form: Fr. *été* yielding French creole *ti*, *te*, etc.; Eng. *been* yielding English creole *bin*, *ben*, etc.; and Pg. *estava* yielding ST (and other Bight-of-Benin creole) *tava*. *Tava/taba* is therefore what one would predict as an anterior marker in the original stage of any Portuguese creole.

Taba is of course well attested for PP, and its distribution is most interesting. Unlike other auxiliaries, it cannot occur alone before a verb, but only in conjunction with nonpunctual *ta:*

/95/ *mi taba lesa
/96/ mi a lesa
      'I read (past)'
/97/ mi ta lesa
      'I am reading'
/98/ mi tabata lesa
      'I was reading'

The fusion of *taba* and *ta* clearly recalls GC *bina*, of similar meaning and origin (i.e., the conjunction of anterior and nonpunctual attested, I believe, for every creole without exception). If *a* had formed part of the original set of auxiliaries, whether with past or anterior meaning, we would have expected to find the form *ata* for past-progressive sentences such as /98/.

We may therefore propose the following scenario for Papia-mentu. Originally, it had *taba* anterior and *ta* nonpunctual, permitting the formation of *tabata* (it is hard to think of any other way in which this form could have been derived). Decreolization then began, via contact between PP and the Spanish of the Venezuelan mainland only a few miles away. Spanish *ya* could have been the model as easily as Pg. *ja;* indeed, for PP-Spanish bilinguals, *ya* and *ha,* the Spanish 3rd pers. perfective marker, could have easily reinforced one another to merge in *a.* The result of borrowing *a* as a past marker would have been to bring Papiamentu, phonologically as well as semantically, more in line with its prestigious neighbor. But by the time *a* entered the language, *tabata* would already have come to be perceived as a single unit (as its modern orthography suggests) and would thus have survived the subsequent disappearance of *taba.* Similarly, *ti pe,* an SC form of comparable meaning, was retained even when some anterior functions of *ti* were taken over by *(fi)n.*

A further argument for an original anterior-nonanterior distinc-tion in Papiamentu comes from the synchronic distribution of zero forms. For example, Goilo (1953:107) observes that stem forms express the present indicative for verbs such as *gusta* 'like', *quier* 'love', *jama* 'be called', etc.—i.e., statives—while all other verbs form the same tense with *ta.* It should be made quite clear that this is not a parallel to the English habitual-progressive distinction. In English, we can have *I write* as well as *I want,* and there exists the opposition *I write/I am writing.* Papiamentu presents quite a different picture:

/99/ mi quier esaquinan
     'I want these'
/100/ *mi ta quier esaquinan
/101/ *mi skirbi buki
/102/ mi ta skirbi buki
     'I write books/am writing a book'

If Papiamentu started life with a simple past-present opposition, expressed by *a* versus *ta*, then the fact that statives in the present cannot take *ta*, while nonstatives must, becomes merely a mysterious anomaly. However, if it began with an anterior-nonanterior opposition, the fact is well motivated. In all such systems, present-reference statives are unmarked (since by definition they cannot take nonpunctual marking), and present-reference nonstatives are obligatorily marked with the nonpunctual morpheme (since any event or action that is ongoing in the present must be either durative or part of a series, whereas, conversely, any punctual event or action must be over, i.e., in the past, by the time it can be referred to!). The distribution of zeros and nonpunctuals in PP is identical to that of synchronic SR or basilectal GC, except for one thing: in the latter, past punctuals, as well as present statives, are zero-marked (again, Bickerton [1975:Chapter 2] explains why this should be so). In Papiamentu, *a* has moved in to fill the "vacuum" created by zero-marked past-reference nonstatives, thereby bringing the PP TMA system closer to European models, but, again, as with *tabata*, leaving clear traces of the more creole system that must have existed at an earlier stage.[12]

We can now turn to Deviation D: the fact that MC and SC contain both *ti* and *(fi)n*, *a* and *pu*.

First, I shall have to comment on the state-of-the-art in Indian Ocean creoles. In MC and SC, and a fortiori in Réunion Creole, that state is perhaps best exemplified by the following pessimistic remarks of Corne (1977:94-95):

> A close study of SC preverbal markers has been made by Bollée, by Papen and by myself, and the results of our efforts do not always coincide . . . . The sociolinguistic background of our informants is to some extent different, and this alone is quite possibly the source of conflicting data. It seems likely that some speakers categorise given markers differently from other speakers.

Methods which make it possible, without invoking extralinguistic data, to systematically order and account for all variations in such systems were publicly presented by DeCamp in 1968 (DeCamp 1971), refined and extended by C.-J. Bailey (1973, etc.), and applied to the analysis of a seemingly far worse preverbal chaos in Bickerton (1975), after they had been proven effective in a number of other areas where creoles showed similar variation (Bickerton 1971, 1973a, 1973b, etc.). The bibliographies of Baker, Bollée, Corne, and other IOC scholars (Carayol and Chaudenson [1977] is a distinguished exception) betray no awareness of any of this work, which I suppose merely reflects the parochialism that afflicts the field. Given this methodological time lag, anything one says about IOC TMA systems must be treated as provisional.

Combinations of markers form the liveliest areas of dispute. According to Baker (1972) and Valdman (1980), *(fi)n* will combine only with *ti* in MC; according to Moorghen (1975), it will also combine with *a* and *pu*. According to Bollée (1977), *(fi)n* will combine with *a* and *pu* in SC, but not with *pe;* according to Corne (1977), *n pe* combinations are found, in addition to the others.

A dynamic analysis can easily reconcile all these apparent contradictions. It was suggested earlier that between the second stage of *(fi)n* incorporation—movement into Aux—and the third stage of *(fi)n* incorporation—free combinability with other preverbal markers—we would expect to find intermediate stages, and the data in the previous paragraph suggest just such stages, preserved synchronically in the Indian Ocean population either by different groups, or at different stylistic levels, or both. If those data are correct, it would appear that the combinability of *(fi)n* began with *ti* in SC, spread to MC, while in SC it extended also to *pu* and *a,* and (for at least some speakers) spread to *pu* and *a* in MC while it was extending to *pe* in SC—a classic demonstration of Baileyan wave theory.[13] This proposal is made all the more plausible by the fact that combinability proceeds from tense, the leftmost Aux constituent, to modal, the second leftmost, to aspect, the rightmost (which, perhaps coincidentally, perhaps not, is a conjunction of two members of the same class, *(fi)n* being a completive, therefore aspectual, and therefore, initially perhaps, being in the same slot as *pe* and thus barred from co-occurring with it).

We are now almost ready to consider what would have been the repercussions of an invasion by *(fi)n* of a classic creole system. First, however, we must note a particular characteristic of TMA systems which, though seemingly obvious, has been ignored by virtually all work up to and including Comrie's (1976) influential study of aspect. Meillet's famous observation that "language is a system in which every-thing keeps its place" has the corollary that if a new element intrudes, everything must shift its place somewhat; while the latter statement may not be true of languages considered as wholes, it is certainly true for tight little grammatical subsystems like those of TMA. A TMA system may be compared to a cake, a cake that is always the same size, for TMA systems, whether simple or complex, all have to cover the same semantic area: every verb has to have some tense, mood, aspect, or combination of these applied to it, for there are (pace some creolists) no such things as "TMA-neutral" sentences.

But a cake may be split up into five, or eight, or ten slices, just as a TMA system can divide its semantic area among five, or eight, or ten TMA markers and/or combinations of markers. If a cake is divided into five slices, while another identical to it is divided into eight slices, there is no way in which each of the slices in Cake A can contain exactly the same amount of material as each of the slices in Cake B. In other words, how much, and exactly what, is contained in each slice will be largely determined by the number of slices. This is exactly the state of affairs in TMA systems throughout language; what each marker of modality, tense, or aspect means will be largely determined by how many markers of these things there are in the system and by what each of the others mean. Facts such as these are, however, ignored by most scholars in the field, who strive to fit all phenomena into the same conceptual straitjacket, and who, when this fails, as fail it must, then seek, like Comrie, some kind of ideal type of the "Progressive" or the "Perfective."

The main point to be grasped here is that if you mark out a cake to be cut into *n* slices, then change your mind and decide to cut *n* + 1, you can only get your extra slice at the expense of one or more of the originals. Thus, if *(fi)n* were introduced as a ninth term into the classic eight-term creole system, it could only be accommodated by robbing the semantic domain of one or more existing markers.

Since *(fi)n* conjoined first with *ti*, it is not surprising that *ti* was its main victim. Admittedly, *ti* held its ground with statives, as we saw in /94/,[14] and in the nonpunctual *ti pe* structure; the picture with punctual nonstatives is more complex. To clarify it, we need to refine the concept of anterior, which we can provisionally define as "prior to the current focus of discourse." But current focus may be explicit (where the times of an earlier and later event are directly contrasted), or implicit (where the relationship between the earlier and later events is simply assumed), or there may be nothing prior to current focus. The situation will become clearer with the following examples:

/103/ Current focus, nothing prior:
      Eng.:   Bill has come/came to see you
      GC: Bil (don) kom fi sii yu
/104/ Prior event, current focus implicit:
      Eng.:   Bill came/*has/*had come to see you yesterday, too
      GC: Bil bin kom/*don kom/*kom fi sii yu yestide an aal
/105/ Prior event, current focus explicit:
      Eng.:   When I got here, Bill had come/*has come/*came
            already
      GC: wen mi riich, bil bin kom/*don kom/*kom aredi

In /104/ current focus is on the present, second visit of Bill implied by *too;* this, English can handle by one of the means available for /103/, but the anterior system of GC cannot. Example /104/ has to be treated exactly like /105/ in GC; /105/ must be treated differently from /104/ in English. This illustrates just one of the many differences between past-nonpast and anterior-nonanterior systems.

Corne (1977:107) has an illuminating minimal pair which shows that SC behaves much more like GC than like English on "current focus, nothing prior" cases like /106/ and "prior event, current focus implicit" cases like /108/; GC translations follow each example:

/106/ mô *n vin* isi pur eksplik . . .
       I COMP come here for explain
       'I have come here to explain (and I'm still here)'
/107/ GC: mi *(don) kom* ya fi ekspleen . . .
/108/ mô *ti vin* isi pur eksplik . . .
       'I came (on a previous occasion) to explain (and then went away again)'
/109/ mi *bin kom* ya fi ekspleen . . .

The implicit current focus is of course the speaker's most recent arrival, since he could not say *I came* unless he were here again.

However, when current focus is explicit, SC and GC part company (SC example from Corne [1977:108]):

/110/ letâ mô ti âtre dâ lasam, i *ti n fini* mâz sô banan[15]
       time I TNS enter in room, he TNS COMP finish eat his banana
       'When I entered the room, he had finished eating his banana'
/111/ wen mi kom iin di ruum, i *bin finish* (*bin don finish) nyam
       i banana

In other words, it is only where there is prior reference with explicit current focus—i.e., when two past events have to be explicitly ordered with respect to one another—that *ti n* encroaches on the domain of anterior *ti*. However, reference of this kind is probably the most perceptually obvious of anterior functions (certainly it is the easiest to teach in creole courses), and its loss to a completive cannot but serve to erode an anterior-based system and tilt it in the direction of a past-based system.

Anterior is further eroded once one begins to get *(ti) a n* and
(ti) pu n constructions. In the classic system, irrealis handles conditionals and there is no distinction between probable and improbable
conditions, so long as they are not counterfactual conditions:

/112/ GC: mi go tel am if mi sii am
        'I'll tell him if I see him' or 'I would tell him if I saw him'

Counterfactuals are expressed by a combination of anterior and irrealis:
anterior because current focus in such cases is always on the consequences of not having done whatever one didn't do; and irrealis because
the action or event in question is an imaginary one:

/113/ GC: if mi bin sii am mi bin go tel am
        'If I had seen him I would have told him'

    In SC, *ti a n* (and less commonly, *ti pu n*) naturally takes over
from a prior *ti a*, the "pastest" among conditions: counterfactuals such
as /113/, yielding sentences such as /114/ (example from Corne 1977:
109):

/114/ mô *ti a n* marie, si mô pa ti mizer
        I TNS MOD COMP marry, if I not TNS poor
        'I would have gotten married if I weren't poor'
/115/ GC: mi *bin go* mari if mi na bin puur

The result of this development is another change in the system. The
coming into existence of *ti a n* does not automatically remove the
former expression of counterfactuals, *ti a; ti a* remains in the language, and what remains in the language has to mean something.
The consequence of the *ti a n* invasion is therefore the shifting of *ti a*
one step down the hierarchy of conditions, from impossible to merely
improbable *(if X, I would Y)*—again, the example is from Corne (1977:
106):

/116/ si u ti aste lavian, i *ti a* mâze
   if you TNS buy meat, he TNS MOD eat
   'If you bought some meat, he would eat it'
/117/ GC: if yu bai miit, i *go* nyam am

A further erosion of anterior terrain is indicated by the structure of
the subordinate clauses in these examples. Note that the subordinate
clause in counterfactual /115/ requires anterior marking but that the
subordinate clause in the merely improbable /117/ does not; this is
classic anterior marking. However, the subordinate clauses in both
counterfactual /114/ and merely improbable /116/ are marked with *ti*,
presumably because subordinate clause marking is dragged down, so
to speak, by the shift of *ti a* main-clause marking from counterfactuals
to improbables.

In other words, once you turn a completive loose in a classic
creole TMA system, the only consequence must be a drastic remodeling
of that system. Some creoles (SR, basilectal GC, HC) have kept their
completives under control either by keeping them out of Aux altogether or by allowing them in but not letting them combine with
other auxiliaries. It is not coincidence that these creoles are ones
which have kept the classic TMA system virtually intact. On the other
hand, creoles that have let the completive have the run of the house—
such as SC, MC, and Krio—have, in consequence, had to change their
TMA systems to a point at which reconstruction of the original system
becomes quite difficult, although not—thanks to the careful work of
Corne and others—impossible.

The curious reader may well ask, "Why is it that some systems
have let loose their completives, while others have not?" I have no
answer to that, at present. Suffice it to say that doing so must remain
an option within any theory of linguistic change; if the option is taken,
certain results must follow, as night, day; if it is not, they will not.
It would be interesting to know why, but the fact that we do not can
in no way affect the validity of the foregoing analysis.

The other main divergence of IOC from the classic model is the presence of two "future" forms, *a* and *pu*. Several things are at issue here. One of them is why either form should be limited to future, rather than being a true irrealis. In fact, on the evidence of Corne (1977:103), *pu* retains conditional meaning, if only in subordinate clauses, and thus still covers a large part of the semantic area of irrealis:

/118/ i pa ti kone ki i *pu* fer
       he not TNS know what he MOD do
       'He didn't know what he would do'
/119/ GC: i na (bin) no wa i *go* du/wa *fu* du

The GC translation is instructive in several respects. First, the optionality of *bin* serves to underscore another characteristic of anterior as opposed to past marking. Expressions like *he didn't know* are ambiguous between 'he didn't know, but he knows now' and 'he didn't know then and he still doesn't know'. In the first reading, *bin* is obligatorily present since this reading represents another instance of prior event (or rather, prior state, in this case) with implicit current focus, i.e., upon the change in state of the person referred to. In the second reading, *bin* is obligatorily absent since the state of not knowing is a continuing one, and there is therefore nothing prior to refer to.

Second, we see again that the range of a true irrealis (GC *go*) parallels at least part of the range of an SC marker. But the third point is perhaps the most interesting. *He did not know what he would do* is semantically close to, if not quite synonymous with, *he did not know what to do*. The GC sentence *i na no wa fi du* more accurately translates the second of these sentences.

Fi (which often takes the form *fu*) derives from Eng. *for*, while *pu* derives from Fr. *pour* 'for'. *Fi* can also be a complementizer, as can *pu*. *Fi* can occur as an auxiliary in its own right:

/120/ mi fi go
       'I should/ought to go'

Note that *fi* is narrowly restricted to a meaning of obligation, while it is a verbal auxiliary. When it is a complementizer, however, it and its cognates in other creoles express irrealis meaning just as *pu* does, see examples /27/-/30/ and /35/-/37/ above.

Fi in general does not combine with other auxiliaries, but in GC it does occasionally occur with *bin*, and it is tempting to claim that it is starting to do just what *(fi)n* did in IOC, i.e., combine first of all with the anterior marker. Thus one can have GC /121/:

/121/ mi bin fu nak am
'I should have hit him' or 'I was about to hit him'

The construction is not common in GC, and native speakers are more or less evenly divided as to which gloss is the more appropriate.

Thus, in basilectal GC, with a classic TMA system, only a slight increase in the semantic range of *fi* and in the syntactic privileges of occurrence is needed for the situation to begin to approximate that of SC and MC. All we have to assume is that a process which is beginning in GC (and which must be latent in any creole since all creoles, presumably—the most drudgingly comprehensive grammars are all too often silent on this score—have an auxiliary of obligation which is ipso facto +irrealis) has been taken a stage or two further in IOC, languages which we already know have a predilection for expanding and complicating Aux.

The rest of the story is simple. As *pu* was graduating as a full-fledged competitor to the original irrealis *a*, *(fi)n* was distorting the classic system in such a way that the irrealis scope of both markers, *a* and *pu*, was losing some of its conditional functions and thus was getting closer to a simple future. In any case, when any two morphemes divide the semantic terrain of "future," it is a highly natural development that they should mark out their boundaries in some way, and that those boundaries, while often vague, should generally distinguish relatively likely from relatively unlikely events (cf. the discussion of *go* versus *gon*, HCE's first mesolectal replacement, Bickerton

[1977:23ff., 181ff.]). In fact, the IOC position is far from clear-cut, and MC and SC seem to have developed rather differently. According to Corne (p.c.), *pu* in MC marks a more definite future. In SC, on the other hand, the precise roles of *pu* and *a* are more vague, although the fact that only *pu* can occur in the scope of negation suggests that here, *pu* may be becoming the less definite of the two.

We have now seen how two very natural developments could have turned a classic creole TMA system into the kind of system we see in IOC today. IOC scholars will doubtless object that the account I have given is a purely conjectural one. That may be; but if it is conjectural, that is only because those scholars have not done the job of tracing the diachronic development of IOC through synchronic residues, as was done in Bickerton (1975) for GC. The most anyone can do who does not have direct and unlimited access to the IOC community is to show that similar developments have occurred or are occurring elsewhere in other creoles, which I have done. There is thus a prima facie case for the scenario outlined above; conclusive evidence can only come through the patient sifting of the highly variable data about which all IOC scholars have complained, but which none of them have yet exploited.

We can now turn to our final deviation—the split between habituals and progressives which, according to Taylor (1971), conflates the former with the "completive" (in the present terminology, zero-marked past punctuals) in JC and HC and with the "future" (in the present terminology, irrealis) in CR and ST. Again, as with anterior versus past marking, we must first ask ourselves if the data on which such claims are made are valid. Again, we must answer that at least sometimes they are not.

For example, Hall (1953:31) describes the HC aspect marker *ap(e)* as "indicating action which is continuing, not yet complete, or future"—in other words, *ap(e)* does not include habituals. This, if true, would indicate that the HC system is not a classic TMA system since in that system the nonpunctual category embraces both continuing and habitual actions. However, the First Law of Creole Studies enables us to find, in Hall's own texts, numerous sentences in which *ap(e)* marks habituals, past as well as nonpast:

/122/ sa k-*ap-fè* mâjé, *ap-fè* mâjé pou-apézé lwa yo
    that which-ASP-make eat, ASP-make eat for appease *loa* PL
    'Whatever they *used to give* it to eat, they *used to give* it to eat to
       appease the African gods'
/123/ tout gasô chak mèkrédi *ap-prâ* bou-t-makak yo
    all fellow each Wednesday ASP-take stick PL
    'Each Wednesday, all the fellows *take* their sticks'
/124/ tout moun sou-latè *ap-chaché* pou-yo viv avèk êtélijâs
    all person on-earth ASP-seek for-they live with intelligence
    'Everyone on earth *tries* to live with a head well filled (with
      knowledge)'

Although some claims may be disposed of in this way, there remains, as with anteriors, a residue of cases where genuine problems need to be resolved. In this particular case, a new factor enters the system: areas of relative indeterminacy in semantic space. In Chapter 4, where we will try to extract the very roots of semantics, it will become apparent that Deviation E represents an inherent point of weakness in the semantic infrastructure of the TMA system; we will see also that such points MUST exist if language is to change and develop. However, since a full account of Deviation E depends on a prior analysis of the nature of semantic space, it will have to be postponed until that chapter.

For the present, then, we can conclude that the bulk of so-called "counterexamples" to our analysis of creole TMA systems arises from one of the three following sources:

1) Inadequate data-gathering and/or acceptance of inaccurate data and/or faulty analysis of data.
2) A slightly longer than normal antecedent period of pidginization, allowing pidgin features to become fixed.

3) Linguistic change, internal or contact-stimulated, subsequent to creolization.

In one or two cases, (2) would distort the normal process of creolization, although we must note that only syntactic, and not semantic, aspects of that process are affected: PP *lo* and CR *ba* retain their predicted meanings, even though they do not assume their predicted place in sentence structure. Being a subsequent development, (3) cannot have any relevance to the process of creolization itself. As for (1), one can only hope that this will disappear as the field continues to develop.

Finally, I shall examine three types of complementation in creoles: complements of perception verbs; factive, nonfactive, and related complement structures; and "serial verb" structures. My aim in doing so will be twofold. First, as in the previous sections of this chapter, I shall seek to show that substantial identities of structure exist throughout creoles, even where these may be masked by ongoing change processes or other factors. But I also want to establish certain facts about the nature of creole syntax—facts which will assume a greater significance when we meet them again in Chapters 3 and 4.

In English, the complements of perception verbs consist of nonfinite sentences from which aspectual markers are excluded, and the subjects of which have undergone raising:[16]

/125/ I saw him leaving the building.
/126/ We can hear them play trombones.
/127/ *I saw he leaving the building.
/128/ *I saw him was leaving the building.
/129/ *We can hear them have played trombones.

While a superficially similar sentence, /130/, is grammatical, it does not contain a perception-verb complement, but a factive complement that has undergone complementizer deletion:

/130/ I saw he was leaving the building.
/131/ I saw *that* he was leaving the building.

In creoles, perception-verb complements are finite, can contain aspect markers, and have subjects which do not undergo raising:

/132/ GC: mi hia drom a nak
       I hear drum ASP beat
       'I heard drums beating'
/133/ GC: dem sii i kom
       'They saw him come'

Although one might be tempted to gloss /132/ as 'I heard *that* drums were beating'—along the lines of /130/—such a gloss would be incorrect; factive complements are introduced by the obligatory particle *se,* which we shall return to later:

/134/ GC: mi hia *se* drom a nak
       'I heard THAT drums were beating'

In /133/, the nominative case of the 3rd pers. sing. pronoun is obligatory; the accusative case is ungrammatical:

/135/ GC: *dem sii am kom

Free occurrence of nonpunctual-aspect *a* and the ungrammaticality of an accusative form such as would result from raising indicate that the embedded sentences in /132/ and /133/ are finite. At least two further arguments point in a similar direction.

     In English perception-verb complements, it is possible not merely to raise the subject of the embedded S, but also to delete it. Thus, alongside /136/ we can have /137/:

/136/ I heard Bill singing.

/137/ I heard singing.

GC will allow the equivalent of /136/, but not of /137/:

/138/ mi hia bil a sing
/139/ *mi hia a sing

It is characteristic of languages in general that while they may allow
zero subjects in nonfinites, they cannot freely delete subjects in finite
clauses, except of course under identity, which does not apply here.

A second argument involves the Propositional Island Constraint
(PIC) as proposed by Chomsky (1977). The PIC affects structure of the
form:

/140/ ... X ...$_\alpha$[... Y ...] ... X ...

and prevents any rule from moving a constituent from position Y to
either position X just in case α marks a finite clause. Let us assume that,
ignoring some nonrelevant details, the structure underlying both
/132/ and its English equivalent is something like /141/:[17]

/141/

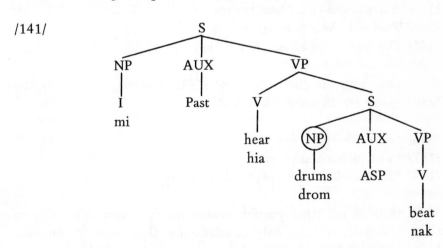

In the case of the English version of /132/, this would yield a derived structure something like /142/:

/142/

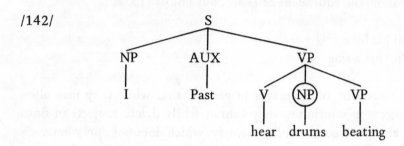

However, in the case of the GC version of /132/, /141/ would represent the superficial as well as the underlying structure.

If we have analyzed these sentences correctly, then it should be possible to extract from the circled node in /142/, since such a move does not violate the PIC, but impossible to extract from the circled node in /141/, which would constitute such a violation since the lower S dominates a finite clause. Extraction from /142/ is fine:

/143/ It was drums that I heard beating.
/144/ What did I hear beating?
/145/ The drums that I heard beating never stopped.

Extraction from the circled node of /141/, however, yields only sentences which are ungrammatical in GC:

/146/ *a drom mi hia a nak
/147/ *a wa mi hia a nak?
/148/ *di drom-dem we mi hia a nak neva stap

Since there is no other possible reason for the ungrammaticality of these sentences, we can only conclude that they are ungrammatical because they violate the PIC, and that therefore the embedded sentence in /132/ is a finite one.

Very few writers on creoles have discussed perception-verb complements specifically, and fewer still have even attempted to analyze them. Thus, the most that can be done at present is to point to a wide range of superficially similar structures and hope that scholars in the various regions will determine whether they show the same constraints on subject deletion and extraction as did the GC examples. Similar structures are found in other English creoles, such as Belize Creole (BC); in French creoles, such as HC and Guyanais (GU); and in Portuguese creoles like ST:

/149/ BC: i onli si di tar a flo:t ina di bailing wata
            'He only saw the tar floating (lit., tar was floating) in the
                boiling water'
/150/ GU: mo we li ka briga
            I see he ASP fight
            'I saw him fighting (lit., he was fighting)'
/151/ HC: li wè tèt Boukinèt ap-gadé li
            he see head Bouquinette ASP-watch him
            'He saw Bouquinette's head watching him (lit., head was
                watching)'
/152/ ST: e be i-ska landa
            he see I-ASP swim
            'He saw me swimming (lit., I was swimming)'

Before leaving perception-verb complements, we should note that there are also some similar constructions which are nonfinite in English but clearly finite in at least one English creole, GC; for example, causative imperatives:

/153/ mek i gowe
      'Make him leave'
/154/ *mek am gowe
/155/ na mek i na wok
      'Don't prevent him from working'

/156/ *na mek am na wok

Note the impossibility of clefting such sentences in GC:

/157/ I prevented him from working.
/158/ It was him that I prevented from working.
/159/ mi mek i na wok
/160/ *a i mi mek na wok

Example /160/ is so bad that it is almost unpronounceable. However, the restriction does not apply to clefting per se since the subject NP may undergo the process:

/161/ a mi mek i na wok
    'It was I who prevented him from working'

The fact that complements of perception and causation verbs appear to constitute finite sentences in creoles suggests the possibility that there might be no such thing as a nonfinite structure in these languages. In fact, I doubt whether there is any creole extant for which such an extreme statement would be true. However, there is a good deal of evidence which suggests that at their earliest stage of development creoles may not have had any nonfinite structures.

It should have become apparent by now that we are not going to get very far with the study of creoles—or of child language acquisition, or of language origins—if we allow ourselves to remain trapped within the static, antiprocessual framework which has dominated linguistics since de Saussure. The emergence of creole languages is a process; language acquisition is a process; the original growth and development of human language was assuredly a process. To apply to processes those methods expressly designed to handle static-synchronic systems is simply absurd; in order to do this, you have to pretend that a process is a state, and ignore exactly those characteristics that render it distinctive. Such a procedure is sometimes defended as an "idealization," cf. Chomsky and Halle (1968:Chapter 8), but the difference between "idealization" and "convenient fiction" seems not to be grasped by these authors. In fact, static generativism, the only kind we have had so far (although there is no a priori reason why there should not be a dynamic generativism), has ignored creoles, ignored language origins, and in the case of language acquisition—something it could hardly ignore since the mystery of language acquisition was what it was originally set up to explain—it has intervened with the sole result of turning off 90 percent of the workers in the field, as we shall see in the next chapter.

If we are going to call a spade a spade and a process a process, we need to make some basic assumptions. One is that previous changes in any language inevitably leave their footprints behind them (Givón 1971). Another is that diachronic changes must be directly reflected in synchronic variation (Weinreich, Labov and Herzog 1968; Bailey 1973; Bickerton 1975). Equipped with these, we shall examine other types of complementation in creoles to determine whether the current state of affairs in perception-verb and causative constructions may at one time have been that of all complement types.

First let us look at a set of sentences which might appear to contain complementizers. In GC, there are three forms that might be taken for complementizers: *se, go,* and *fu/fi.* We have already glanced at the second two in connection with the realized/nonrealized complement distinction. The first, *se,* introduces complements of verbs of reporting and "psychological" verbs:

/162/ i taak se i na si am
　　'He said that he didn't see it'
/163/ i tel mi se i na si am
　　'He told me that he didn't see it'
/164/ mi no se i na si am
　　'I know that he didn't see it'

Clearly, the complements that *se* introduces are finite Ss, just as are those introduced by Eng. *that*. However, it does not follow from this that *se* is a complementizer.

Doubt arises in the first place because *se*, unlike complementizers in general, is nondeletable. A sentence like *mi hia se i a kom* means 'I heard (that) he was coming'; *mi hia i a kom,* however, cannot be synonymous with this, but can only mean 'I heard him coming'. In other cases, such as *mi taak se i a kom* 'I said that he was coming', deletion yields only ungrammatical sentences: **mi taak i a kom.*

Further, there is the fact that *se*-clauses cannot be generated in subject position. In English, *that*-clauses can be generated in subject position and then undergo optional rightward movement by a rule of extraposition; thus, /165/ would be assumed to be closer to its underlying structure than /166/, derived from the same underlying structure via extraposition:

/165/ That John has left isn't true.
/166/ It isn't true that John has left.

However, a similar generalization could not be true for GC since while there is a grammatical equivalent for /166/, there is no grammatical equivalent for /165/:

/167/ *se jan gaan na tru
/168/ na tru se jan gaan

Not only can *se*-clauses not be generated in subject position, they cannot be moved to sentence-initial position by any rule. There is no creole passive that would turn *Everybody knows that he won* into *That he won is known by everyone.* Clefting and pseudoclefting will front simple NP objects of verbs like *no* 'know' but not *se*-clause objects:

/169/ mi no dis
     'I know this'

/170/ a dis mi no
    'It's this that I know'
/171/ dis a wa mi no
    'This is what I know'
/172/ mi no se dem gaan
    'I know that they've left'
/173/ *a se dem gaan mi no
/174/ *se dem gaan a wa mi no

True, neither clefting nor pseudoclefting works in English either, unless there is a head noun:

/175/ *It's that they've left that worries Bill.
/176/ It's the fact that they've left that worries Bill.

But English can front via topicalization:

/177/ I knew already that they'd left.
/178/ That they'd left I knew already.

GC cannot:

/179/ mi no aredi se dem gaan
/180/ *se dem gaan mi no aredi

    Now, it is true that this datum, taken in isolation, says nothing directly about the status of *se*. It merely suggests that *se*-clauses cannot be dominated by an NP node since if they were, they would presumably be eligible for movement rules that affect NPs and would also constitute possible expansions of subject NPs. If we assumed that *se*-clauses were generated under an $\overline{S}$ node which in turn was immediately dominated by VP (or S_0, if VP is not a constituent in GC grammar), all the above data would follow.
    However, there are some facts that suggest the possibility of

an alternative analysis. In English, there are pairs of sentences such as:

/181/ I'm glad *that they've left.*
/182/ *That they've left* makes me glad.

These sentences are perhaps slightly less than synonymous, and they certainly would not be regarded as transformationally related; since we have already established that *se*-clauses cannot be base-generated in subject position, it will come as no surprise that the GC equivalent of /181/ is grammatical, while the GC equivalent of /182/ is ungrammatical:

/183/ mi glad se dem gaan
/184/ *se dem gaan mek mi glad

Yet /185/ is grammatical:

/185/ dem gaan mek mi glad
       lit., 'They've left CAUSE I glad'

Example /185/ cannot be derived from /184/ by *se*-deletion since, as we saw, *se* does not delete. It could only be derived by embedding S under the subject NP node.

   Again, these facts, taken in isolation, might not seem to constitute evidence against the status of *se* as a complementizer. Since we have already suggested that *se*-clauses could be introduced under $\overline{S}$ not dominated by NP, all we need in order to accommodate /185/ is a rule that will expand NP as S, but not as $\overline{S}$. However, the picture would change somewhat if we could show one or both of two things:

   1) That GC required a rule NP → $\overline{S}$.
   2) That *se*-clauses could not be generated under $\overline{S}$.

In order to examine these possibilities, let us look at another quasi-complementizer, *fi/fu* (henceforth referred to as *fi,* for the sake of convenience, since *fi* is the more basilectal, if nowadays rarer, form).

In the GC lexicon, *fi* must be entered both as a preposition and as a modal auxiliary of obligation:

/186/ mi du am fi meri, na fi ayu
  'I did it for Mary, not for you (pl.)'
/187/ mi fi go tumara
  'I ought to go tomorrow'

However, there are also sentences such as:

/188/ mi waan fi go
  'I want to go'
/189/ mi waan i fi go
  'I want him to go'

In /188/, *fi* looks like a complementizer, more or less the equivalent of Eng. *to.* The likelihood that, unlike *se, fi* is a genuine complementizer is increased by the fact that *fi* in /188/ will delete without change of meaning:

/190/ mi waan go
  'I want to go'

Unfortunately, /189/ seems at first sight to suggest a quite different analysis. Complementizers normally precede the sentences they introduce, but /191/ is ungrammatical:

/191/ *mi waan fi i go

Complementizers may follow subjects of embedded sentences if raising (or whatever you believe in if you don't believe in raising) has taken place, as in *I want him to go;* however, as with perception-verb complements, a morpheme-for-morpheme translation of such sentences is ungrammatical:

/192/ *mi waan am fi go

However, *fi* in its /189/ location is nondeletable:

/193/ *mi waan i go

This contrasts with the status of *fi* in /188/, and suggests that while *fi* in /188/ is a complementizer, *fi* in /189/ is a modal auxiliary.

There would seem to be two possible analyses of /188/ and /189/. In the first, *fi* is really a modal auxiliary in both cases—in /189/ for the reasons already given, and in /188/ because /188/ is simply derived from /194/ by equi-deletion (obligatory since /194/ is ungrammatical without it):

/194/ *mi waan mi fi go

This first solution would be tempting but for /190/: modal auxiliaries do not normally delete without loss of meaning. We might then wish to choose the second analysis, which would derive /189/ from /195/ via obligatory complementizer deletion since without such deletion /195/ is simply ungrammatical:

/195/ *mi waan fi i fi go

However, there still lurks in the background the possibility that, despite /190/ and /195/, the prepositional role of *fi* might somehow be involved (cf. the claim by Koopman and Lefebvre [1981] that HC *pu*, a close relative of *fi* "can introduce final complements, either infinitival . . . or tensed").

To choose out of these three possibilities—complementizer, modal verb, preposition—we need to examine sentences in which constituents are extracted from *fi*-clauses. Let us look first of all at a sentence such as:

/196/ Where did he want to go?

This has the GC equivalent:

/197/ wisaid i waan fi go?

We should note also that sentences like /198/ have exact English equivalents:

/198/ wisaid i waan mi fi go?
      'Where did he want me to go?'

In all three sentences /196/-/198/, a constituent, WH-place, is moved out of an embedded S—in the case of /198/ presumably a tensed S.

If *fi* in /198/ is a modal verb, and no complementizer or preposition has been deleted, /198/ must have an underlying structure (ignoring irrelevant detail) something like /199/:

/199/

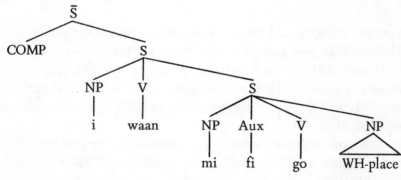

WH-movement would then move WH-place under the COMP node. However, such movement would violate the PIC, since it moves WH out of a tensed S. Similarly, if a deleted prepositional *fi* introduced *mi fi go* in /198/, the latter sentence would have an underlying structure something like /200/:

/200/

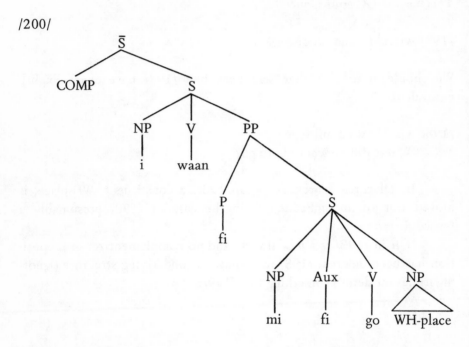

Example /200/ would involve a rule which would expand PP as either P NP or P S; just such a rule is proposed for HC by Koopman and Lefebvre (1981), on rather similar evidence, involving prepositional *pu* and its tensed complements. However, movement of the WH-constituent from the right-hand NP node to COMP would again involve violation of the PIC.

If, on the other hand, *fi* is a complementizer, no violation need ensue. In this case, the underlying structure of /198/ would be something like /201/:

/201/

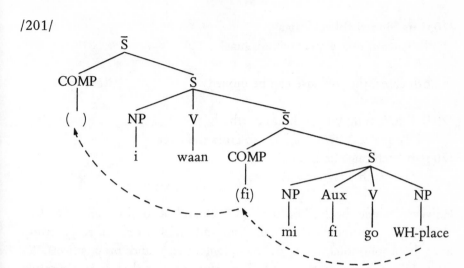

Complementizer deletion, optional in /188/, is, as we have seen, obligatory in /189/ and /198/. However, once *fi* is deleted, we have an
empty COMP node (the one dominating the *fi* in parentheses in /201/).
Chomsky (1977) has argued that WH-movement, being a cyclic rule,
can move constituents from COMP to COMP, thus forming a "bridge"
over the barrier of the PIC. In /201/—but not in /199/ or /200/—
there is a lower COMP node to which WH can be moved on the first
cycle, allowing the second cycle to move it to the higher COMP node,
as indicated by the dotted line in /201/. Thus, in contrast with /199/
and /200/, WH-movement in /201/ does not violate the PIC.

If the foregoing analysis is correct, GC does contain an $\bar{S}$ structure in some complements. However, there was no motivation in /201/
for assuming $\bar{S}$ to be dominated by NP, so we have yet to prove condition (1) (p. 108).

In order to prove condition (1), we need another set of *fi*-
sentences. Unlike perception-verb complements, which cannot have
zero subjects (*mi hia dem a sing* versus **mi hia a sing*), *fi*-clause complements can:

/202/ yu gafi kraas di riba fi miit tong
'You have to cross the river in order to get to town'

/203/ na bin iizi fi kech taiga
  'It wasn't easy to catch a jaguar'

In both cases, the *fi*-clause can be moved:

/204/ fi miit tong yu gafi kraas di riba
  'To get to town you have to cross the river'
/205/ fi kech taiga na bin iizi
  'To catch a jaguar wasn't easy'

However, since both Woolford (1979) and Koopman and Lefebvre (1981) give arguments that Tok Pisin and Haitian Creole, respectively, have homophonous pairs of complementizers and prepositions (TP *long,* HC *pu*), we cannot automatically assume that *fi* is a complementizer in /202/-/205/ just because it was in /198/. To show this, we have to question the NP in /203/:

/206/ a wa na bin iizi fi kech?
  'What was it that wasn't easy to catch?'

If *fi* were a preposition in /203/, /203/ and /206/ would have the underlying structure of /200/; but we saw in our analysis of /200/ that if WH-movement were applied to that structure, a violation of the PIC would result. To avoid such violation, *fi* would have to be a complementizer, and /203/ and /206/ would have to have the underlying structure of /201/. Since /206/ is grammatical, *fi* must be a complementizer.

    If this is the case, /205/ must contain an $\overline{S}$ directly dominated by NP, as in /207/:

/207/

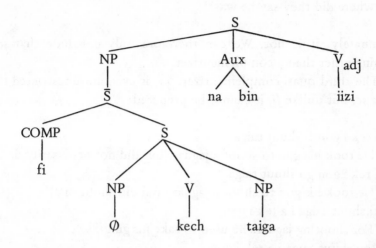

Thus, the exclusion of *se*-clauses from subject position, which we noted in discussing /184/ above, cannot be due to the absence of a rule rewriting NP as S̄ (COMP S). The ungrammaticality of /184/ must, therefore, result from the fact that *se* is not a complementizer, and consequently cannot be inserted in structures such as /207/.

We can now turn to condition (2) (p. 108). The fact that *se* cannot be a complementizer, suggested by the foregoing analysis, would of course also make it impossible for *se*-clauses to be generated in S̄ complements. But let us assume for the moment that *se* is a complementizer. If this were so, a sentence such as /208/ below would have a structure similar to that of /201/:

/208/ dem taak se i de a tong
 'They said that he was in town'

In other words, the complement S̄ would contain a COMP node which would permit COMP-to-COMP WH-movement and hence permit questioning of the rightmost NP. We would then have to predict that /209/ would be grammatical:

/209/ *wisaid dem taak se i de?
      'Where did they say he was?'

Unfortunately, it is not. We can therefore only conclude that *se* is
something other than a complementizer.

The third quasi-complementizer, *go*, is even more restricted than
se. Like *se*, but unlike *fi*, it cannot be preposed:

/210/ i tek i gon fi shuut taiga
      'He took his gun to shoot a jaguar (but did not necessarily do so)'
/211/ i tek i gon go shuut taiga
      'He took his gun to shoot a jaguar (and did shoot one)'
/212/ fi shuut taiga i a tek i gon
      'For shooting jaguars he used to take his gun'[18]
/213/ *go shuut taiga i a tek i gon

Unlike both *fi* and *se*, *go* cannot occur with adjectival verbs:

/214/ mi glad fi sii yu
      'I'm glad to see you'
/215/ mi glad se yu kom
      'I'm glad you came'
/216/ *mi glad go sii yu

As with *se* (but not *fi*), complement constituents cannot be extracted:

/217/ i gaan a tong go sii dakta
      'He's gone to town to see the doctor'
/218/ *a hu i gaan a tong go sii?
      'Who did he go to town to see?'
/219/ *di dakta we i gaan a tong go sii de bad an aal
      'The doctor he went to town to see is sick too'

We can assume, as with *se*, that extraction is blocked because COMP-to-

COMP movement is impossible; therefore, *go* is not a complementizer either.

The claim that *se* is a serial verb in Krio has been argued strongly by Larimore (1976), but since there are some minor differences between the grammars of Krio and GC, not all her arguments apply to the latter language. I shall assume without further argument that *se* and *go* are both serial verbs. If this assumption is correct, then *se* and *go*, if not *fi*, really belong with the verbs that we will discuss in the next section on serialization. But because *fi* may be a complementizer synchronically, it by no means necessarily follows that *fi* always was a complementizer.

Washabaugh (1979:Example 9) cites the following sentence:[19]

/220/ ah waan di rien kom fi ah don go huoam
       'I want the rain to come so that I won't have to go home'

This sentence, from Providence Island Creole (PIC), a variety similar in many ways to GC, is of a type claimed by Washabaugh to be "rare in most contemporary varieties of [Caribbean English creoles], but . . . frequent enough in older texts." Washabaugh does not analyze this sentence, so we do not know whether the following sentence would be rejected by Providence Islanders:

/221/ ?wisaid ah waan di rien kom fi ah don go?

It would almost certainly be rejected by speakers of other Caribbean English creoles.

The most likely structure of /220/ would be one similar to that of /185/, reproduced here for convenience:

   dem gaan mek mi glad

That structure is illustrated in /222/:

/222/

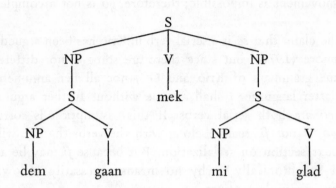

Here, *mek* functions rather like the abstract verb CAUSE once posited by generative semanticists. In /220/, *fi* would have a meaning something like SHOULD CAUSE, with *di rien kom* as its subject and *ah don go huoam* as its object.

On present evidence we cannot determine for sure whether *fi* was once exclusively a serial verb. However, it seems reasonable to suppose that in GC and other creoles, serial verbs may be turning into complementizers. Such a process certainly exists in some West African languages (Lord 1976), and we shall shortly examine evidence from Sranan which indicates that serial verbs there may be undergoing a rather similar kind of reanalysis.

The boundaries of serial verb constructions are not easy to define, nor is it easy (or perhaps even desirable) to distinguish them from other superficially similar constructions such as "verb chains" (Forman 1972). Here, I shall simply concern myself with those serial constructions which are equivalent to multi-case sentences, i.e., which mark oblique cases (dative, instrumental, etc.) with verbs rather than with prepositions or with other types of formal devices. Examples of such structures would include:

/223/ Directionals:

      SR: a *waka go* a wosu
           he walk go to house
           'He walked home'

/224/ Benefactives:
    GU: li *pote* sa *bay* mo
       he bring that give me
       'He brought that for me'
/225/ Datives:
    ST: e *fa da* ine
       he talk give them
       'He talked to them'
/226/ Instrumentals:
    Djuka (DJ): a *teke* nefi *koti* a meti
            he take knife cut the meat
            'He cut the meat with a knife'

Sentences such as /223/-/226/ are by no means always the only ways in which those creoles that have them can express case relations. Alongside /226/, Djuka has /227/:

/227/ a koti a meti anga nefi
    he cut the meat with knife
    'He cut the meat with a knife'

According to Huttar (1975), sentences like /227/ occur more frequently in speech than sentences like /226/.

Which of such pairs represents the most conservative creole level? Serial verbs form a more marked means of expressing case relations than do prepositions. It is, therefore, relatively unlikely that a language which already had prepositions to mark case would develop serial verbs (except in certain circumstances which could hardly apply to creoles and which will be discussed later). On the other hand, it is relatively likely that a language which originally had only serial verbs as a case-marking device would subsequently develop prepositions, either by a type of reanalysis already attested for West African languages (Lord 1976), or by direct borrowing from a high-prestige language with which it was in contact (probably the case in any creole that has undergone even a relatively small amount of decreolization). We are therefore justified in assuming that serial verb constructions represent extremely conservative varieties of those creoles in which they are found.

Serial verbs are usually interpreted as the result of African substratum influence on creoles, but creolists seldom if ever ask how those West African languages which have serial verbs (by no means all of them) happen to have come by them. Despite lip service to linguistic equality, a dual standard is still applied to creoles: if a creole has a feature, it must have borrowed it; but if a noncreole language has the same feature, it is assumed to be an independent innovation— at least in the absence of clear evidence to the contrary. In fact, I would claim that creoles and West African languages invented verb serialization independently, but for slightly different reasons.

Wherever serial verbs are found outside creoles, a change in word order is always involved (see Li and Thompson [1974] for Chinese; Givón [1974] and Hyman [1974] for West African languages; Bradshaw [1979] for Austronesian languages in New Guinea). Sometimes the change may be contact-influenced, as in New Guinea; sometimes it may come from purely language-internal developments, as with the Kwa languages of West Africa. Precise explanations of why SOV-SVO (West Africa) or SVO-SOV (New Guinea) changes involve serialization are still controversial. Givón (1974) suggests that serialization results from the decay of postpositional case marking, an explanation challenged by Hyman (1974); Bradshaw (1979) suggests serialization eases parsing problems in a period of transition by generating sentences that can be parsed as either SVO or SOV without any semantic confusion (we shall return to this point at the end of Chapter 4). However, there seems to be no serious ground for doubting that serialization and word-order change are involved with one another in some kind of way.

Word-order change cannot have been a factor in creolization since most of the languages in contact, as well as the resultant creoles, have been SVO. However, the problem that word-order change creates—

that of unambiguously identifying case roles while the change is under way—must have been a problem in creolization too, if we assume what must almost certainly have been the case in at least some pidgins, i.e., that the latter did not contain (or at least did not contain a full range of) prepositions. Without prepositions and without inflectional morphology, how else could oblique cases be distinguished if not by serial verbs?

More specific doubts about the viability of substratal accounts, as well as the seeds of an explanation as to why creoles differ so much in the extent to which they exhibit serialization, are suggested by the following data on the Surinam creoles (Djuka, Sranan, Saramaccan). In these languages, instrumental constructions (as expressed via equivalents of 'He cut the meat with a knife') have the following range:

/228/ DJ: a koti a meti anga nefi
/229/ SR: a koti a meti nanga nefi
/230/ SA: a koti di gbamba ku faka
/231/ DJ: a teke nefi koti a meti
/232/ SR: a teki nefi koti a meti
/233/ SA: ?a tei faka koti di gbamba

A sentence similar to /233/—*a tei di pau naki en,* lit., 'He took the stick hit it', i.e., 'He hit it with the stick'—is cited in Grimes and Glock (1970) but footnoted to the effect that the authors have since become highly doubtful as to its status in SA. In Glock (1972), which deals explicitly with case phenomena, there is no mention of sentences like /233/, although sentences like /230/, as well as serialization of other cases, are cited and discussed; nor is SA credited with *tei*-serialization in Jansen, Koopman and Muysken (1978), although, again, there is no explicit discussion. It is thus impossible to tell whether Saramaccan has this kind of serialization, although the present balance of evidence seems to be against it.

Saramaccan is well known as being, among the three Surinam creoles (or, for that matter, among all the Caribbean creoles), the one which best preserves African lexical and phonological characteristics (note, in the preceding examples, *gbamba* 'meat', a word of presumably African origin which preserves the coarticulated and prenasalized stops characteristic of many West African languages but of no other creoles, compared with DJ and SR *meti* from Eng. *meat*). This being so, and if serial constructions also reflect African influence, one would expect to find that SA had more of such constructions than DJ and SR, rather than the reverse.

But while there is no explanation for the pattern in terms of substrate influence, an explanation can be provided in terms of interaction between the antecedent pidgin and its superstrate. It seems reasonable to assume that if a creole can acquire prepositions from its antecedent pidgin (as HCE did), it will not need to develop serial verbs for case marking. The only question is, why should some antecedent pidgins acquire prepositions while others do not?

Clearly, one factor is population balance, while another factor is the type of social structure; between them, these will determine the accessibility of the superstrate language and hence help to determine how many superstrate items the pidgin will absorb. However, these are by no means the only factors involved. Other things, including social conditions, being equal, structural differences between superstrate features may determine whether a pidgin will or will not absorb these features.

For a superstrate feature to be accessible to a pidgin, that feature must be more or less unambiguous with respect to meaning, more or less free from mutation with respect to phonological structure, and as close as possible to the canonical form of CV(CV). The superstrate prepositions of instrumentality available to the three languages were: for SR and DJ, Eng. *with;* for SA, Eng. *with* and Pg. *com*—phonetically, [kõ] or [kū] in many contemporary dialects. The former, with its initial semivowel (a marked segment) and final labiodental fricative (an extremely marked segment), is remote from the canonical pattern; the latter, in the form in which it is perhaps most frequently realized, fits it exactly. The relative difficulty of acquiring *com* and *with* may best be pictured if the reader imagines that his linguistic competence is limited to African languages and then attempts to segment the following synonymous utterances:

/234/ vai com aquele homem
/235/ go with that man

Word boundaries in the Portuguese utterance are fairly un-ambiguously marked; in the English one, it would be hard to determine where the verb ended and the preposition began, or where the preposition ended and the demonstrative began—or even to be sure that there was a preposition there at all. It is hardly surprising, therefore, that neither Sranan nor Djuka could absorb *with,* but had to adopt a serializing device in order to express instrumentality, and that only later did they develop their own preposition, *(n)anga,* of uncertain origin; whereas, on the other hand, Saramaccan, like all Portuguese creoles, easily acquired *ku* and thus did not need a serial construction for instrumentality.

The underlying structure of serial-verb constructions has been a subject of some controversy (see Williams [1971, 1975], Roberts [1975], Voorhoeve [1975], Jansen, Koopman and Muysken [1978] for some differing views on this subject). I suspect that varying analyses are due at least in part to inherent conflicts in the data, and that these conflicts, in turn, are due to ongoing developments in creoles which have the result of complicating the original creole syntax and introducing categories which formed no part of the original grammar. If we are to understand what creoles are, and make comparisons between particular creoles without allowing ourselves to be misled by subsequent and irrelevant accretions, we must—to cite the words of Koopman and Lefebvre, on which I could not hope to improve—"restrict the notion of syntactic expansion to changes leading to the acquisition of features that are part of core grammar up to the time of creolization and to consider the emergence of other features as regular cases of syntactic change" (Koopman and Lefebvre 1981:218).

Koopman and Lefebvre assume, as I do, that pidgins begin with nouns, verbs, and very little else. They assume that VP is a pidgin category, but do not defend it as such. For reasons given in the discussion of GC movement rules above, I do not think VP is a category in most early creoles, although of course creoles may acquire it later, either through decreolization or regular syntactic change (reanalysis). The only rule creoles would then require to generate any of the complement types, serial or other, discussed so far (with the exception of *fi*-clauses) would be /236/:

/236/ S → NP Aux V (NP) (S)

If in fact VPs were developed initially, two rules would be required:

/237/ S → NP Aux VP
/238/ VP → V (NP) (S)

Not a great deal depends on which analysis is correct; therefore, since crucial evidence will be taken from Sranan, and since Sranan scholars generally assume a VP (although, once again, without explicit discussion), I shall accept /237/ and /238/ as specifying the earliest and most basic level of creole syntax, while continuing to suspect that /236/ may be a more accurate representation of it.

The evidence consists of judgments by native speakers of Sranan cited in Jansen, Koopman and Muysken (1978). The parenthesized asterisks before certain sentences indicate that while some speakers found them grammatical, others did not.

/239/ Kofi teki a nefi koti a brede
       'Kofi cut the bread with the knife'
/240/ san Kofi teki koti a brede?
       'What did Kofi cut the bread with?'
/241/ (*) san Kofi teki a nefi koti?
       'What did Kofi cut with the knife?'
/242/ na a nefi Kofi teki koti a brede
       'It was the knife that Kofi cut the bread with'

/243/ (*) na a brede Kofi teki a nefi koti
   'It was the bread that Kofi cut with the knife'
/244/ na teki Kofi teki a nefi koti a brede
   '*With* the knife, that's how Kofi cut the bread'
/245/ (*) na koti Kofi teki a nefi koti a brede
   '*Cut* it, that's what Kofi did to the bread with the knife'

In /241/ and /243/, some speakers can extract the most deeply embedded NP, while others cannot. In /244/, a rule similar to the GC verb-
focusing rule copies the higher of the two verbs, for all speakers;
but in /245/, while some speakers can copy the more deeply embedded
verb, others cannot.

   These facts can be accounted for if we assume that the two
sets of speakers have different types of underlying structures for these
sentences, as represented in /246/ and /247/, respectively:

/246/

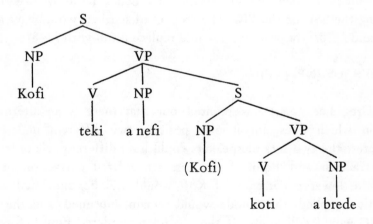

/247/

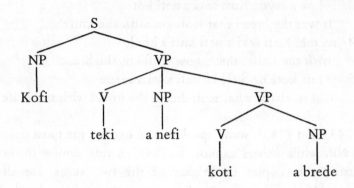

Speakers who rejected /241/, /243/, and /245/ would have /246/ as an underlying structure. Here, both the Specified Subject Condition (SSC: Chomsky 1973) and the PIC would block movement out of sites dominated by the lower S. Speakers who accepted these three sentences would have /247/ as an underlying structure. Since /247/ contains no tensed S, specified subject, or bounding nodes that would block extraction, all constituents could be moved without violating the SSC or the PIC. The first set of speakers would have rules /237/ and /238/; the second set would replace /238/ with /248/:

/248/ VP → V (NP) (VP)

Greg Lee (p.c.) has pointed out that there is an alternative solution which does not involve positing two different underlying structures: the two sets of speakers could have different rule orderings for extraction and Equi. If the first set ordered extraction before Equi, the lower occurrence of *Kofi* would still be undeleted when extraction applied, the S-node would remain unpruned, and the SSC and PIC would still apply. If the second set ordered Equi before extraction, the offending S-node would be pruned to give /247/ as a derived structure, and no constraints would then inhibit movement.

This is true, but it means that both sets of speakers would then have the more primitive phrase-structure rules—/237/ and /238/—that would yield /246/ as the underlying structure for /239/. I shall show in a moment that even if speakers did not have underlying structures like /247/ for serial *teki* sentences, they would require them for other types of serial-verb constructions. In any case, I know of no evidence that would point to differences in rule ordering among Sranan speakers; indeed, it is very hard, in creole grammars, to find any clear cases in which rule ordering is crucial.

A second set of native-speaker judgments concerns Sranan directional constructions, for example /223/, repeated here for convenience as /249/:

/249/ a waka go a wosu
     he walk go to house
     'He walked home'

Here, in contrast with the previous examples, there are no disagreements; either verb can be fronted by the same verb-focusing rule that led to disputes over the status of /245/;

/250/ na waka a waka go a wosu
     'He *walked* to the house (rather than ran to it)'
/251/ na go a waka go a wosu
     'He walked *to* the house (rather than away from it)'

Thus there is no possibility that speakers could assign to /249/ a structural description like that of /246/, where the existence of a tensed S would prohibit extraction of the lower verb; rather, /249/ must have a structure similar to /247/, as illustrated in /252/ on the following page:

/252/

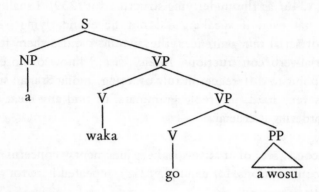

Finally, Sranan speakers disagree again over sentences involving datives and benefactives expressed with *gi*, which has an independent existence as a main verb with the meaning 'give'. Differences may be illustrated by the following sentences:

/253/ Meri tek watra gi den plantjes
      Mary take water give the plants
      'Mary brought water for the plants'
/254/ gi san Meri tek watra?
      'What did Mary bring water for?'
/255/ (*) san Meri teki watra gi?
      'What did Mary bring water for?'
/256/ Meri teki a buku gi mi
      'Mary gave me the book'
/257/ (*) na mi Meri teki a buku gi
      'It was me Mary gave the book to'
/258/ (*) na gi Meri teki a buku gi mi
      'Mary *gave* the book to me'

Sranan does not strand prepositions. For those who find /255/ and /257/ ungrammatical, *gi* must be a preposition, and they must have, instead of /248/, the rule /259/:

/259/ VP → V (NP) (PP)

For those who find the two sentences grammatical, *gi* must be a verb, and such speakers must have rule /248/. The verb-focusing rule that applies in /258/ cannot front prepositions, so, again, those who find /258/ ungrammatical must consider *gi* as a preposition, while those who find it grammatical must consider *gi* a verb. Differences of this kind are only comprehensible if the set of speakers who find all three sentences grammatical assigns to /253/ and /256/ a structure similar to /252/, with VP expanded as in /260/ below; while the set of speakers who find all three sentences ungrammatical (and therefore regard *gi* as a preposition) analyzes the same VP as in /261/ below:

/260/

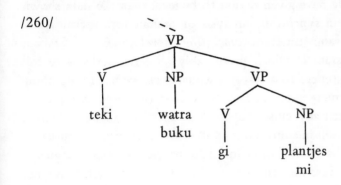

/261/

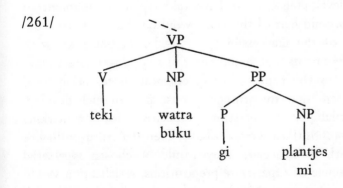

In other words, there are three distinct ways in which Sranan speakers analyze serial-verb constructions:

/262/ VP → . . . . (S)
    (some speakers for *teki* instrumentals)
    VP → . . . . (VP)
    (some speakers for *teki* instrumentals; all speakers for *go* directionals; some speakers for *gi* dative/benefactives)
    VP → . . . . (PP)
    (some speakers for *gi* dative/benefactives)

If the first of these stages represents the most primitive level of creole development, as we have given reason to believe, then the data shown here, drawn from a *synchronic* analysis of Sranan verb serialization, represent at the same time the *diachronic development* of Sranan, from an original state in which presumably all serial verbs were full verbs in tensed sentences to a stage in which these verbs are beginning to be reduced to mere prepositions. Note that this process serves to bring Sranan structurally closer to the high-prestige language, Dutch, with which it has been in continuous contact for over three centuries.

Thus, there is good reason for claiming, across creole languages generally, that the vast majority of embedded sentences are finite and tensed, and that where exceptions to this generalization can be found, they constitute developments that have taken place subsequent to creolization. The second half of this claim would be hard to prove convincingly because of the inaccessibility of evidence; but I know of neither facts nor arguments that would point in an opposite direction.

With regard to the types of complementation featuring serial verbs, it would seem that the strongest constraint on such developments was the availability of superstrate prepositions for case-marking purposes. Where prepositions were available, even if African influence was strong (as with Saramaccan), they would be chosen over serial models. In the absence of superstrate prepositions, serialization would always be chosen. I suspect that it was reinvented, rather than selected, in most if not all cases; but if not, if it was indeed selected out of a range of substrate alternatives, the present theory would remain unaffected. This theory claims that verb serialization is the only answer to the problem of marking cases in languages which have only N and V as major categories. Thus, if such structures were selected from a substratum, they were selected because they offered the only answer, not merely because they happened to be present in the substratum; and, in those cases where they were not present in the substratum (as may have been the case in creoles that drew heavily on Guinean or Bantu rather than Kwa languages), readers of Chapter 1 should have little doubt as to the power of creole children to invent such structures, should the language they were developing require these.

However, before leaving serial verbs, a word is in order on HCE. Substratomaniacs will naturally wish to attribute the absence of serial-verb constructions in HCE to the absence of an African substratum rather than to the presence of prepositions. In fact, though no true serial constructions have developed as a consistent part of the synchronic grammar, sporadic residues of such constructions are to be found both in synchronic speech and in the literature. For instance, instrumental and directional uses of verbs would occur occasionally in the speech of the very oldest HCE speakers:

/263/ dei wan get naif pok yu
      'They want to stab you with a knife'
/264/ dei wawk fit go skul
      they walk feet go school
      'They went to school on foot'

Moreover, decreolization in Hawaii began so early and progressed so rapidly that there is good reason to believe that other similar forms were already lost by the early seventies. For instance, in basilectal GC, *take it* and *bring it* are regularly rendered as *ker am go* (lit., 'carry it go') and *bing am kom,* a fact usually explained by pointing to a similar structure in Yoruba. Smith (1939), listing the commonest "mistakes" made by children in Hawaii—most early sources of HCE have this deplorable pedagogical bias—mentions *take om go* and *bring om come*, only this time the origin is given as Chinese! (In fact, the majority of children listed as using it are non-Chinese.) However, similar forms did not occur in any of our recordings (although the children of Smith's study would only have been in their forties when those recordings were made), and they would seem today to have disappeared entirely. Yet their existence, for however brief a period, can leave little doubt that HCE could have and would have invented regular serial-verb constructions if no other means of marking case had been available.[20]

We have now surveyed a wide range of creole structures across a number of unrelated creole languages. We have seen that even taking into account the, in some cases, several centuries of time that have elapsed since creolization, and the heavy pressures undergone by those creoles (a large majority) that are still in contact with their superstrates, these languages show similarities which go far beyond the possibility of coincidental resemblance, and which are not explicable in terms of conventional transmission processes such as diffusion or substratum influence (the ad hoc nature of the latter should be adequately demonstrated by the opportunism of those who attribute a structure to Yoruba when it appears in the Caribbean and to Chinese when it appears in Hawaii). Moreover, we find that the more we strip creoles of their more recent developments, the more we factor out superficial and accidental features, the greater are the similarities that reveal themselves. Indeed, it would seem reasonable to suppose that the only differences among creoles at creolization were those due to differences in the nature of the antecedent pidgin, in particular to the extent to which superstrate features had been absorbed by that pidgin and were therefore directly accessible to the first creole generation in the outputs of their pidgin-speaking parents. Finally, the overall pattern of similarity which emerges from this chapter is entirely consonant with the process of building a language from the simplest constituents—in many cases, no more than S, N, and V, the minimal constituents necessary for a pidgin.

In theory, given these basic constituents, there are perhaps not infinitely many but certainly a very large number of ways in which, one might suppose, a viable human language could be built—at least as many ways as there are different kinds of human language. This would certainly be the conclusion to which any existing school of linguistic theory would lead one. It would, however, be an incorrect conclusion. The fact that there appears to be only one way of building up a language (with some, but relatively few and minor variations, of course) strongly suggests that when this problem was originally faced, whether thirty thousand years or thirty thousand centuries ago, it might have had to be solved in a very similar way, and we shall further explore this possibility in Chapter 4.

Our original aim in this chapter was to show that the "inventions" of HCE speakers illustrated in Chapter 1 were not peculiar to them, but followed a regular pattern of "invention" which emerged wherever human beings had to manufacture an adequate language in short order from inadequate materials. Now, if all children can indeed do this—and it would be bizarre indeed if the capacity developed only when it was needed—they can only do so as the result of the factor which is responsible for all species-specific behavior: genetic transmission of the bioprogram for the species.

The idea that there is a bioprogram for human (and other species) *physical* development is wholly uncontroversial. No one supposes that human beings have to learn to breathe, eat, yell when they are hurt, stand upright, or flex the muscles of finger and thumb into what is the purely human, species-specific "precision grip." We speak of children "learning to walk," and we characteristically help them in their first stumbling efforts, but no one seriously imagines that if we neglected to do this, the child would go crawling into maturity. The term "learning" is used here in a purely metaphorical sense.

Yet the idea that there is a bioprogram for human *mental* development still meets with massive resistance, despite the fact that Piaget and his disciples have shown how human cognitive development unrolls in a series of predetermined and invariant stages,[21] and despite the fact that, at an ever-increasing rate over the last few decades, experiences long believed to be due to some unanalyzable entity called "mind" —if they were indeed more than subjective illusions—have been shown to be conditioned and in some cases entirely determined by electrochemical events in the brain. The mind-body dualism that has so long dominated Western thought is beginning to seem more and more like an artifact of armchair philosophers operating in blissful ignorance of the laws of reality; and yet the idea *that there is an innate bioprogram that determines the form of human language* is still vigorously if often quite illogically resisted, threatening, as it seems to, free will, mental improvement, and the whole galaxy of human dreams and desires.

I shall return to these fears in the final chapter. In the next chapter I want to pursue what would appear to be an inevitable corollary of the language bioprogram theory. If it is the case that the creole child's capacity to create language is due to such a bioprogram, then, as noted above, it would be absurd to suppose that this bioprogram functions only in the rare and unnatural circumstances in which the normal cultural transmission of language breaks down. Forces that are under genetic control simply cannot be turned on and off in this way. Therefore, if our theory is correct, it should be the case that the acquisition of language under *normal* circumstances should differ considerably from what has hitherto been supposed.

Briefly, the theory predicts that instead of merely processing linguistic input, the child will seek to actualize the blueprint for language with which his bioprogram provides him. We should note from the outset that there are numerous differences between the present theory and earlier Chomskyan theories of linguistic innateness, although the latter are often so vague that such differences are not always clear. One point that should be made is that in the present theory, the child is not supposed to "know" the bioprogram language from birth—whatever that might mean—any more than we would suppose that a child at birth, or even at six months, "knows" how to walk.

Rather, the bioprogram language would unfold, just as a physical bioprogram unfolds; the language would grow just as the body grows, presenting the appropriate structures at the appropriate times and in the appropriate, pre-programmed sequences (I shall have more to say about the mechanisms by which this might be accomplished when we come to Chapter 4).

However, the vast mass of human children are not growing up in even a partial linguistic vacuum. There will be a ready-made language which their elders will be determined that they should learn. Thus, almost (but not quite) from the earliest stages, the evolving bioprogram will interact with the target language. Sometimes features in the bioprogram will be very similar to features in the target language, in which case we will find extremely rapid, early, and apparently effortless learning. Sometimes the target language will have evolved away from the bioprogram, to a greater or lesser extent, and in these cases we will expect to find common or even systematic "errors" which, in orthodox learning theory, will be attributed to "incorrect hypotheses" formed by the child, but which, I shall claim, are simply the result of the child's ignoring (because he is not ready for it) the data presented by speakers of the target language and following out instead the instructions of his bioprogram.

Clearly, then, it should be possible to examine existing studies of child language acquisition and reinterpret them in light of the theory outlined above. If that theory is correct, we expect to find a wide variety of evidence that would arise directly from the interaction of bioprogram and target language, and hopefully, be able to account for phenomena of acquisition which have remained mysterious in all previous theories. Accordingly, the next chapter will present just such a survey of the existing literature on language acquisition.

Chapter 3
ACQUISITION

In recent work, a number of scholars (e.g., Bruner 1979, Snow 1979) have summarized the development of acquisition studies over the last two decades. In the mid-sixties, the field, which had previously been atheoretical and somewhat underdeveloped, came to be dominated by a type of innatist theory. This theory, derived largely from generative grammar, and in particular from works such as Chomsky (1962), held that the child acquired language through simple exposure to linguistic data, much of which was "degenerate"—i.e., consisted of sentence fragments, mid-sentence reformulations, and many types of performance error which would render natural speech a very unreliable mirror to mature native-speaker competence. Somehow the child had to sift the wheat from the chaff, and he could only do this, it was claimed, if he had some kind of inbuilt Language Acquisition Device (LAD). A LAD would contain a set of linguistic universals, presumed to be innate and genetically transmitted. These universals would not, however, precisely specify a particular potential language, as in the theory described at the end of the last chapter; rather, they would define somewhat narrowly the limits on the forms which human language might take, thereby drastically reducing the number of hypotheses that the child could make about the structure of his future native tongue and rendering it correspondingly easy for him to select the correct hypothesis.

Since it is well known that children, whatever else they may do, do not in fact instantly and unerringly make correct hypotheses about adult structures, but rather approximate to those structures by means of a fairly regular and well-defined series of stages, the innocent observer might have expected the next step to consist of an examination of the initial (and often incorrect) "hypotheses" made by the child, to determine why it was that that particular hypothesis, rather than any other, was originally selected. Further steps might have consisted of determining in what ways the child discovered the falsity of his original hypothesis and how he subsequently modified it (or selected an alternative) in order to approximate more closely to the linguistic models available to him.

Unfortunately, nothing of the kind was done. The founders of generative theory remained grandly aloof from the hare they had started, claiming that real-world acquisition processes were still too chaotic and ill understood to constitute a legitimate object of study and taking refuge in the "idealization of instantaneity" described in Chomsky and Halle (1968:Chapter 7). Workers in the field were not simply left to their own devices; they were continually harassed by endless revisions of the theory. Doing acquisition work along Chomskyan lines became rather like playing a game in which every few minutes the umpires revise the rules.

Bearing this in mind—and bearing in mind too that workers in the field not only had no training in the analysis of variability and dynamic process generally but also had been given no reason even to think that such training might be necessary—it is not surprising that their results were somewhat unrevealing. In general, as shown, for example, in Brown and Hanlon (1970), Brown (1973), Bowerman (1973), etc., the predictions that generative theory seemed to make about acquisition were simply not borne out: young children did not show conclusive evidence that they knew S → NP VP or other basic PS rules; syntactic structures were not acquired in the order that was dictated by their relative complexity, and so on.

At the same time, and inspired at least in part by the meager results of generative-oriented work, many scholars began to question the assumptions on which this work was based. Was the input really degenerate? Was learning as rapid as had been claimed? Did it take place in the cognitive vacuum that at least seemed to be implied, if not actually asserted, in most generative writing? Upon examination, a number of these assumptions appeared to be partly or even wholly incorrect. Thus, there came about in the early seventies a very rapid and extreme swing of the pendulum, leading to an all but universal consensus among those working directly on acquisition which persists, with relatively minor variations, up to the present.

This consensus, while not ruling out entirely the possibility that some kinds of innate mechanisms may be involved in acquisition, systematically plays down and degrades the role of such mechanisms, often regarding them as constituting no more than a "predisposition" to acquire language, whatever that might mean (they never do say). The consensus holds, however, that prelinguistic communication and extralinguistic knowledge (acquired, naturally, through experience) play crucially important roles in acquisition, but that perhaps the most critical role of all is that of the interaction, paralinguistic as well as linguistic, which takes place between the child and the mother (or other caregiver). The mother, it is claimed, models language for the child, adapting her outputs to his linguistic level at every stage. Far from being degenerate, the data she provides are highly preadapted, highly contextualized, and patiently repeated. "Mothers *teach* their children to speak," Bruner (1979) states. When all these factors are taken fully into account, the consensus claims, the need to posit an innate component in language acquisition shrinks to near zero or even disappears altogether.

Unfortunately, the whole position of this consensus is based on a fallacy—a fallacy that should be readily apparent to all readers of the two previous chapters. That fallacy is perhaps most concisely expressed by Snow (1979:367) when she remarks that "Chomsky's position regarding the unimportance of the linguistic input was unproven, since *all children*, in addition to possessing an innate linguistic ability, *also receive a simplified, well-formed and redundant corpus*" (emphasis added). This is quite simply untrue. The input that the first creole generation in Hawaii received was over-simplified rather than simplified, and was as far from being well formed as anyone could imagine; and we can assume that in other areas where creoles formed, the same state of affairs must have existed. Mother could not teach *these* children to speak, for the simple and inescapable reason that Mother herself did not know the language—the language didn't exist yet. But even so, without Mother, those children learned how to speak.

In addition to this fallacy of fact, the Bruner-Snow position is based on a simple logical fallacy. If we accept that in the vast majority of circumstances mothers do teach and children do learn, it by no means follows that children learn BECAUSE mothers teach. It would be logically quite possible to argue that there is no connection whatsoever between mothers' teaching and children's learning, any more than there is between children's walking and uncles' dragging them around the room by their fingertips. If it could be shown that without well-formed input from the mother the child could not learn to speak, then we might indeed assume a causal connection. In fact, we have shown the reverse: well-formed input from the mother cannot constitute even a necessary condition for children to acquire language; for, otherwise, creoles could not exist.

But our argument, though logically correct, need not be pushed to its logical extreme. I am perfectly willing to accept that if mother did not teach her child English, that child might have a much harder time learning it—even that the child might never acquire a perfected form of the language, but might significantly distort it in the direction of the kind of pattern we reviewed in the last chapter. All I want to claim is that if we persist in believing that the child must have input in order to learn, we shall continue to misunderstand completely the way in which he does learn a developed, natural language. Just as the child does not need mother in order to learn, so he could not learn even with a myriad of mothers if he did not have the genetic program that alone enables him to take advantage of her teaching.

In fact, the evidence we reviewed in the first two chapters of this book has simply never been taken into account in studies of child language acquisition. The vast majority of scholars in the field evince no awareness whatsoever of the existence, let alone the possible significance, of pidgins and creoles; an honorable exception is Slobin (especially Slobin 1977). Unfortunately, the data available to Slobin at the time were by no means as ample as those given in the present volume; moreover, he makes the common mistake of supposing Tok Pisin to be paradigmatic of normal pidgin-creole development. Still, even limited access to pidgin-creole data is better for acquisitionists than none, and in consequence we shall find the work of Slobin and his associates illuminating on a number of points in the pages that follow.

Meanwhile, in the absence of the insights provided by creolization, the current paradigm has provided us with much information that we lacked before—on the nature of input to the child and of child-caregiver interaction; on the acquisition of turn-taking, conversational routines, and the kind of social appropriateness summed up under Hymes's concept of "communicative competence"; on "acquisition strategies" based on contextualization, semantic and pragmatic clues to the function of novel structures, etc., etc.—and yet, as more and more thoughtful scholars are realizing, the gathering of this information has merely served to conceal the fact that the central question of acquisition, the question with which the early generativists did at least struggle, however unsuccessfully, is simply not being answered:

How can the child acquire syntactic and semantic patterns of great arbitrariness and complexity in such a way that they can be used creatively without making mistakes?

Cromer (1976:353), for instance, observes that the concept of "acquisition strategy" "has made us aware of some of the ways by which the child may possibly 'get into' the linguistic system. It has shown us the importance of perceptual mechanisms for interpreting utterances, and how as adult speakers with full linguistic competence we nevertheless rely on a number of short cuts to understanding . . . . The concept of language acquisition strategies has told us much—except how the child acquires language." Bowerman (1979), who cites this passage with approval, further points out that while such strategies may enable children to understand utterances which still lie outside their developing grammars, those strategies do not and indeed cannot, in and of themselves, assign structural descriptions to these novel utterances. Yet children must achieve this kind of structural knowledge if they are subsequently to use such utterances themselves in a productive and creative way—understanding something is miles away from manipulating that something freely and voluntarily. In other words, strategies belong in the realm of performance, and the problem is, how do you get from performance to competence? Small wonder that so many supporters of the current consensus seek to downgrade, ignore, or even abolish the competence-performance distinction. But real problems cannot be defined away.

I propose, therefore, to review the literature on acquisition as it concerns certain core syntactic and semantic structures, in particular some that we have had occasion to deal with in earlier chapters, to see whether what we know of the acquisition process supports or fails to support the hypotheses advanced at the end of the last chapter. To the extent that these hypotheses are supported, the general theory of a human language bioprogram will tend to be confirmed. To the extent that these hypotheses fail to be supported, doubts will be cast upon the theory, although the reader should perhaps be reminded that not even the most thorough refutation, in the arena of child language, would make the initial problem which led to the theory—the fact that creoles are learned without experience—miraculously go away. At worst, such refutation would merely drive us back to a reconsideration of that problem.

But before commencing this review, three words of caution are in order: the first concerning the data; the second concerning the reviewer; the third concerning the theory.

From our point of view, the data suffers from two defects. First, much of it has been presorted in ways that automatically diminish its utility. There are a variety of reasons for this, but I shall deal with only one in detail, since it is fairly typical. Around 1970, when acquisitionists were still concerned with proving (or disproving) generative predictions about acquisition, it appeared that one way of doing this would be to see whether features of a language were acquired in an order which conformed to some kind of hierarchy of grammatical complexity—simplest first, most complex later on. But in order to do this, it was necessary to determine exactly what one meant by "acquisition of a feature." Children are such messy creatures; instead of quietly going to bed one night without a feature, and waking up with it, as the Chomskyan idealization of "instantaneous acquisition" suggests they should, they stubbornly insist on alternating presence and absence of that feature in appropriate contexts, not to mention absence and presence of that feature in inappropriate contexts, for periods of weeks, months, and occasionally even years.

Not only that, but the little beasts do not even proceed as reason dictates they should, gradually and cumulatively diminishing inappropriate usages as they increase appropriate ones; on the contrary, a graph of their appropriate productions zigzags up and down like a malaria victim's temperature chart, before finally leveling off at or near the 100 percent mark. The innocent observer might think that the most interesting thing you could do in acquisition study would be to figure out *why* this happens, but as usual, he would be disappointed. Fashion and expediency dictate that order must be imposed on disorder: to determine the order of acquisition—a "need" dictated merely by current theory—Brown (1973) established a purely arbitrary "criterion" for acquisition, i.e., a 90 percent production rate in appropriate environments, maintained over three consecutive recording sessions. The reign of the criterion merely reinforced what has always been a trend in acquisition studies, and a deplorable one: to look to the goal rather than the path, to ask "What has the child acquired?" rather than "How has he acquired it?" In consequence, masses of potentially valuable data, which would be required by any interesting acquisition theory, were simply flushed down the drain.[1]

In addition to deficiencies of this nature, we have to remember that all the data collected to date were collected for very different purposes than the present one. It is a general law applicable to all research that one tends to find what one is looking for, and not to find what one is not looking for. Hence, it would be unrealistic if we expected to find massive quantities of unambiguous evidence pointing toward the truth of our theory, which had yet somehow been missed by previous observers. The most that one can ever hope for from data collected under other assumptions and for other purposes than one's own are oblique hints, gaps that one's own hypotheses might fill, puzzles set aside that might begin to make sense in the context of a different framework. However, if one finds any of these at all, it is a reasonable assumption that a purposeful search of raw data sources would reveal much more—something comparable to the invisible eight-ninths of the iceberg.

With regard to the second word of caution, I can lay claim to no special expertise in the field of child language. In creoles, I have fourteen years' experience, most of them spent in direct contact with native creole speakers, so that I can speak in that field with some degree of confidence. In language acquisition, I can claim to be no more than an assiduous reader of the literature, and in consequence, both my knowledge and my understanding may be at fault sometimes. On the credit side, I can only offer complete uninvolvement in any of the controversies that have racked the field (for, as we shall see, my position, although innatist, is really no closer to the orthodox Chomskyan one than it is to the "motherese" school), and the freshness of perspective that a novel viewpoint may on occasion bring. So be it: the facts will decide.

Finally, a word of caution about the theory. Straw-man versions

of innatist theories abound, and in particular, those which claim that
to stress the function of an innate component in acquisition is automatically equivalent to completely writing off all other modes of
learning and all other aids to learning. In the present case, this particular straw man has even less substance than usual. The language
bioprogram theory is, as we shall see in Chapter 4, an evolutionary
theory, and the bioprogram itself is an adaptive evolutionary device.
Now, it is the nature of such devices that they are facilitatory, not
pre-emptive; that is to say, their whole adaptive function is lost if
they force a species into a position where that species is dependent
upon them and upon them alone, by inhibiting the action of other
adaptive processes. In addition to whatever we may have in the way
of innate language equipment, we also have a wide variety of learning
strategies and problem-solving routines which are applicable to a
range of situations far broader than language. It would be absurd to
suppose that in the presence of data classified as "linguistic," all these
routines and strategies should simply switch off.

It would be equally absurd to suppose that they and the innate
language component would be always and necessarily at war with one
another. Sometimes their respective promptings may combine, sometimes they may point in opposite directions; which way is an empirical
issue at any given point. But their interaction must form the core of
any complete description of language acquisition. If I have ignored
other resources in the present study, and have concentrated solely on
the innate component, that is for strategic purposes only; besides,
general cognitive processes have had far more than equal time in the
last decade, and the turn of hardcore syntax and semantics has come
around again. But I believe that in order to acquire language—a feat
which is, so far as we yet know, without parallel in the entire universe—
we need every ounce of help, particular or general, innate or acquired
through experience, that we can get. To pit one kind against another
simply demonstrates a failure to understand how complex language
really is.[2]

With these preliminaries disposed of, we can begin our review. The evidence we shall consider will fall into two quite separate classes. One class will consist of the "incorrect hypotheses" which, in the course of language acquisition, children often make, yet which often seem to have no simple explanation either in the structure of the input the child receives or in any general theory of acquisition. The similarity between such "hypotheses" and the structures which actually emerge as part of the grammars of creole languages is often quite striking, and when I first contemplated writing this chapter, I felt certain that examples drawn from this class would constitute by far the strongest evidence in favor of the bioprogram theory. After writing the first draft of this chapter, however, I became much less certain, not so much because of the weakness of the original evidence—although there are some phenomena, as I shall show, which may allow alternative explanations—but because of the growing impression that a much subtler and less obvious class of evidence made on me.

As the "incorrect hypotheses" suggested, there were many things in language which children seemed to find quite difficult to learn, often spending years before they acquired full control over the structures concerned. On the other hand, there were certain other things which seemed to give them no trouble at all, which they learned very early in the acquisition process and/or without any of the "mistakes" which arose so frequently in other areas. On principle, one might suppose that these differences correlated with some kind of scale of relative difficulty, and yet it was extremely difficult to see exactly what objective factors might constitute such a scale. Indeed, from a commonsense linguistic viewpoint, some of the things that were easily and effortlessly acquired looked a lot more difficult to learn than some of the things that gave so much trouble.

But obviously, to talk about things being "difficult" or "easy" from an adult standpoint is totally irrelevant in an acquisition context. What is "difficult" or "easy" for the child is all that is of interest, and one might therefore conclude that what seems "difficult" to us might seem "easy" to the child, and vice versa. However, a moment's thought should show that it was not so much the adult viewpoint as the use of the words "easy" and "difficult" themselves that was at fault in our original formulation.

Terms like "easy" and "difficult" imply an act of evaluation which in turn depends on the capacity to compare one task with another, which in turn depends on prior experience of tasks with differing levels of difficulty. Thus, when we acquire a second language, we can say that its derivational morphology, for example, is difficult to learn, while its relativization processes, say, are relatively easy. Such remarks are meaningful only because we already know a language and can measure features of the second language against those of the first. If we had not previously learned a language, we would have no standard of comparison; moreover, it is at least in part the nature of what we have already learned that determines whether what we are now about to learn will turn out easy or difficult for us.

Now, if we say that something is easy for a two-year-old to learn, we cannot possibly mean any of this; all we can mean is that the child is somehow preadapted to learn that thing, rather than other things, or that in terms of the present theory, he is programmed to learn it. If, as we shall see is the case, the things that children learn early, effortlessly, and errorlessly turn out repeatedly to be key features of creole languages, which the children of first creole generations acquire in the absence of direct experience, we can then assume that such early, effortless, and errorless learning results, not from characteristics of the input, or from the efforts of the mother—since the features involved are often too abstract to be known to any but the professional linguist—but rather from the functioning of the innate bioprogram which we have hypothesized.

I find evidence of this second class to be even more convincing than that drawn from systematic error, and will accordingly begin by considering some examples of it. The first concerns the learning of the specific-nonspecific distinction (henceforth SNSD) by English-speaking children. This distinction, as we saw in Chapters 1 and 2, is explicitly represented in all creole grammars by the opposition between zero and realized determiners. It is expressed in English too, but much more obliquely, as we will see.

The most comprehensive study of the acquisition of English articles is that of Maratsos (1974, 1976), who confirmed by means of ingenious experiments the naturalistic observations of Brown (1973), i.e., that the article system is mastered at a very early age. Some of Maratsos' findings have been questioned in subsequent work (Warden 1976, Karmiloff-Smith 1979), but such criticisms relate only to the earliness with which the definite-nondefinite distinction is acquired. No one has challenged Maratsos' finding that the SNSD is handled virtually without error by three-year-olds, well ahead of the earliest date by which the child masters the definite-nondefinite distinction.

At first sight, this is an odd finding since the latter distinction is clearly marked in English, while the SNSD is not. In English, "definite" really means presumed known to the listener, whether by prior knowledge (*"the* man you met yesterday"), uniqueness in the universe (*"the* sun is setting"), uniqueness in a given setting (*"the* battery is dead"—cars do not usually have more than one battery), or general knowledge that a named class exists (*"the* dog is the friend of man"). "Indefinite" really means presumed unknown to the listener, whether by absence of prior knowledge (*"a* man you should meet is Mr. Blank"), nonexistence of a nameable referent ("Bill is looking for *a* wife"), or nonexistence of any referent ("George couldn't see *an* aardvark anywhere"). In other words, the two classes are systematically distinguished by the distribution of *the* and *a/an.*

Specific and nonspecific, however, are not systematically distinguished. Consider the following:

/1/   If you're sick, you should see *the doctor* (NS).
/2/   Call *the doctor* who treated Marge (S).
/3/   *The doctor* may succeed where the priest fails (NS).
/4/   *Dogs* are mammals (NS).
/5/   *The dog* is a mammal (NS).
/6/   *A dog* is a mammal (NS).

/7/   *A dog* just bit me (S).

/8/   Mary can't stand to have *a dog* in the room (NS).

In fact, the only way in which English distinguishes specifics from nonspecifics is in constructions with at least two articles. If a given referent is specific, it will receive *a* on first mention and *the* on second and subsequent mention:

/9/   Bill bought *a cat* and *a dog,* but the children only like *the dog.*

If a given referent is nonspecific, it will receive *a* on first mention and on second and subsequent mention:

/10/   Bill wanted to buy *a cat* and *a dog,* but he couldn't find *a dog* that he really liked.

Maratsos constructed an ingenious set of stories which his child subjects were asked to complete. In some of the stories, reference was made to a specific entity; in others, to a nonspecific entity; in both cases, naturally, the entity was introduced into the story as *a* NP. However, the completion task required the child to produce *a* NP just in case the entity was nonspecific, and *the* NP just in case the entity was specific, in accordance with the rule illustrated in /9/ and /10/ above (for full texts of the stories and a more complete description of the experiments, see Maratsos 1976).

The success rate in this experiment was almost 90 percent for three-year-olds and over 90 percent for four-year-olds. In order to maintain these high rates, the children had to determine that out of some NPs identically marked, half had specific real-world referents and half had not. The stories were original and contained no contextual clues as to the status of the referents. How did the children succeed so often?

Maratsos himself was surprised and impressed by his subjects' capacities, and he discusses the implications of his experiments at some length and with great insight. He notes that the high frequency of articles in adult speech is often regarded as an adequate explanation of the relative earliness and lack of error shown in the acquisition of articles. He points out, however, that "although the frequency of [articles'] use may somehow serve to bring them to the child's attention and provide data for him, he must still select and attach to the articles just those abstract differences in the circumstances of their use that correspond to the specific-nonspecific distinction. One clear requirement is that he have available some conceptual understanding of such matters as the difference between the notion of any member (or no member) of a class and that of a particular class member. This understanding must be sufficiently well articulated for the child to perceive just this difference in the circumstances of use of the definite and indefinite morphemes and construct the meaning of the terms accordingly" (Maratsos 1974:453).

Let us try to reconstruct the process or processes by which the child might arrive at this perception. We will ignore the problems that arise from the child's original isolation and recognition of articles, although these are far from trivial (especially with *a,* so frequently reduced to an unstressed schwa and so closely linked to its following NP that morpheme boundary perception becomes quite difficult), and deal solely with how, having recognized them, he determines their functions. If the conventional accounts are correct, the child can do this in only two ways—through linguistic context or through extralinguistic context.

The nature of the problems involved can be better understood if we compare the acquisition of articles with the acquisition of plural marking, which occurs at roughly the same age (a very few weeks later, according to Brown 1973). The plural morpheme marks a single, straightforward distinction—one/more than one—and it does so bi-uniquely, that is to say, in a one-morpheme, one-meaning relationship: when the morpheme is present, one meaning is entailed; when it is absent, the other meaning is entailed. Articles are, from a purely formal viewpoint, much more complex than that. Three articles, *the, a,* and zero, represent two distinctions—supposed-known-to-listener / supposed-unknown-to-listener and specific-referent / no-specific-referent—but without the biuniqueness that relates semantics to surface representation in the case of plurals. Instead, with regard to the second distinction only (the SNSD), there are two morphemes with one meaning (both *a* and *the* can have specific reference) and one morpheme with two meanings (*a* can be both specific and nonspecific).

Let us suppose that the child can first factor out the distinction between *a* and *the* (although in fact he cannot even rely on this aid; Warden [1976] and Karmiloff-Smith [1979] show that it will be several years before he is able to overcome this potential distraction). He then has to distinguish specific from nonspecific *a*. One might think he could do this by distinguishing between linguistic environments. For instance, the scope of negation is often crucial in determining whether a given occurrence of *a NP* is specific or nonspecific: the difference between *I saw a dog* (S) and *I didn't see a dog* (NS), for instance. So is the scope of desiderative verbs: the difference between *I want a dog* (NS) and *I have a dog* (S). Those who put their trust in extralinguistic context will, however, point out, quite correctly, that things like desiderative scope and negative scope are themselves extremely abstract relations, unlikely to be capturable by two-year-olds.

But in fact the problem is even tougher than we have suggested; there are many cases in which a mere tense switch marks the SNSD:

/11/ When you see *a dog* (NS), are you frightened?
/12/ When you saw *a dog* (S), were you frightened?

Since the child's control of tense is, at the appropriate age, highly questionable at best, it is implausible to suppose that he could utilize such clues.[3] Again, there are cases when desiderative scope alone is insufficient to mark the distinction:

/13/ Your little sister wants *a dog*—any kind of dog (NS).
/14/ Your little sister wants *a dog*—and it's that one (S)!

In fact, the only reliable indicator of the SNSD is not a single article use, but a series of articles uses; an *a-a* sequence, as in /10/ above, as opposed to an *a-the* sequence, as in /9/ above.

However, as Maratsos (1976:95) again points out, it is at least highly questionable whether the child can take advantage of clues provided by sequences, especially when members of such sequences are not necessarily adjacent—as they are in /9/ and /10/—but may be separated by several sentences: "It is easy to forget that the child, to the best of our present knowledge, does not have an extensive corpus of data at any one time with which to work. He probably cannot record numerous long stretches of conversation and all of the contextual information that accompanied them, as can an adult linguist investigating a novel language."

We must therefore conclude that a child would be, at best, highly unlikely to derive the SNSD from analysis of purely linguistic context.

Yet is it any more likely that he could learn it from physical experience or any other kind of extralinguistic source? As noted above, recent studies have concentrated heavily on the here-and-nowness of speech aimed at children, and on the child's prelinguistic experiences in the world of objects. It is hard to see just how either of these could help with the SNSD. As Maratsos (1976:94) remarks, "specific and nonspecific reference are connected in no clear way with external physical attributes or relations of perceived objects." For example, nonspecific reference is usually (although not always) made in the absence of any member of the referent class: *we don't have a doggy, Daddy's looking for a doggy for you, a doggy would be nice to play with, wouldn't it?* and so on. But specific reference is made just as often in the absence of the referent: *a dog bit Jessie yesterday, I saw a dog you'd really have liked in town today,* and so on. How does the child determine that of the two absent sets of referents one is concrete while the other is only hypothetical? If he did not do so, he would score no better than chance on Maratsos' tests.

While it is true that many concepts are formed by the child prior to language learning, these are generally concepts which relate to physical objects which the child can see, touch, etc. Moreover, it is reasonably clear that such concepts ARE arrived at by interaction with experience rather than by merely processing language input. If the child only processed linguistic tokens of *dog,* for example, he would presumably apply the term only to members of the appropriate species; whereas, as is well known, the initial meaning of *dog,* for the child, is likely to be 'any four-legged mammal'. Thus, we know that the child reaches out ahead of linguistic experience, so to speak, in order to derive ways of talking about the world.

But how could the child derive knowledge of purely abstract relationships from direct experience? A comparison with plural-marking acquisition is again very much to the point. Plural marking is directly associated with relations that the child is physically able to observe. He can see and feel at any given time whether he has one toy or several, whether he is allowed only one cookie or more than one; the grammatical marking of nouns correlates directly with manifest and obvious differences in his perceptual field. But the distinction between an actual member of a class (which more often than not is not physically present) and an imaginary representative of that same class is in no way one that can be determined by the organs of perception, or inferred from any kind of direct experience. The SNSD involves comparisons, not between physical entities, but between purely mental representations; one can only marvel that a child, for whom the boundaries between real and unreal are notoriously vague, should be able to make it at all, by *any* means.

Indeed, that he should even hypothesize such a distinction—as would, presumably, be claimed by those who believe in a hypothesis-forming, hypothesis-testing LAD—is highly implausible. Even about possible functions of *a* and *the,* there are many possible hypotheses that might be made. Since definites tend to be subjects while indefinites tend to be objects, one might hypothesize that *the* marks agents and *a* marks patients. Since *the* often co-occurs with NPs that are physically present and *a* with NPs that are physically absent, one might hypothesize that *the* and *a* mark poles of some kind of proximal-distal distinction. In fact, so far as we know, such hypotheses are never made. In any case, they would affect only *a* and *the;* with regard to *a* alone, why on earth should the child even start by hypothesizing that there are really two kinds of *a*? Moreover, since two-year-olds use few or no articles, and the SNSD is acquired by about the age of three, it would have to be just about the first hypothesis the child makes— there would hardly be time to frame and discard any other. To say that the child invariably forms a correct hypothesis about the SNSD as his first hypothesis is simply an issue-dodging way of saying that he is programmed to make the SNSD.

Indeed, we can only conclude that the SNSD would be quite impossible to learn, by means of linguistic data, or of experience, or of any hypothesis-forming process, or of any feasible combination of these. For the child to make the SNSD as early and as successfully as he does, he would have to be somehow preprogrammed to make it.

This proposal is strongly supported by the creole data reviewed in Chapters 1 and 2. We saw there that the SNSD was made by the first creole generation in Hawaii (even though none of their HPE-speaking parents made it) and that it is made consistently, and always by the same means, in all creole languages. If we assume a language bioprogram that includes the SNSD in its specifications, the problem of how the child acquires that distinction in English becomes a manageable one. The child knows of the distinction in advance and is therefore looking out (at a purely subconscious level, of course) for surface features in the target language that will mark it. If no other feature is preprogrammed for NP, which is likely, then the fact that the SNSD constitutes the child's first "hypothesis" is no longer bewildering, but an automatic consequence of the theory.

The skeptical reader may, however, ask: if creole children following the bioprogram universally mark the SNSD by allotting zero marking to nonspecifics, how is it that children learning English, prior to correctly interpreting the two *a*s, do not mark, or at least attempt to mark, nonspecifics with zero, as creole children do? The answer is that we do not know that they do not.

Earlier, I referred to deficiencies in the data due to excessive concentration on the goals rather than the paths of acquisition. Here is a case in point. Even as conscientious and insightful a scholar as Maratsos confesses (1974:450) that "only full noun phrases of the form article plus noun were counted; answers which included no article, such as *boy*, were not counted in the analysis." Another careful investigator, Brown (1973), who allots some sixteen pages to a discussion of articles in early child speech, makes no reference to zero forms, and in what he claims is a "full list of errors in definite and nondefinite reference for Adam, Eve and Sarah from Stages IV and V" (1973: Table 51) includes only cases of *a* where *the* is indicated, and cases of *the* where *a* is indicated—no zeros at all. Yet from what Maratsos says, and from mere common sense, one knows there *must* have been zeros; after all, the child has no articles at the two-word stage, and obviously does not acquire the surface forms overnight.

The present theory predicts that when a substantial body of early child language is properly examined, there will be found to be a significant skewing in article placement, such that a significantly higher percentage of articles will be assigned to specific-reference NP, while zero forms will persist in nonspecific environments longer than elsewhere. Such examination affords a simple and straightforward means of empirically testing the claims made about the innateness of the SNSD in this chapter.

We will now examine another distinction which is made even earlier and without, apparently, even a single reported case of error. This is the distinction between states and processes, including under the latter rubric verbs of experiencing as well as action verbs (hereafter referred to as the state-process distinction, or SPD). The SPD is directly involved in the acquisition of the English progressive marker *-ing*.

In general, the acquisition of novel morphology by the child is attended by cases of over-generalization, a number of which are discussed in Cazden (1968). Thus, the consistency in the final segments of possessive pronouns leads to production of the aberrant form *mines, while plurals such as *sheeps, *foots (or *feets), *mouses, etc., and past-tense forms such as *comed, *goed (or *wented), *buyed, etc., occur in the speech of most, if not all, child learners of English.

The -ing form is acquired even earlier than the -ed form (before any of the other thirteen morphemes studied in Brown [1973], and as early as the second year in at least some cases). Also, just as there are verbs that do not take -ed, there are verbs that do not take -ing (with certain qualifications, see Sag 1973), such as like, want, know, see, etc. These verbs are quite common in children's speech, probably as common as many of the irregular verbs to which children incorrectly attach -ed. Yet, apparently, children never ever attach -ing to stative verbs.

Kuczaj (1978) has argued that the two cases are not really commensurate since with the past tense there are other ways of marking than -ed (just as with plurals there are other ways of marking than -s), whereas in the case of -ing, English has no alternative way of marking progressive aspect. This argument is somewhat disingenuous since zero can be a term in a subsystem, and it is hard to see what the difference would be between, on the one hand, adding -s to sheep to make sheeps or -ed to put to make putted, and, on the other hand, adding -ing to like to yield I am liking you. A more pertinent observation would be that verbs which do not take -ing, as opposed to verbs which do not take -ed or nouns which do not take -s, constitute a natural semantic class; we shall return to this point in a moment.

In fact, Kuczaj undercuts his own argument by observing that children do indeed over-generalize -ing, but not to stative verbs— rather, to nonverbal items, as in /15/:

/15/   Why is it weathering?
        (presumably, 'Why is the weather so bad?')

Note that, in fact, *weather* is a plausible candidate for admission to the list of "climatic" verbs that yield expressions such as *it is raining/snowing/thundering,* etc. But all these verbs have in common the fact that they are nonstatives, as *weather* would be also if it were a verb in the sense of /15/. The fact that children will generalize *-ing* even to nouns IF AND ONLY IF SUCH NOUNS HAVE A PLAUSIBLE NONSTATIVE READING makes their abstemiousness with respect to stative verbs even more significant.

Brown (1973:326ff.) rightly regards it as remarkable that children should be "able to learn a concept like involuntary state before they [are] three years old," and explores several hypotheses which might account for such learning. In the case of one child, Eve, he was able to show that many nonstatives, as well as statives, were unmarked by *-ing,* and that the unmarked nonstatives were precisely those which Eve's mother seldom used with progressive aspect; on the other hand, the nonstatives which the mother did use frequently with *-ing* were precisely those which appeared with *-ing* in Eve's speech. However, a similar relationship did not hold for the other children in Brown's study; and as Brown himself pointed out, even if it had held, it would not have provided a solution. For anyone who claimed that children delayed applying *-ing* to a verb until they learned from experience that it was "*-ing*able" would then be forced to explain why a similar caution and restraint was not applied to other morphemes, like *-ed* and *-s,* where over-generalizations abounded.

Brown next considered the possibility that the SPD was learned from imperatives and transferred to progressives, since the verbs that will not take *-ing* are just those that cannot be used in the imperative. Against this possibility, Brown argued that it would depend also on imperative usage being errorless; and it was simply impossible to tell whether this was the case since, especially in Stage I, children's imperatives are often formally indistinguishable from their declaratives (*want cookie* looks like an imperative, but is probably no more than the child's version of 'I want a cookie').

A stronger argument against the "imperative transfer" hypothesis, not made by Brown, involves first recognizing that Brown's argument is in error; children could learn imperatives through trial and error and, having learned at last the list of verbs which could not be imperatives, simply apply that knowledge to the learning of -*ing*. But trial-and-error learning of imperatives is more implausible than errorless learning of imperatives, and for the following reason: in trial-and-error learning, the child must correct himself simply through observing that others produce forms different from his (we know that overt correction of grammar, as opposed to content, is rare among parents). Thus, the child who says *drinked* eventually becomes aware that others say *drank,* and revises his grammar accordingly. If such things did not come to his attention, he would presumably go on saying *drinked* indefinitely.

But negative evidence cannot function in this way. Let us suppose that the child who said *want cookie* really was urging someone else to desire a cookie. Would the fact that he did NOT hear others saying **want some chocolate* or **hate naughty bunny* deter him? It is hardly likely. I know of no facts which would indicate that a child needs positive reinforcement, as well as an absence of counterexamples, in order to maintain his current grammar. The child may be diverted from that grammar by the existence of contradictory forms to which he is obliged to pay attention; we can hardly expect him to pay attention to something that is NOT happening.

Moreover, on a purely pragmatic basis, trial-and-error learning of imperatives is unlikely. A child's early imperatives are all action-oriented, aimed at getting people to pick him up or put him down, bring nice things to him and take nasty things away. It would be bizarre if he sought instead to influence the thought-processes and emotions of others by commanding them to want, need, know, etc. In fact, the likeliest possibility is that children do not acquire the SPD from imperatives, either errorlessly or by trial and error, because they themselves would only ever need nonstative imperatives for pragmatic reasons. They would not know whether statives could be used as imperatives because the opportunity for such use would simply not have occurred—unless of course they were already programmed with the SPD, and thus "knew" that such uses were impossible, without requiring experience to prove it.

But whereas the use of imperative statives might seem bizarre, the use of progressive -ing with statives would surely appear, to a child not programmed with the SPD, to be the most natural thing in the world. For -ing is applied to verbs with present reference, and when a child wants or sees or likes something, it is right now that he does it. *I wanting teddy (now) or *I seeing pussy (now) would surely appear, to such a child, every bit as grammatical as I playing peekaboo (now) or I sitting potty (now). Nobody could claim that the distinction emerged from experience, or from context; on the contrary, both experience and context would point in a contrary direction.

Finally, Brown considered the possibility that the distinction is innately known. However, he rejects this possibility because of what he claims are "fatal difficulties." Since neither he nor other scholars who have discussed the issue (e.g., Kuczaj 1978, Fletcher 1979) have advanced any serious alternative to the innatist suggestion, we should examine Brown's "difficulties"—bearing in mind that they arose out of a theory of innateness quite different from this one—and see whether they are really as "fatal" as he believes.

The first difficulty is that, according to Brown, children do not behave as innatist theory predicts with respect to categories other than state-process. If they came equipped with a full set of syntactic and/or semantic subcategories, "they ought to attempt to order regular and irregular inflections in terms of one or another of the innate subcategories. They should test the hypothesis that verbs that take -d [sic] in the past are all transitives and the others intransitives or that those that take -d are animate actions and the others not, or something of this kind" (1973:328). Of course, this does not happen, and because it does not happen with distinctions other than the SPD, Brown concludes that the SPD cannot be innate.

Now this argument makes sense only if you assume, first, that children are born with all the subcategorization features of an *Aspects* grammar in their heads (a view Brown specifically attributes to McNeill [1966]), and second, that children, like junior linguists, acquire grammars by formulating and testing hypotheses. The present theory assumes neither of these things. Thus, the fact that other distinctions were treated differently from the SPD could never constitute an argument against the innateness of the SPD, unless it could be shown that those other distinctions also formed part of the bioprogram. To do that, it would be necessary to show that those distinctions were formally marked in creole languages. In creoles, animate actions are not formally distinguished from other types of action, and transitive verbs are not formally distinguished from intransitive verbs—quite the reverse, indeed, as we saw in the section on Passive Equivalents in Chapter 2, and as we shall see again later in this chapter. Thus, the child hypotheses Brown suggests would not make any kind of sense in light of the present theory, even if that theory supposed that children test hypotheses—which it does not.

Brown's second difficulty is that the SPD is "a poor candidate for innateness" because it is "very far from being universal in the world's languages." The problems foreign learners have with English progressives and a claim by Joos (1964) that English is "unique or almost unique" in possessing the SPD are adduced as evidence for this contention.

Again, in the present theory, whether or not a given feature is common to all the world's languages is quite irrelevant. All previous universals theories have been static theories, which assume that language is always and everywhere the same; if one accepts this, it follows that only features that occur in all languages can really qualify as candidates for innateness. But the present theory is a dynamic, evolutionary theory which assumes that language had a starting point and a sequence of developments, which are recycled, in rather different ways, in both creole formation and child acquisition, as well as perhaps in certain types of linguistic change (consideration of which would take us beyond the scope of the present volume). What is innate is therefore

what was there at the beginning of the sequence, and thus there is
not the slightest reason to suppose that innate features will automatically persist and be found in the structure of all synchronic languages—
indeed, given the nature of dynamic processes, this would be an extremely unlikely result.

In other words, the SPD is presumed to be innate, not because
of its universality, which may well be as low as Brown suggests, but
because it plays a crucial role in creole grammars. There, statives are
distinguished from nonstatives by the fact that the nonpunctual marker
never attaches to the former; but that is by no means the only significant difference between the treatment of the two categories. The SPD
causes a characteristic skewing of the creole TMA system, not explicitly
treated in the present volume, but discussed at some length in Bickerton (1975:Chapter 2). Briefly, there is a significant difference between
creole and Indo-European systems which takes the following form.
In the latter, the same morphological marking applies to both statives
and nonstatives in any given tense; this seems so obvious that it is
never even remarked on. In creoles, however, present-reference statives
and present-reference nonstatives cannot be marked in the same way,
and the same applies to past-reference statives and nonstatives. The
pattern for GC, which we may take as typical in this respect, is given
in Table 3.1 below:

	Stative	Nonstative
Present reference	∅	a
Past reference	bin	∅

Table 3.1
Stative-nonstative distinctions in GC

Thus, without a clear understanding of the SPD, the creole TMA
system would be quite unworkable.

Since Brown believed that universality was the criterion for
innateness, while the criterion for the bioprogram theory is emergence

in creole grammar, his second objection to the innateness of the SPD is also deprived of its force.

However, Brown's claim that, if a distinction were genuinely innate, it might be generalized to inappropriate environments (cited above in discussion of his first objection), is a reasonable one if it is made with respect to distinctions found in the bioprogram (as opposed to distinctions supposedly innate by the standards of other theories). An example which looks, from the data available so far, somewhat like an inappropriate generalization of the SPD is found in data on the acquisition of Turkish in Slobin and Aksu (1980).

Turkish has two morphemes used for marking past-reference verbs: *-dI* and *-mIs*. These are used in adult speech to mark direct experience (events personally observed by the speaker) and indirect experience (events reported to or inferred by the speaker), respectively. According to Slobin and Aksu, *-dI* is usually acquired by age 1:9, and *-mIs* about three months later (i.e., about the same age as *-ing* is acquired). But "at first the *-dI* and *-mIs* inflections differentiate between dynamic and static events . . . . (C)lear differentiation of the two forms [according to their adult meanings, D.B.] is not stabilized until about 4:6."[4]

The delay in acquisition is even more significant since most features of Turkish verb morphology are fully acquired at age 3:0. Although "evidential" tenses are found elsewhere (for example, in some American Indian languages such as Hopi), they are completely unknown in all creoles. From these two facts, we may conclude that the direct/indirect experience distinction does not form part of the bioprogram, and we may further hypothesize that non-bioprogram distinctions that have emerged in natural languages are particularly vulnerable to reinterpretation in the course of the acquisition process. Such reinterpretation would naturally involve the assumption that the surface markers of a non-bioprogram distinction were really marking a distinction established in the bioprogram—which is exactly what seems to be happening in the Turkish case. Certainly, any case of unusually delayed acquisition may turn out to be evidence as conclusive of the workings of the bioprogram as are cases of early and errorless acquisition, once the mechanisms of interaction between bioprogram and target language are adequately understood.

We may therefore place the SPD alongside the SNSD as a second semantic distinction (with important syntactic consequences) which is innately programmed. But consideration of the SPD naturally prompts the question: since among the most distinctive features of creoles is their distinctive TMA system, should it not be the case that this or a similar system emerges at some stage of acquisition, if indeed a universal genetic program generates such a system?

This question will serve to focus more sharply on the nature of bioprogram-target interaction, briefly mentioned two paragraphs above. In the present volume, emphasis is placed on the first member of the pair, for obvious reasons: until students of acquisition are convinced that a bioprogram is really operative, it is premature to talk too much about how such a bioprogram might interact with other components of the acquisition process. But such emphasis can lead all too easily to a familiar straw man: the innate component which is supposed to roll like some irresistible juggernaut through the years of acquisition, sweeping all other influences aside. After the all too easy demolition of this travesty, the empiricist thinks he has disposed of innatism.

In fact, no innate program could or should behave in this way. From one viewpoint, the child is a biophysical organism evolving along the genetic lines laid down for its species, but from another and equally valid perspective, the child is a sociocultural organism growing up into membership of a particular human community. The pressures from the second side of being human must inevitably mold the impulses of the first—the more so since biophysical characteristics are typically more general and cultural characteristics more highly specified. Thus, from an early age—certainly from age two upward—we would expect that in a "natural" acquisition situation, as distinct from a pidgin-creole one, the pattern of the bioprogram would be gradually shifted in the direction of the target-language pattern.

Such shifting must inevitably affect the formation of a TMA

system. Since virtually all the relevant literature deals with acquisition of particular pieces of such systems, rather than with such systems as wholes, it is difficult to say at what age the child fully controls the TMA system of his mother tongue; but it is highly doubtful whether such control is achieved prior to age four, and likely that it may come considerably later than that. This means that the acquisition of TMA must spread over at least two years, two years during which the pressure of the target grammar on the evolving bioprogram is steady and continuous. It would therefore be highly unrealistic to expect any child at any stage of acquisition to exhibit anything like a fully-developed creole TMA system. The most that we could expect would be that acquisition of the earlier features of TMA systems would be influenced in rather oblique ways. However, if the results of such influence should prove mysterious to other theories of acquisition, yet follow logically from the present one, even such oblique evidence would be significant.

Accordingly, I shall re-examine two of the most influential papers on the acquisition of tense: Bronckart and Sinclair (1973) and Antinucci and Miller (1976); and I shall show that some puzzling features of those studies become immediately clear once we assume that while the subjects of these studies appear to be merely learning French and Italian, respectively, the bioprogram decisively influences the progress of their acquisition.

One point must be made first, however. With few exceptions, students of acquisition assume that when a child uses a past-tense form, he uses it because he fully understands, and deliberately intends to mark, pastness of reference.[5] True, it is often admitted (e.g., by Antinucci and Miller [1976]) that the child's concept of past may be restricted as compared with the adult's, and may extend only to past events that leave presently-observable consequences; but it is still assumed, without question, that where past marking appears, some sort of concept of past must be there too.

This by no means necessarily follows. All we can say is that during the period in which past tense is being acquired, some past-reference verbs are tense-marked while some are not. There are several possible explanations of why this is so, none of which can be ruled out a priori. The child may have acquired a full past rule but may apply it unpredictably because of lapses of attention, phonological difficulties, etc. The child may have acquired a partial past rule which applies only to a subset of past-reference verbs. The child may have acquired a rule that has nothing at all to do with pastness or non-pastness, but which just happens, coincidentally, to mark a certain percentage of past-tense verbs. Which of these explanations is the correct one can only be determined by empirical investigation in each individual case.

Since the study of variable data is much further advanced in decreolization than it is in acquisition, it should be instructive to look at another situation where variable past-morpheme insertion takes place. In creoles, past tense is not a category. But when creoles begin to decreolize, past-tense markers begin to be introduced, occurring sporadically just as they do in child acquisition.

At first, one might interpret such data just as similar child language data have been interpreted—the speakers have an established past category but do not always mark it. However, analyses of decreolization in both Guyana and Hawaii (Bickerton 1975:142-61; 1977:36-51), with a data base of a thousand past-reference verbs in both cases, suggest quite a different picture.

On the assumption that speakers had a past category, one would have to conclude that decreolizing GC speakers randomly inserted past morphemes 27 percent of the time while decreolizing HCE speakers did so 30 percent of the time. However, when all past-reference verbs were divided into two categories—those that referred to SINGLE, PUNCTUAL EVENTS, and those that referred to iterative or habitual events—insertion rates were shown to vary widely between the two categories, as shown in Table 3.2:

		Punctual	Nonpunctual
	GC	38%	12%
Past-marking rate			
	HCE	53%	7%

Table 3.2
Past versus punctual in decreolization

In other words, what was being marked in both sets of data was not really pastness, but rather punctuality.

The punctual-nonpunctual distinction (henceforth PNPD) is related to, yet distinct from, the SPD, and is of equal importance in creole grammar. Since both decreolization and acquisition involve the introduction of "past" marking where none was before, it should at least be worthwhile examining acquisitional data to see whether punctuality plays the same role in the second as it does in the first. We should certainly do well to bear this possibility in mind while we reconsider previous findings on past-tense acquisition.

We may now turn to the first of the two papers cited above, Bronckart and Sinclair (1973). The authors' starting point was their informal observation that when children were asked to describe past events, their choice of tense often seemed to be influenced by the nature of the event: if the latter was one of some duration, like washing a car, they would tend to use *il lave la voiture* 'He washes/is washing the car', rather than *il a lavé la voiture* 'He washed the car'; whereas if the event was a punctual one, like kicking a ball, they would use *il a poussé la balle* 'He kicked the ball', and seldom if ever substitute *il pousse la balle* 'He kicks/is kicking the ball'.

Normally, the opposition between *il lave* and *il a lavé* is treated as a simple past-present opposition, but of course this is not the case. The "present" tense in French is in fact a nonpunctual aspect which does not extend into the past (unlike that of creoles); but, like a creole nonpunctual aspect, it embraces both iterative and durative events.

Similarly, the "past" is not a simple past in the sense of English simple past. English simple past is applicable to past-punctual and past-iterative (but not always to past-durative) reference; French *avoir* + participle is limited to past punctuals, while past iteratives and past duratives are rendered by the so-called "imperfect" form, e.g., *il lavait* rather than *il a lavé*.

In other words, when French children use different verb forms for different kinds of past events, they are doing exactly the same as creole speakers, who always mark nonpunctual pasts differently from punctual pasts.

Bronckart and Sinclair confirmed and quantified their original observation by asking 74 children to describe (after the event) different types of actions which the investigators performed with the aid of a series of toys. Ages of the children ranged from under 3 to nearly 9. Eleven actions were performed. Of these, six were actions which had a clear goal or result (e.g., "a car hits a marble which rolls very rapidly into a pocket"), while two were actions which had no perceptible goal or result (e.g., "a fish swims in the basin [circular movement]"). The three remaining "actions," which consisted merely of cries of differing types or duration supposedly uttered by various toys, can be disregarded for our purposes.

Of the six goal-directed actions, some were durative and others were not. While the French *passé composé* was used more frequently for these six than for the two goalless actions, there was a significant difference (p < .01) between durative and nondurative actions, the former having a much higher probability of being marked with a nonpast (= nonpunctual) verb. The authors concluded that "the distinction between perfective and imperfective events seems to be of more importance than the temporal relation between action and the moment of enunciation. Imperfective actions are almost never expressed by past tenses, and for perfective actions the use of *présents* is the more frequent the greater the probability of taking into account the unaccomplished part of the action. This probability is partly determined by duration, frequence [*sic*], and maybe other objective features we have not investigated."

In terms of the present study, Bronckart and Sinclair have clearly shown that the PNPD overrides the past-nonpast distinction until at least the age of six. However, the situation in French acquisition may be even more creole-like than the authors suggest.

First, they fail to mention the possibility that even when their subjects seem to be marking +past, they are in fact marking +punctual. French-speaking children, like all other children, start out using the bare stem of the verb for every kind of reference, past or nonpast, punctual or nonpunctual, realis or irrealis. Then, at an age when developmental studies suggest that they have only the vaguest idea of past time, they encounter a form (the *passé composé*) which has exclusively punctual reference. Note that, semantically, the categories of past and punctual overlap. While all pasts need not be punctuals, all punctuals must be pasts—if they were not, they would still be happening, and if they were still happening now, they would be nonpunctual by definition. Which is likelier—that they would interpret *passé composé* in terms of a distinction that they barely yet grasped (past-nonpast), or that they would interpret it in terms of a distinction which would be apparent to them from their own direct observation of actions and events (punctual-nonpunctual)?

Second, there are a number of facts about the Bronckart and Sinclair data that the authors themselves either skim over or ignore altogether. In order to understand the significance of these facts, we shall have to re-examine their study rather minutely.

Let us begin by describing the six goal-oriented actions used in the study and then coding them in terms of type of action, duration, and iteration (where applicable). The actions (Bronckart and Sinclair's 1-6) are as follows:

/16/ A truck slowly pushes a car toward a garage.
/17/ A car hits a marble which very rapidly rolls into a pocket.
/18/ The farmer jumps over ten fences and reaches the farm.
/19/ The farmer's wife jumps in one big jump over ten fences and reaches the farm.

/20/   The cow jumps over five fences and does not reach the stable.
/21/   The horse jumps over one fence and does not reach the stable.

Sentences /19/ and /21/ are single jumping movements which take two seconds and one second, respectively, so we will call them J-2 and J-1; /18/ and /20/ are repeated jumping movements which take ten seconds and five seconds, respectively, so we will call them Jx-10 and Jx-5; /16/ and /17/ are single pushing movements which take ten seconds and one second, respectively, so we will call them P-10 and P-1.

The authors present (their Figure 1) a graph which shows the percentages of *passé composé* used to describe each of the different actions by members of five age groups, average ages of each group being as follows: 1, 3:7; 2, 4:7; 3, 5:6; 4, 6:6; 5, 7:8. Like all the acquisition charts I have ever seen, this one does not show a consistent and steady rise from low to high percentages of correct forms; rather it shows the familiar fever-chart zigzags before coming to rest, at age 7:8, with fairly uniform percentages of past marking across all action types. In Bronckart and Sinclair's presentation, I think quite unintentionally, the amount of zigzagging is reduced by showing two different graphs for durative and nondurative events; thus, certain very interesting crossover phenomena, which are not accounted for in the authors' conclusions, may very easily be overlooked.

In order to display these phenomena, I shall recast Bronckart and Sinclair's data into the form given in Table 3.3 on the following page. In this table, the six actions, /16/-/21/, are ranked for each of the first four age groups. Rank order is based on percentage of past-tense assignment; thus, in each column the event at the head of the column is that which is most frequently assigned past marking, while the event at the foot of the column is that to which past marking is least frequently assigned. The nondurative items are circled in the table for easier reference:

Rank	Age Group 3:7	4:7	5:6	6:6
1	P-1	P-1	J-1	J-1
2	J-2	J-1	J-2	(Jx-5)
3	J-1	(Jx-5)	(Jx-5)	J-2
4	(Jx-5)	J-2	P-1	(Jx-10)
5	(Jx-10)	(Jx-10)	(P-10)	P-1
6	(P-10)	(P-10)	(Jx-10)	(P-10)

Table 3.3
Rank orders for past-marking frequency

Table 3.3 presents a picture rather different from that which appears in Bronckart and Sinclair's tables and analyses. At the earliest age, actions seem to be ranked entirely on the basis of their duration, the shortest being the most likely to be past-marked. The authors' Figure 1 shows that the difference between the three highest ranks in the first column (i.e., those actions that have a duration of two seconds or less) is less than ten percentage points, while there is a gap of over twenty percentage points between the lowest of the nondurative actions and the highest of the durative actions (Jx-5).

However, this picture gradually and progressively changes, through the next three age groups: jumping actions irrespective of duration tend to rise in rank, while pushing actions sink to the bottom of the table. The final column shows durative and nondurative actions regularly interspersed, but the four jumping actions are now all placed higher than the two pushing actions. The authors' Figure 1 shows that the stratification between jumping and pushing is quite sharp: while the four jumping actions in the 6:6 column are grouped in a narrow range around the 90 percent past-insertion mark, the higher of the two pushing actions is separated from the lowest jumping action by a span of more than twenty percentage points.

Far from there being an overall rise in past marking of pushing actions, past-marking percentages for these show an absolute decline between ages 4:7 and 6:6, at the same time as past-marking percentages for jumping actions are rising fairly steadily. It stretches the imagination to suppose that children between these ages begin to perceive pushing actions as LESS past and jumping actions as MORE past; yet if we really believe that past tense is all that the children are acquiring, we have no alternative but to believe in improbabilities such as this.

Bronckart and Sinclair note some of the fluctuations mentioned here, but attempt to account for only one of them, and that, perhaps, the least significant: the drop in rank for J-2 (their "event 4") between ages 3:7 and 4:7. The explanation they offer is that "this action took objectively more time (2 sec.) than the others (1 sec.)." By "the others" the authors mean, presumably, J-1 and P-1, but they are a little disingenuous here because they fail to note that the past-marking rate for J-2 ALSO FALLS BELOW THAT FOR Jx-5—which takes more than twice as much time as J-2! Moreover, the rate for J-2 is only a point or two higher than that for Jx-10, which is five times longer! Relative length of time, therefore, cannot be the factor involved.

Let us see if we can really determine what underlies the phenomena illustrated in Table 3.3. From the first column, it would appear that children in the lowest age group do indeed discriminate between events on the basis of pure length. However, as they grow older, the criterion of durativity is replaced by another which is also related to the PNPD.

For the punctual-nonpunctual opposition must also be marked in the semantic features of individual verbs. That is to say, some verbs are inherently punctual, while others are inherently nonpunctual. If you hit something for five minutes, it must be that you hit it many times; similarly, if you jump for five minutes, you must jump many times; both *hit* and *jump* express inherently punctual actions. But on the other hand, if you push something for five minutes, you do not necessarily push it more than once, and if something rolls for five minutes, it does not necessarily roll more than once; both *push* and *roll* express inherently nonpunctual actions (although of course a compound verb like *roll over* is inherently punctual).

In other words, although the PNPD is crucial throughout the acquisition of past-tense marking, the way in which punctuality and nonpunctuality are interpreted changes as children mature. At first, they merely register the relative length of events, and do not distinguish either the inherent characteristics of different actions or any difference between iterative and durative events. Note how, in column 1 of Table 3.3, the two Jx events, which are sequences of punctual events, are grouped with P-10, the only truly durative event. Thus, their judgment of what is nonpunctual at age 3:7 accords with the commonest creole judgment of what is nonpunctual: that is, a merger of the iterative (habitual) with the durative (progressive).

However, as time goes by, the two Jx events are reinterpreted as sequences of events, each one of which, considered individually, is brief and inherently punctual. Thus, iteratives are removed from the nonpunctual category (which now contains only duratives) and reassigned to the punctual category. This judgment—merging of iteratives with punctuals—corresponds to the minority creole pattern found in Jamaican Creole and perhaps a few others referred to under the heading of Deviation E in Chapter 2 (p. 78). It is certainly intriguing to speculate that at least some of the relatively few real differences in creoles could result from their having been "finalized," so to speak, at slightly different age levels by the inventing generation—but of course we can only speculate at this stage.

What is of more immediate interest is the insight that we can derive, from the process described above, into the way in which a bioprogram would evolve. Some scenarios for Chomskyan innatism seem to suggest that every neonate already has a full *Aspects* grammar curled up in Broca's region. This literalistic reading of "innate" has no place in a bioprogram theory. A true bioprogram would grow, develop, and change just as the physical organism that houses it grows, develops, and changes. Increases in the child's cognitive abilities (which of course also form part of the bioprogram in its widest sense) would interact with the linguistic component and progressively modify it.

For the French-speaking child, the shift in the nature of the nonpunctual category would have the effect of moving more events into the punctual category, thus making more events available for past marking. It would, in other words, help the child in his transfer from predominantly punctual marking to predominantly past marking—although whether this result issues from the hand of a beneficent providence, or is merely an accidental bonus, it is far too early to tell.

The suggestion that children may have been marking punctuality when they seemed to have been marking pastness may still seem bizarre to some readers. Let us, therefore, see how well it stands up in light of another well-known study of tense acquisition—that of Antinucci and Miller (1976).

Antinucci and Miller found that the earliest tense form used by their sample of Italian-speaking children was the past participle. At first this always agreed in number and gender with the sentential object, suggesting that the children regarded the participles as adjectives rather than verbs. Then, around age two, they dropped the agreement rule and began to use the participles in ways suggesting that they now perceived them as true past-tense verbs (the usual past tense in Italian consists of auxiliary plus participle, *ho venuto* 'I came', but the children almost always omitted the auxiliary).

However, the verbs which children used in this way appeared to be somewhat restricted in number. The authors divided verbs into three classes: activity verbs (where the action has no end result), stative verbs, and change-of-state verbs (such as *close, fall, give,* etc.) which describe actions as a result of which "an object changes its state." They found that with very few exceptions, children's past forms were found with verbs of the last class only, and they concluded that the child could only assign past tense to an action when something presently in his physical environment—a toy that had been broken, some milk that had been spilled—remained behind as a concrete result of that action.

Now, it happens to be the case that change-of-state verbs are all inherently punctual; the rare, apparent exceptions are often due to purely technological developments, as in *the abandoned astronaut fell toward the planet for several hours.* But even sentences like that can be seen to be underlyingly punctual if we apply another test for inherent punctuality: the question, "If you stop halfway through *Ving,* have you *Ved?*" Thus, if you stop halfway through closing, you have not closed, and if you stop halfway through giving, you have not given; similarly, if the abandoned astronaut stopped halfway through falling, he would not have fallen, although he might have lost altitude. But with activity verbs, which are inherently nonpunctual, the converse applies: if you stop halfway through playing, you have played, if you stop halfway through writing, you have written, and so on. If, as the Bronckart and Sinclair study suggests, the more an action is regarded as punctual, the more likely it is to be given past-tense marking, then the verbs in Antinucci and Miller's change-of-state list may be given past marking because they are punctual, rather than for the reason the authors suggest.

It is true that in the Bronckart and Sinclair study the first criterion for the PNPD was raw duration, and that inherent characteristics of verbs did not become dominant until an age long past that of the Antinucci and Miller subjects. However, the Bronckart and Sinclair data are drawn from experiments, whereas the Antinucci and Miller data are drawn from naturalistic observation; moreover, Bronckart and Sinclair do not include any change-of-state verbs in their study. The two studies are therefore not comparable at the fine-grained level of, "Just how do children interpret punctuality at age X?"; they do, however, seem to be in agreement that some kind of PNPD is involved.

There are other clues in Antinucci and Miller's study which

suggest that a punctual analysis may account for the facts better than a change-of-state one. Early in their third year, Italian children generally acquire a second Italian past tense, the imperfect. This is used with activity verbs, but is not extended to change-of-state verbs, which continue to be past-marked with participial forms (with or without auxiliary):

/22/ (Antinucci and Miller's 82)
Mamma *e andato* (participial) al parco e io *stavo* (imperfect) a casa
'Mommy *went* to the park and I *stayed* home'
/23/ (Antinucci and Miller's 90)
Li *ha messi* (participial) nel saco e dopo gli altri bambini *piangevano* (imperfect)
'He *put* them in a sack and then the other children *cried*'

In other words, imperfects and participials are in complementary distribution, the first being used for punctual verbs, the second for nonpunctual ones. Note that this does not reflect anything in Italian grammar; all Italian verbs, whether punctual or nonpunctual, activity or change-of-state verbs, have both perfective and imperfective past tenses.

Antinucci and Miller's explanation for this state of affairs is far from satisfactory. They note that the imperfect appears first during story-telling, and suggest that the child uses it to distinguish "pretend" from real events. But if this were really the case, we would expect use of the imperfect to be extended to all types of verbs, including change-of-state verbs; for surely change-of-state (or punctual) verbs can be used to describe imaginary events as easily as activity (or nonpunctual) verbs. Moreover, in the examples that Antinucci and Miller themselves cite, such as /22/ and /23/ above, the events of *staying* and *crying*, rendered by the imperfect, are no more (or less) "pretend" events than the events of *going* and *putting*, which are rendered by the participial form.

It is therefore highly possible that the connection observed by the authors between "pretend" events and the imperfect is merely a partial and coincidental one. It is hard to tell, since they present no statistical data that would serve to quantify the distribution of participial and imperfective forms in realis and irrealis contexts. And if their hypothesis is falsified even by the few sentences they themselves choose to cite, and if both tenses are past-reference in adult speech, then there is nothing but the PNPD to prevent children from generalizing the more regular, imperfect form to change-of-state verbs, just as English children generalize -ed to irregular pasts.

Indeed, how is it that English children generalize in this way when Italian children do not? If everyone has the same bioprogram, how come everyone doesn't learn the same way? Let us explore this problem in some depth, for by so doing we will not only answer these and other questions, but we will also better understand how the same bioprogram can yield superficially different results when it interacts with two languages that differ in structure.

First, let us dispose of a possible objection. It might be argued that the two processes—Italian-speaking children learning first participles, then imperfects; English-speaking children learning first irregular, then regular pasts—are not really commensurate. So they are not, from an adult point of view. But the child does not have an adult point of view, and for the child they must be completely commensurate. The adult knows that Italian has two tense forms with different meanings, whereas English has only a single form, expressed in diverse ways. But there is no way a child could know this unless he were born with a comparative grammar of Indo-European in his head, as well as *Aspects*. Remember, the children we are talking about are under three. Not only can they not have the slightest idea what the mature tense system of their languages will eventually look like, but even on the most favorable accounts, they can have only the vaguest notion of what past means, and by some accounts, they can have no notion at all.

What must really happen is something like the following. Around age two, the child who happens to be learning Italian becomes aware of a set of rather irregular forms, which are past-reference forms in adult grammar (the Italian participles), whereas the child who happens to be learning English also becomes aware of a set of rather irregular forms, which are also past-reference forms in adult speech (the English "strong" past tenses). Shortly afterward, the child learning Italian encounters a set of quite regular forms, once again past-reference forms in adult speech (the Italian imperfective), while, around the same time, the child learning English also encounters a set of regular forms that are past-reference forms in adult speech (the English "weak" past tenses).

Up until this point, the experiences of the two children have been, from their point of view, identical. I defy anyone to explain how those experiences could be differently interpreted by the two children—except in a single respect, which we shall deal with shortly. From the child's point of view, in both cases he has begun by finding some irregular forms that mean past (from the traditional perspective) or punctual (from the perspective of this volume), and he has gone on to find some regular forms that also mean past (from the traditional perspective).

But now, the Italian learner and the English learner part company. The Italian learner keeps the two sets of forms, the regular and the irregular, completely separate, applying one set to one class of verbs and the other to another. The English learner, on the contrary, proceeds to generalize the regular set to the irregular set, applying "weak" tense endings to "strong" verbs in defiance of adult grammar rules. Why? Why doesn't the Italian learner make a similar generalization? Or, to put it differently, why doesn't the English learner make the same kind of distinction as the Italian learner, maintaining the irregular forms (like *came, went, bought, sold, gave, broke*—all good changes-of-state, note) for punctual verbs, and saving the *-ed* affix for activity verbs?

To understand the answer, we have to get used to looking at the acquisition process in a way it has not been looked at hitherto—even though everything we know about language points to that way as the most logical and fruitful. Alas, the "order of acquisition" gambit set child language studies back fifteen years by concentrating exclusively on the acquisition of isolated features. Small wonder if, as we have seen, the sterility of this approach sent acquisitionists gamboling off across the meadows of pragmatics, cognition, "motherese," etc., which were not much more irrelevant to the central problem of syntax acquisition, but a good deal less dull. For what both groups forgot was that language is a tight system composed of even tighter subsystems. Children do not learn individual morphemes in isolation from one another; they build up subsystems and at the same time integrate those subsystems into an overall system.

The situation was not helped any by the primitive state of the art in TMA studies, in spite of (I would prefer to say, because of) work in the field from Reichenbach (1947) to Comrie (1976) and Woisetschlaeger (1977). We shall return to this issue in Chapter 4; for the moment, suffice it to say that an approach like Comrie's, which tries to extract some kind of Platonic core meaning from terms like "perfective" and "imperfective," totally ignores the fact that the units of grammatical subsystems cannot be defined independently of those systems—that, in consequence, what "perfective" and "imperfective" mean, in any subsystem where such labels are applicable, is entirely determined by how many other units that subsystem has and what the other units mean.

Once this viewpoint is established, we can proceed to look at the acquisition of TMA systems AS SYSTEMS, bearing in mind all the while the injunction of the bioprogram: "Make sure that punctuals and nonpunctuals are adequately differentiated." We may then represent the acquisition process for English and Italian learners as in Figure 3.1 on the following page:

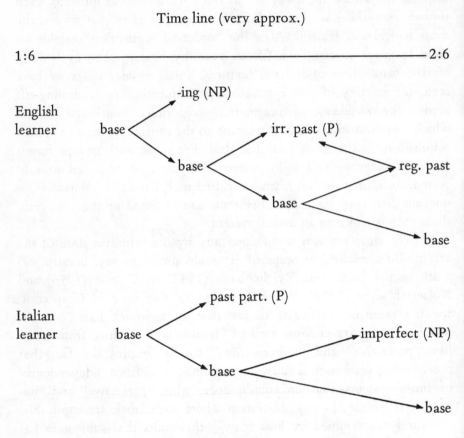

Figure 3.1
Comparative TMA acquisition (Italian versus English)

Both English and Italian learners begin with a single undiffer-entiated base form which at first has to cover all intended forms of TMA reference (in fact, the Italian base form is really a series of forms differentiated for person, but this and similar details will be ignored here for the sake of clarity of presentation). As new forms are added, the semantic scope of this base form contracts until it evolves into the adult, so-called "present tense" in both languages. Note, however, that the scope of this "present tense" differs in English and Italian; in English it includes habitual and iterative reference only, whereas in Italian it includes progressive and durative reference also. The child, needless to say, cannot foresee these facts, but they exert a profound influence on the acquisition process, as the following paragraphs will show.

The question of what determines the order in which new forms are acquired is too complex to be explored fully here.[6] However, it seems likely that the difference between Italian and English present tenses determines the first addition to the system. English has a distinct (and frequent) form for present progressives; Italian has not. Therefore, the first new term that English learners add is a nonpunctual one. But since there is no similar form in Italian, the first new form that Italian learners add is a past form—the participle—which they interpret as a punctual one.

The second new form acquired by English learners is the irregular past, which they interpret as marking punctuality. They are therefore now able to mark both sides of the PNPD. But shortly afterward they become aware of a third form—regular past -ed. Since they already have markers for punctual and nonpunctual, they cannot accommodate this new form by assigning to it its own semantic scope; they therefore assume they were wrong in choosing irregular past as a punctual marker, and proceed to extend -ed to those past punctuals which had previously been allotted irregular forms.

However, the second new form acquired by Italian learners is the imperfect. This, like the past participle, is used for past reference by adults, and if Italian learners were really using participles to mark past reference, they would surely generalize the imperfect form to verbs of all types, just as English learners generalize -ed—for, as noted above (p. 176), the Italian participial/imperfect opposition and the English irregular/regular past opposition must look formally identical to the child learner. The reason why they do not do this can stem only from the unique difference between the situations of the two sets of learners: English learners have already marked both sides of the PNPD, while Italian learners have marked only one side. For them, nonpunctuals are yet to be marked, so instead of generalizing the imperfect, they seize on it as their nonpunctual marker and keep it carefully separate from their marker of punctuality, the participial form.

Note that without the bioprogram the differences in behavior between Italian and English learners are quite inexplicable. In virtually identical circumstances, the English learner over-generalizes, while the Italian learner under-generalizes. However, once we see that English and Italian learners are equipped with an identical program, but still satisfying the requirements of that program in a different order—an order determined by the interaction of the bioprogram with two different languages—such differences are not merely explicable, but follow inevitably from the theory presented here.

Now we can better understand what the child of a first creole generation does. When that child is around 18 to 21 months old, his TMA "system" and the TMA "system" of his parents' pidgin exactly coincide; both consist of the "universal base" shown at the left-hand side of Figure 3.1. The only difference between the child's trying to learn a pidgin and the child's trying to learn French or Italian is that the latter will be offered a variety of verb forms which he can then interpret according to the specifications of his bioprogram, while the former will not be offered anything new in the way of forms. The creole child therefore decides to mark the nonpunctual side of the opposition.

Two questions may be asked here: why does the creole child decide, apparently without exception, to mark nonpunctuals rather than punctuals, and why does he not mark both terms of the opposition, as I have claimed that both English and Italian children do?

I think that nonpunctuals rather than punctuals are marked because, from a pragmatic viewpoint, nonpunctuals represent the marked case in a Jakobsonian sense: in the real world, more actions are punctual than nonpunctual; punctual actions constitute the background against which nonpunctual actions stand out. Regarding the second question, we should rather ask, why do noncreole children mark both terms? The answer to that clearly is because noncreole children receive, if anything, too great a variety of forms—greater, certainly, than any two-year-old can incorporate into a coherent system. The child feels obliged to assign some kind of significance to terms with which he is constantly bombarded, so he assumes that in the language confronting him both sides of the PNPD are formally marked.

But, of course, both sides of an opposition do not have to be formally marked—it serves to distinguish them if you formally mark one term and zero-mark the other. Considerations of parsimony alone would indicate such a choice, if the opportunity presents itself (and for the creole child, it does). It is quite enough trouble for the creole child to select, from the pidgin, one content-word (like HPE locative *stei*) to mark one term of the opposition, without having to search out another to mark the other. In both cases, albeit by different means, the demands of the bioprogram are satisfied.

I have little doubt that when acquisitionists begin to study TMA acquisition from a dynamic, systems-oriented standpoint, and with the tools of variation analysis already available from decreolization studies, many more of the effects of the bioprogram will become visible. For the present, we must leave that area and survey rather more briefly some others in which resemblances between creoles and acquisitional stages are to be found. We shall look at just four areas: complement Ss, questions, negatives, and causatives.

A recent overview of complex sentence acquisition (Bowerman 1979) draws heavily on Brown (1973) and Limber (1973), which appear to be the major, if not the only, sources in this area. If true, this is surprising, since Brown devotes less than a page (p. 21) to sentential complements, and Limber's only slightly longer (six-page) treatment leaves many crucial questions unasked. However, much of what is said by these scholars is highly suggestive.

Brown cites four examples only of complement Ss produced by children:

/24/ I hope *I don't hurt it.*
/25/ I think *it's the wrong way.*
/26/ I mean *that's a D.*
/27/ You think *I can do it?*

Brown comments that "the embedded sentence appears exactly as it would if it stood alone as an independent simple sentence." He observes that there are other types of complement S of which this is not true, such as:

/28/ It annoys the neighbors *for John to play the bugle.*

He does not state whether or not the children in his sample produced sentences like /28/, but the implication is that they did not. He does observe, however, that "there is also a complementizer *that*" which can occur in sentences like /24/-/27/; but "the children did not use it."

Limber's data are more problematic in that it is not always clear from his treatment whether a given example is an actual child utterance or one presented for heuristic purposes. Thus, although Limber states that "marked infinitive" is acquired early, this is not clearly the case from the example given: *I want to go.* If, as seems probable, this is just an orthographic regularization of the actual utterance, *I wanna go* (a likelihood increased by the fact that Limber himself includes a similar form, *hafta,* in his Table 1), then it is not at all clear *from the viewpoint of what the child (as opposed to the adult) knows* that the child has acquired marked infinitives. Consider the following sentences, which few children can have failed to hear or failed to produce themselves:

/29/ I wanna cookie (unambiguous noun).

/30/   I wanna drink (ambiguous between noun and verb).
/31/   I wanna go (unambiguous verb).

Faced with such data, the most reasonable conclusion on the part of
the child would be that the canonical form of the verb was *wanna*
rather than *want*—or that, at the very least, *hafta, liketa, wanna* should
be entered in the lexicon as variant (perhaps phonologically conditioned) forms of the verb stems concerned. Such, certainly, is the
assumption made by Brown (1973:54) when establishing rules for the
calculation of mean length of utterance: "*gonna, wanna, hafta*...
[were] counted as single morphemes rather than as *going to* or *want
to* because evidence is that they function so for the children."
     The following series of examples represents, with one exception,
all the sentential complement forms cited by Limber which we can
assume to be examples of actual child speech:

/32/   I want *mommy do it.*
/33/   I don't want *you read that book.*
/34/   Watch *me draw circles.*
/35/   I see *you sit down.*
/36/   Lookit *a boy play ball.*

     If we look at these five examples together with the four cited
by Brown (and these, strange to say, seem to be virtually the only
complement-S constructions cited in the literature), we will note
first that not one of them has an overt complementizer, and second,
that with the exception of /34/ the complements could stand on their
own as independent simple sentences. Moreover, since *me* as subject
has been widely reported for black children, it is by no means certain
that for the speaker of /34/, *me draw circles* would be ungrammatical;
and even if it were, the analogy with *watch me, mommy!*—an utterance
surely developmentally prior to /34/—may be what is operative in this
case.
     It is true that we cannot point to the same kind of evidence

we used in Chapter 2, when the same question of finite versus non-finite analysis was at issue; we cannot point to the presence of markers of tense or aspect in the embedded sentence. But it would be illegitimate to expect such evidence, since at the ages from which Limber's examples are taken (1:6 to 3:0), the vast majority of children's verb forms consist of unmarked stems anyway.

The only example of Limber's which was not cited above is:

/37/   I all done eating.

This might at first seem like a clear case of a nonfinite complement S. But Limber himself explicitly observes that in his recordings there is no trace of "a variety of *-ing* complements; for example, *I like eating lollipops* in contrast to the very common *I like to eat lollipops*" (which, as already suggested, is more probably a case of a quasi-modal *liketa*). He further comments that nonfinite *-ing* forms (as distinct from the "finite *-ing*" discussed in a previous section) occurred only in sentences like /37/, i.e., "with *finish* or *all done.*" Although Limber himself does not explicitly draw it, it would seem legitimate to draw the conclusion that *finish* and *all done* are interpreted by the child either as quasi-modals followed by "finite *-ing*" or as main verbs followed by NP. Either way, /37/ would not be relevant to the present discussion.

Limber goes on to "informally summarize" the major developments in complex sentences prior to age three in the following manner: "An N-V-N sequence is the common simple sentence . . . . [children] expand (or substitute) an N-V-N sequence for certain noun phrases . . . [but] do not apply syntactic operations to any subject NPs." Brown (1973:21) also observed that sentences of the type of /38/ below did not occur in child speech:

/38/   *That John called early* annoyed Bill.

Stated more formally, Limber's study would suggest that children have only the following major PS rule (assuming that Aux is not yet established and that there is no evidence, as there seems not to be, for any VP constituent):

$$/39/ \quad S \rightarrow NP \quad V \quad (\left\{ \begin{array}{c} NP \\ S \end{array} \right\})$$

Similarities between the foregoing account of complement Ss in child speech by Limber and Brown and the account of complement Ss in creoles given in Chapter 2 are quite striking. They include:

1) The absence of embedded sentences in subject position.
2) The absence of complementizers.
3) The identity of form between embedded and nonembedded sentences.
4) The absence of nonfinite and subjectless embeddings.

In addition, we may note the similarity of /39/ to the major creole PS rule /236/, Chapter 2, hypothesized on quite independent grounds for all early-stage creoles, and repeated here for convenience as /40/:

$$/40/ \quad S \rightarrow NP \; Aux \; V \; (NP) \; (S)$$

Rule /40/ is merely a slightly more sophisticated version of /39/, as would befit its more mature users, differing only in that it admits an established Aux and allows for object NP as well as complement S in the same sentence, instead of only admitting these as alternatives.

Of the similarities listed, the first three are self-explanatory, but perhaps a word should be said about the fourth, which relates to the absence from child speech of sentences like *I like eating lollipops* and from creoles of sentences like /41/ or /42/:

/41/   GC: *mi hia a sing
              'I heard singing'

/42/   GC: *mi laik a sing
          'I like singing'

(Sentences whose complements have overt subjects, such as *mi hia i a sing* 'I heard him singing', are of course in another class entirely.) In fact, more is involved here than there is space to discuss—/42/ involves equi-deletion while /41/ involves deletion of an unspecified subject, so the reasons for their ungrammaticality cannot be the same—but I would like to suggest a reason why both creoles and children should reject sentences on the model of *I like doing X*.

If children learned language primarily on the basis of analogy, the absence of such sentences would be mysterious. The child would observe some specific questions and answers:

/43/   What are you eating? Cookies.
/44/   What are you playing with? My ball.

Answers to such questions fit well into the frame, *I like . . .*:

/45/   I like cookies.
/46/   I like my ball.

Once the child had acquired "finite *-ing,*" he would be able to answer slightly less explicit questions with *-ing* forms:

/47/   What are you doing? Eating cookies.
/48/   What are you doing? Playing ball.

By analogy with /45/, /46/, these ought to yield:

/49/   I like eating cookies.
/50/   I like playing ball.

Of course, children do not learn primarily by analogy; analogical forms may crop up from time to time, but not when (as here) they would conflict with important structural aspects of the grammar. For *eating cookies* in /47/ is not the same as *eating cookies* in /49/. In /47/, it expresses a particular nonpunctual action in realis time; in /49/, it expresses the abstract concept of an action, not necessarily either punctual or nonpunctual, in irrealis time. The superficial identity of the forms involved is an illusory one, and the child, for all the little he is supposed to know of language, is not fooled by it. For both child and creole, nonpunctual means nonpunctual, nothing more, and because of the form-meaning biuniqueness that characterizes both child speech and creoles, the form chosen to mark nonpunctual cannot be assigned any other function.

We may justifiably conclude, then, that the mechanisms of child language and creoles for incorporating sentences within sentences are highly similar, with one exception: children show no evidence of verb serialization (at least in existing accounts; I would not rule out the possibility that it might turn up if people started looking for it). But then, the reasons why child language doesn't have verb serialization are probably the reasons why some creoles don't have it: because prepositions are available in the input, and therefore serialization is not needed to differentiate case roles.

Let us now turn to questions. Children acquire questions early— certainly by the two-word stage, and probably earlier even than that. The acquisition of question forms was first studied intensively by Klima and Bellugi (1966), and although some subsequent observers have found more variation in question development than these authors recognized, their principal findings have not been seriously challenged.

Among English learners, yes-no questions are at first distinguished from statements only by a rising intonation contour, and WH-questions only by a sentence-initial WH-word; in neither type is there any trace of Subject-Aux inversion. This state of affairs changes only very slowly. Sentences grow longer and more complex, all the question words are acquired, but yes-no questions retain the form of /51/ and /52/:

/51/   This can't write a flower?
/52/   You can't fix it?

At a later stage, when inversion begins to appear in yes-no questions, it is still absent from WH-questions:

/53/   Why he don't know how to pretend?
/54/   Where the other Joe will drive?

This last stage is all the more puzzling because children who remain in it are often at the same time producing sentences which indicate mastery of rules seemingly more complex than those required for correctly forming English WH-sentences, such as the following:

/55/   You have two things that turn around (relativization).
/56/   I told you I know how to put the train together (double comple-
          ment embedding plus embedded nonfinite WH-clause).
/57/   Let's go upstairs and take it from him because it's mine (co-
          ordination and subordinate-clause causative construction).

Why do children at this level of development persist in using structures so different from the many well-formed questions which they must have heard?

      Clark and Clark (1977:354) suggest that "WH-questions may be more difficult because they require *two rearrangements: movement of the WH-word from where it would have been* to initial position in the sentence and inversion of the subject and auxiliary verb" (emphasis added). This claim assumes (rather uncharacteristically for these authors) that children actually carry out, in the processing of sentences, the operations which a generative grammar of English would apply to derive WH-questions. Erreich et al. (1980), writing from an orthodox generative standpoint, make the same assumption. However, the latter note that if children do really derive WH-questions in this way, one would expect to find errors resulting from incomplete application of the process, such as *you doing what?* or *what you doing what?* in place of the expected *what you doing?;*[7] with a candor as rare as it is commendable, they observe that such errors have not as yet been reported and that it will constitute counterevidence to their claims if those errors do not in fact occur. If indeed there is no evidence to support the two-rearrangement argument, the only reason for supposing that WH-questions are psychologically complex is that they take longer to acquire. In other words, the whole explanation becomes circular.

An alternative explanation is suggested by Ruth Clark, who claims that uninverted WH-questions are modeled on the embedded WH-clauses produced by mothers and other caregivers (Clark 1977). For example, the child who asks *where Teddy?* may often be answered by *I don't know WHERE TEDDY IS.* Clark argues that children are sure to listen with special attention to the answers to their own questions; in this way, they acquire the uninverted structures which they subsequently use to form questions of their own. Clark's explanation is implausible on several grounds.

First, the productive use of analogy it entails has little support in acquisition studies generally, and we have just noted one specific case ("nonfinite *-ing*") where the predictions it makes are not in fact fulfilled. Second, if there is anything children can do with language, it is to tell the difference between a question and a statement; according to Halliday (1975), they learn to do this productively, by applying appropriate intonation contours to some of their earliest one-word utterances, around the age of fifteen months. In the two years or so that may elapse between that time and their final mastery of English WH-questions, they must receive countless well-formed tokens of the type to which—since the consequences of inattention may in some cases be acutely dysfunctional for them—they must listen as acutely as they do to answers to their own questions. It is well known that children try, wherever possible, to maintain "one form, one function" in the very teeth of "natural" languages which insist on having two forms for one function and two functions for one form. In the face of all of this, why should children take a form that clearly belongs in answers and use it to make questions?

If we assume a language bioprogram, however, a much more reasonable explanation emerges. The bioprogram would enjoin just that biuniqueness in form-function and form-meaning relationships which children strive for and which creoles, with a large measure of success, attain. In this, it merely follows the pattern of genetic programs in general, which do not prescribe sets of alternative routines, but leave open the possibility of adapting given routines for other purposes.

One resource in the bioprogram is constituent movement. We will not directly consider movement rules in this chapter, although we considered them in the first two, simply because not enough work has been done on the acquisition of movement rules for any valid comparisons to be drawn. But it would appear from creoles that movement has, as the overall model would suggest, only one function—expressing shifts from the expected pattern of focus and presupposition. Certainly no creole rule that I know of moves any constituent for any other reason than this.

English, therefore, goes contrary to the bioprogram when it uses a movement rule—subject-aux inversion—to distinguish between questions and statements. The child, therefore, either fails to hear correctly or simply ignores the sentences that depart so radically from his expectations. Eventually (perhaps as a result of misunderstandings; it would be interesting to have some "caregiver interaction" data on this) the child observes that subject-aux inversion is required in yes-no questions. Two factors could reasonably be expected to delay the generalization of this rule to WH-questions. First, WH-questions are unambiguously marked by the initial WH-word, so that misunderstanding is correspondingly less likely to occur. Second, the fact that WH-questions are already formally distinguishable from statements could well deter the child from applying what, to him, would be a quite redundant rule—why mark a question as a question twice over?

Finally, of course, he has to capitulate; the child learning a creole does not. The yes-no questions of children in Klima and Bellugi's second stage and the WH-questions of children in their third stage are identical with the yes-no and WH-questions cited in Chapter 2.

Let us turn to negation where, again, the findings of Klima and Bellugi (1966) have hardly been superseded (except, again, that they may not have paid enough attention to individual differences). At the earliest stage of negation, a negative morpheme—occasionally *not,* most often *no*—is placed at the beginning or end of the utterance. These forms persist into the second stage, but here, one or two specialized negative forms, such as *don't* or *can't,* are also acquired. Since *cannot* and *do not* never appear at this stage, we can conclude that for the child, *can't* and *don't* constitute monomorphemic utterances. Also these forms seem to be more restricted in distribution than they are in adult language; *don't* seems to be confined (in Klima and Bellugi's examples, at least) to stative verbs and imperatives.

Can't and *don't* are, presumably, superimposed on the bioprogram by sheer force of parental repetition; I know of no statistics on the subject, but casual observation alone suggests that these must be among the most frequent words addressed to small children—perhaps to creole speakers too; for I cannot resist interrupting this account to describe two striking similarities between acquisition and, this time, decreolization.

It may seem illogical at first to compare acquisition with decreolization in a study whose main thrust is the comparison of acquisition and creolization; but regarding later stages of acquisition, such comparisons are apt and pertinent. The position of the bioprogram-activating child vis-à-vis the target-language-enforcing adult is highly comparable to the position of the creole speaker vis-à-vis the superstrate speaker. Both adult and superstrate speaker believe that both child and creole speaker are speaking merely a "broken" form of their own "proper" language. Both child and creole speaker are eventually forced to modify their natural behavior by the bombardment from above.[8] With regard to changes in negative forms, the results seem to be identical. Both basilectal GC and basilectal HCE order Neg before Aux in surface structure; in the decreolization of both languages, the thin end of the wedge of English negative placement (i.e., in surface structure as the second member of Aux) consists of adoption of the negative form of *can* (GC *kyaan*, HCE *kaenat*) to replace, respectively, GC *na kyan*, HCE *no kaen. Kyaan* and *kaenat* are both perceived and treated as monomorphemic units. In GC, *kyaan* is first acquired, and *doon* (the equivalent of *don't*) is acquired second and some time later in the decreolization process; in HCE, *kaenat* and *don* are acquired around the same time. In GC, exactly as in child language, *doon* is initially applied to statives, imperatives, and little else (see Bickerton [1975:Table 3.9], where these two types account for 84 percent of the output of early *doon* users); comparable figures are, unfortunately, unavailable for HCE.

We return now to the normal evolution of child negatives. Around the time that *don't* and *can't* make their first appearance, there also appear sentences such as the following:

/58/ That no fish school.
/59/ He no bite you.
/60/ I no want envelope.

These sentences find exact parallels not in decreolization, but in the classic form of creole negative sentences. As in creoles, the negative morpheme is identical with the morpheme of denial. As in creoles, the negative morpheme is inserted directly after the subject, before any verbal or auxiliary element, rather than sentence-externally (as in the first phase of child negation) or after a first auxiliary or verbal constituent (as in English). This second similarity is maintained even after *no* begins to be replaced by *not:*

/61/ He not taking the walls down.
/62/ Ask me if I not made mistake.

In part, at least, these developments are natural, perhaps inevitable. At the two-word stage there is nowhere the child could put a negative except sentence-externally. Moreover, since *no* is heard as an isolated unit with heavy emphasis, while *not* often occurs in contracted forms which may be unrecognizable to the child, it is hardly surprising that *no* rather than *not* is selected for sentence negation.

It is less clear why negative placement in longer sentences takes the position it does. To judge from the examples cited above, that placement involves post-subject, rather than preverbal, placement—inapplicable in /58/ which has no verb—or second position in sentence—ruled out by /62/ where a subordinate clause is negated. Yet there is no support for a "post-subject" hypothesis in English. One might claim that the child knows roughly where the negative should go but doesn't yet have any auxiliary to place in front of it, so he arrives at post-subject placement by default, so to speak. This may sound plausible at first. But note that post-subject placement is arrived at BEFORE the child acquires *not*—*not* merely usurps the place staked out by *no*. Just how would the child know "roughly where the negative goes" in English if that child has not yet succeeded in even IDENTIFYING *not?* Recognition of the "English position" for Neg-placement depends crucially on the ability to realize that *not* (all that ever occurs in that position) is the marker of negation. Those who would argue for the "commonsense" explanation of how children acquire negative placement will have to explain how you can learn what a form means and where it is placed WITHOUT ACTUALLY LEARNING THE FORM ITSELF.

There is empirical evidence, too, to confirm that people can't and don't learn in this way. I have already suggested some ways in which child acquisition is somewhat like decreolization: or, to put it more precisely, the child's actuation of the bioprogram is like creolization, and the child's modification of bioprogram specifications is like decreolization. Now, as I abundantly demonstrated in Bickerton (1975), decreolization proceeds by acquiring new forms first and new functions later.[9] Newly acquired morphemes are at first assigned meanings and functions that already exist in the speaker's grammar; in other words, these morphemes have to be stripped of the meanings and functions which they had in the superstrate before they can be incorporated into the existing creole grammar. Only later, as that grammar itself changes, do they reacquire all or part of their original superstrate meanings and functions. I know of no counterexamples to this empirical finding, nor has it been challenged in the literature. We should therefore be highly skeptical of any claims about child acquisition which involve the assumption that meanings and functions can be acquired in the absence of the formal units which act as bearers of those meanings and functions.

Another puzzle concerns the slow spread of *don't*. If *don't* is acquired at the same time as post-subject *no,* how is it that the child does not straight away adopt the hypothesis that *don't* is the "real" negative marker, and spread its use to all environments? In fact, *don't* MUST be perceived simply as an alternative to *no,* rather than *do +* negative, since the child has no independent *do* at this stage or for some time to come. If a child applied this hypothesis just to the examples /58/-/62/, he would score two almost correct sentences out of the five—*he don't bite you, I don't want envelope*—as opposed to only three incorrect ones: **that don't fish school, *he don't taking the walls down, *ask me if I don't made mistake.* This is better than five out of five incorrect, which is what he now has.[10]

Resemblances to creole structures are not exhausted even when the child has fully mastered the negative placement rule. McNeill (1966) reports the case of a child who uttered /63/ on eight consecutive occasions, despite overt parental correction:

/63/   Nobody don't like me.

Such sentences, though not reported from all children so far studied, are by no means uncommon at age four or thereabouts. We saw in Chapter 2 that the use of negative subjects with negated verbs is common to a number of creole languages, although it would appear to be uncommon in languages generally.

It could be argued that sentences like /63/ are nothing more than a result of the order in which *somebody, nobody,* and *anybody* are acquired. It is hardly surprising that *somebody,* the only one that can have a concrete referent, is learned first. In consequence, children slightly younger than those who produce sentences like /63/ often say things such as *I don't see somebody* rather than *I don't see anybody.* Since *nobody* is learned before *anybody,* it tends to replace *somebody* in sentences like this, giving *I don't see nobody.* At the same time, when *nobody* is first used in subject position, it would be unrealistic to expect the child to realize immediately that no further formal marker of negation is required; unreasonable, too, to expect him to abandon at once, in sentences like /63/, the system of verbal negation which, as we have just seen, cost him so much difficulty to acquire. On this showing, sentences like /63/ would issue, not from some command of the bioprogram to produce multiple negatives, but rather from factors inherent in the process of learning English.

This argument stands up much better than most others which seek to explain away creole-like structures in child language. However, it is by no means immune to question. It depends crucially on independent motivation for the fact that *nobody* is acquired before *anybody,* which may be as common or more common than *nobody* in adult input. It leaves mysterious both the frequency of negative subject/negative verb in creoles and the greater frequency of double predicate negation in languages generally. There must be some way in which multiple negation is more natural than single negation, despite the pedagogues and logicians.

Here is a case where fuller and more carefully collected data may help to resolve the issue. In creoles, negative subject/negative verb is by no means restricted to generic indefinites like *nobody, no one, nothing.* It also involves *Neg + NP* as in the following GC sentence:

/64/   non dag na bait non kyat
      no dog not bite no cat
      'No dog bit any cat'

I have not seen any reports of sentences like /64/, but that in itself is no indication that they never occur in child language. If they do not occur, then the "commonsense" argument given above could well be the answer. If they do occur, then an argument based on the order of acquisition of negative indefinites cannot account for all the data, and in light of the creole evidence, the workings of the bioprogram must again be suspected.

For our fourth and final area of creole acquisition comparison, we will look at the acquisition of causative constructions.

First (for we shall be drawing evidence from the acquisition of more than one language in this area), we must bear in mind that there are many different ways of making the causative-noncausative distinction (henceforth the CNCD). This distinction may be marked on the subject (as in ergative languages) or on the verb. In either case, there may be several different types of marking, especially where verb-marking is the option chosen. English excludes subject marking, but marks the CNCD on the verb in several ways.

The simplest way of marking the CNCD is by using the same verb for causative and noncausative versions of the same event—i.e., for cases where the subject must be the causative agent but also for cases where the subject is the patient, experiencer, or whatever. These cases are differentiated only by transitivity versus intransitivity: causative-agent cases will have both subject and object NP, noncausative cases will have only subject NP.

/65/   The door opened.
/66/   Bill opened the door.

There are other cases in which the same verb is used for both causative and noncausative versions, but where the noncausative version must be marked by use of the passive:

/67/   *The tree planted.

/68/ The forester planted the tree.

/69/ The tree was planted (by the forester).

In yet other cases, a different lexical verb is required for causative and noncausative versions:

/70/ The sheep *ate* (noncausative).

/71/ John ate the sheep (≠ John caused the sheep to eat).

/72/ John *fed* the sheep (causative).

In a fourth set of cases, no appropriate lexical alternation exists, and for causative versions a periphrastic structure must be used:

/73/ Mary *suffered* (noncausative).

/74/ John suffered Mary (≠ John caused Mary to suffer).

/75/ John *made* Mary *suffer* (causative).

Yet another verb-marking method, not used by English but found, for example, in Turkish, is to employ the same lexical verb in both cases but differentiate them by means of a verbal affix. Ergative languages, too, generally use the same lexical verb, but mark causative subjects only with the ergative case-marker; subjects of noncausatives are marked, like objects of causatives, with the accusative case-marker. The particular strategy or selection of strategies chosen by any language to make the CNCD will, of course, reflect the typology of that language. But the function of all of these varying devices is identical.

Some methods of expressing the CNCD would seem to be more easily acquired than others. Slobin (1978) reports a cross-linguistic experiment on the interpretation of causative constructions in which the subjects were child learners of English, Italian, Serbo-Croat, and Turkish. Subjects were required to act out with toy animals sentences such as *the horse made the camel run*. In English, Italian, and Serbo-Croat, such sentences have rather similar structures, involving two distinct verbs, one of them a lexical causative like *make* (Slobin did not include examples of the three other English ways of marking the CNCD). Turkish, however, uses single verb + affix:

/76/   At deveyi koştursun
       horse-nom camel-acc run-causative-optative-3rd pers.
       (lit., the horse ran the camel)
       'The horse made the camel run'

The task was performed with almost 100 percent accuracy by Turkish-speaking children before the age of three. Serbo-Croat speakers, however, did not reach this level until they were four or over, while even at age four the English and Italian speakers averaged between only 60 and 80 percent.

This finding is hardly surprising in light of the fact that the Turkish causative suffix is learned and used productively and correctly by the age of two—another of those cases of "errorless learning" we discussed earlier in this chapter. Equally early and errorless marking of the CNCD is reported by Schiefflin (1979) for Kaluli, an ergative language of Papua-New Guinea. Here, the suffix which is applied to causative agents is fully acquired and appropriately used by age 2:2, without ever being generalized to nonagentive subjects.

The fact that CNCD strategies that involve marking of causatives by bound morphemes and single-clause structures (the case in both Turkish and Kaluli) are acquired earlier and more easily than structures involving two clauses and a causative verb casts strong doubts on those generative-semanticist analyses that would assume something like *Bill caused the door to become open* as the underlying structure of sentences like /66/. We shall return to this point shortly when we discuss the treatment by Bowerman (1974) of the acquisition of English causatives.

First, however, we should ask how the cases of Turkish and Kaluli relate to the creole case. We saw in Chapter 2 that out of the six potential strategies for expressing the CNCD described above (case-marking, verbal affixation, causal-verb periphrasis, passivization, lexical alternation, and simple transitive-intransitive alternation), creoles use only the last named. The examples given—/86/-/91/, Chapter 2— were identical in structure with the English examples in the present chapter, i.e., /65/-/66/. Notoriously, creoles avoid bound-morphology solutions. Is it not then counterevidence to the language bioprogram that the bound-morphology solutions of Turkish and Kaluli are so quickly acquired?

The answer is: not in the slightest. To provide counterevidence of any value, one would have to show that Turkish-type or Kaluli-type solutions were acquired BEFORE the simple transitive-intransitive alternations of the kind that creoles make. This is a most unlikely finding because, in fact, the Turkish and Kaluli solutions ARE ALREADY transitive-intransitive alternations which are simply underlined, as it were, by the addition of a further marker. Moreover, English causatives of the *door opened/Bill opened door* type are certainly acquired at an equally early age; it is the three other types of causative that create problems, as we shall see.

Far from being counterevidence, the Turkish and Kaluli cases are confirmatory. If there is a language bioprogram, then children are programmed with a set of basic distinctions which they expect that their native tongue will implement somehow. It is less clear whether, or to what extent, they are specifically programmed with the means to realize these distinctions should their native tongue fail to meet their expectations (as is the case, most drastically, if they are born into a pidgin-speaking community). I suspect that the bioprogram may turn out as follows: both distinctions and means for implementing them are programmed, but are not necessarily conjoint in the program. We have already claimed that the bioprogram is not present at birth, but unfolds progressively during the course of the first four years or so of life. The distinctions would then be programmed to emerge prior to two, possibly around eighteen months or earlier, while the means of implementation would not necessarily emerge until the third or fourth year. Thus, children would start early searching for means to express the distinction, and only if they failed to find any would they need the implementation part of the program.

Put like this, without any supporting evidence, the structure of the bioprogram may look too much like some bizarre kind of providentiality, as if a well-meaning deity had foreseen the consequences of European imperialism and specially equipped his creatures to circumvent them. However, the picture will change considerably in the next chapter, when I shall discuss the ways in which the bioprogram may have come into existence. Creole languages will then appear not as a case of divine foresight and beneficence, but rather as the quite accidental consequence of a much vaster design.

As for those who claim that the causative-noncausative distinction is one that is salient to the child and important in his interaction with his environment (and therefore easily learnable from experience), it does not follow, even if the claim is correct, that he can learn from this alone that the CNCD is marked in the language he is learning. There are innumerable facts about the real world that a child has learned by age two, and many of them are extremely important to him, but extremely few of them are explicitly coded in language. How, without prior knowledge, can he know which is to be coded and which is not? And this is without even considering other kinds of problems involved in correct learning of the various CNCD expressions, some of which we will review after discussing English acquisitions.

One of the things that facilitates acquisition of Turkish and Kaluli causatives is that they are uniform; there is but one way to form causatives, and the morpheme involved is unique and undergoes only phonologically-conditioned forms of variation. The picture in English, with its four ways of expressing the CNCD, is at an opposite extreme. Since conflicting evidence is not much better than no evidence at all, the theory would predict that English learners would treat English, in this respect, just as creole children treat a pidgin; that is, having failed to extract from their input a consistent way of expressing the CNCD, they would generalize the simplest transitive-versus-intransitive solution, already available to them from *open*-type verbs, to other classes of verbs. And this is, in fact, exactly what they do.

Bowerman (1974) observed that from around 2:3 on, but more particularly around the age of three, children would employ intransitive (noncausative) verbs in causative sentences:

/77/   Mommy, can you stay this open?
       (sc., make this stay open, keep this open)
/78/   I'm gonna fall this on her.
       (sc., make this fall on her, drop this on her)
/79/   She came it over there.
       (sc., made it come over there)
/80/   How would you flat it?
       (sc., make it flat, flatten it)

Note that this creative process extends to adjectives as well as verbs (/80/), and that the line between adjectives and verbs may therefore, at this stage, be as thin as it is in creoles.

This process does not limit itself to intransitives. Transitive verbs like *eat* which are restricted to noncausative meanings (see /70/, /71/ above) and hence, except where cannibalism is practised, to nonhuman objects are also treated as if they were potential causatives:

/81/   Child (pretending to feed doll): See, she can't eat!
       Mother: Just pretend, honey.
       Child: But I can't eat her!
         (sc., make her eat, feed her)

Clark and Clark (1977:511), in discussing these developments, explicitly compare them with the child's over-generalization of regular plural forms. Indeed, what is significant about these cases is precisely that they constitute a generalization to English of the regular creole strategy. But a good deal more is involved than that.

Let us suppose that children learn language by adopting a series of "strategies"; whether learned or innate is immaterial here. Such strategies would clearly include generalization, one of the best-attested concomitants of acquisition. The strategy of generalization might be informally defined as follows:

Step 1: Look for any regular form with a consistent core of meaning.

Step 2: Apply that form in all possible environments.

Step 3: Compare output with input, and note cases (if any) where these do not match.

Step 4: Remove the exceptions (if any) which appear when Step 3 is applied.

This strategy would be applied in a wide variety of cases: in English pluralization, past tense, and, again, in causatives. The child would note the existence of a number of pairs like *X opened/Y opened X* (Step 1); he would generalize this, yielding pairs like *X ate/Y ate X* (Step 2); he would note counterevidence such as *Y fed X* (Step 3); he would then gradually substitute "irregular" forms like *Y fed X* for false "regular" forms like *Y ate X* (Step 4).

Let us suppose that the Kaluli learner applied a similar strategy. He would first observe that a number of nouns in subject position had an ergative affix (Step 1); he would then generalize the affix to all NPs in subject position (Step 2); he would then note that in fact a number of subjects had a different kind of affix (Step 3); he would then work toward a correct distribution of the ergative and accusative affixes (Step 4).

Unfortunately, while the generalization strategy provides an exact description of what English learners do about causative marking, it provides a completely inaccurate description of what Kaluli learners do about their causative marking. If Kaluli learners applied the same strategy, then we should find large numbers of ergative case-markers applied to experiencer or patient subjects which, according to Schiefflin, we do not do. Why is the generalization strategy chosen in one case, but not in the other?

A simplistic answer might be: because the two cases are not really comparable. In Kaluli, there is a semantic and pragmatic distinction between subjects that cause things to happen and subjects that do not. In English, no such distinction is involved. The sets of verbs that take simple transitive-intransitive alternation, as opposed to those that take lexical alternation, passivization, or causal-verb periphrasis, is not a natural semantic class; nothing but experience could tell one that *the jockey walked the horse* and *the jockey galloped the horse* are grammatical, but *the jockey ran the horse* is not.

It is true that the two cases are not comparable from the standpoint of an adult who knows something of the grammar of both languages—but from the CHILD's viewpoint? How is the child supposed to recognize that semantic sets are involved in one case, but not in the other, unless he already knows what the relevant semantic sets are? He cannot construct semantic sets from experience alone until he has at least experienced the full range of semantic classes that the language contains (if then!). Each lexical item has so many parameters of meaning, could fit into so many partially overlapping classes, that one could never say for certain, given any body of partial data, whether semantic classes did or did not coincide with the formal differences perceptible in those data. But production does not stand still until the child has mastered all possible semantic classes in the language confronting him. The child is under pressure to talk, whether he is ready or not.

If the child formed hypotheses, as so many suppose, then there would be many different hypotheses that the Kaluli child might make. He might assume that ergative and accusative case-markers are merely subject markers that happened to be in free variation, or that the ergative marker marked subjects that happened also to be topics, or that stativity was involved somehow (since many causatives are non-statives, while many statives are noncausatives, this hypothesis might be a very attractive one). But wrong choices of hypothesis would inevitably yield misplaced case-markers, and this does not seem to happen. Miraculously, somehow the first "hypothesis" is the right "hypothesis."

Similar considerations apply to the acquisition of Turkish, except that here the child's task is made more complex by the fact that the causative marker is only one of a string of verbal suffixes which frequently co-occur: suffixes which indicate reciprocity, negation, person, number, tense, and the direct/indirect knowledge distinction which, as we saw above, is the only one that seems to cause problems. These strings of suffixes present two quite distinct kinds of problems. The first is a problem of segmentation, which the child presumably solves by some kind of substitution-in-frame process. The second—figuring out what each of the suffixes means, once they have been segmented— is less often considered, perhaps because it looks easy to the adult, who can "look in the back of the book," so to speak. In fact, it is much more difficult than the first, and the fact that speech to children is strongly oriented toward the here-and-now, often urged as a reason why children do not need an innate component, in reality makes the task harder rather than easier; every situational context is composed of innumerable factors, any of which, for all the child is supposed to know, could be directly reflected in linguistic structure, and sets of contextual features are seldom constant from one situation to another. The child who tried to figure out which semantic factors were marked grammatically—assuming that a two-year-old mind would be remotely capable of this, even at an unconscious level—would be in the position of someone who tries to solve a maze problem; he would have to take the most promising-looking path, pursue it until it was blocked, then retrace his steps to the beginning again and repeat the process. But when we consider that the same semantic factors are marked grammatically over and over again across the range of human languages, that in effect languages select out of a very short list of semantic primes the ones that they are going to mark, much as they select their phonological inventory from the set of distinctive features, it becomes more reasonable to assume that the child has advance knowledge of the contents of the category "grammatically-markable semantic feature."

Thus, both a "strategies" approach and a "hypothesis-forming" approach fail to account for the learning of the CNCD in English, Turkish, and Kaluli. A "strategies" approach fails to explain why the child over-generalizes in the case of English causatives but not in the case of Kaluli causatives—unless it introduces some "hyperstrategic" device which would tell the child which strategy to use in which case.[11] A "hypothesis-forming" approach fails because it cannot show how, out of a wide range of hypotheses that the child could form about the nature of Turkish and Kaluli morphemes, that child invariably picks the correct one the first time around. A language-bioprogram approach is able to deal with both problems. It has no strategies, so the first problem is a ghost problem. It specifies the set of distinctions to be marked, so the second problem does not arise.

However, before leaving causatives we should consider an observation made in Bowerman (1974) that while "correct" causatives like *Mommy open door* are acquired before periphrastic causatives like *Billy make me cry*, "incorrect" causatives do not appear until AFTER the emergence of correct *make* sentences. From these facts, Bowerman argued (and the argument sounded a lot better in the days when generative semantics was still alive) that although the child at an early stage might PRODUCE sentences like *Mommy open door*, he would not yet be able to "break down" such sentences into "a cause proposition and an effect proposition." However, once he had acquired *make* sentences, which do formally divide the sentence into these propositions, he could then analyze sentences with *open*, etc., in just the same way; and, once this reanalysis was complete, it could be generalized to both transitive and intransitive causatives, as we saw in examples /77/-/81/.

There are several problems with this argument. It is far from certain that two distinct propositions do underlie *X-open-Y* sentences: the mere existence of *make-X-do-Y* sentences is not itself evidence one way or the other. Certainly, the results of Slobin's experiments, discussed above, suggest that the latter sentences are perceptually more complex than the former, therefore intrinsically unlikely candidates for underlying forms.

But a more serious objection stems from Slobin's (1978) work

Slobin found that even at age four, English learners often could not act out *make-X-do-Y* sentences correctly, which suggests that even at that age, they understood them only imperfectly. If this is the case, then it is hardly likely that children a little over two could understand them structurally in the way that Bowerman claims. Of course, Bowerman could not be expected to foresee Slobin's results, but she assumes that children understand *make* sentences on the basis of no evidence whatsoever.

Let us suppose that children could analyze sentences as she suggests. In that case, why do they not generalize *make-X-do-Y* to newly acquired noncausatives, instead of going back to *X-open-Y* and generalizing that? If they took this surely very plausible step, they would produce perfectly grammatical sentences like *can you make this stay open?, I'm gonna make this fall on you*, etc., in place of the ungrammatical /77/-/81/. The fact that they do not do this, viewed in light of Slobin's results, suggests that the earliest periphrastic *make* causatives are acquired as idiomatic chunks which are not yet analyzed and therefore not yet generalizable. If they are not analyzed, their analysis cannot be what triggers the spread of incorrect *open*-type causatives. Bowerman's argument is simply the logical fallacy *post hoc, ergo propter hoc.*

As for the alleged delay in the appearance of incorrect *open*-type causatives, this could be due to nothing more complex than the interaction of communicative need with available vocabulary. As long as the child can handle his needs with a relatively small vocabulary, the need to "invent" new causatives simply will not arise. But when the number of things he wants to (and potentially can) say is expanding more rapidly than his vocabulary, which is the case as he gets deeper into his third year, he will need to express concepts like those expressed by *drop, flatten*, etc., before he has had the opportunity to acquire the appropriate lexical items. And it is from this period, say 2:6 to 3:3, that most of Bowerman's examples are drawn.

We have now reviewed a wide range of evidence, dealing with the acquisition of a number of widely different features in several different languages, which cannot easily, if at all, be accounted for by existing theories of language acquisition, but which follow naturally if we assume the existence of an innate bioprogram for language. Moreover, the view of acquisition which this assumption provides is more satisfactory on a commonsense level. Hitherto, we have had to assume that small creatures who could barely control their own bowel movements were capable of learning things—whether you choose to call them "rules" or "behavior" is quite irrelevant at this level—of such abstractness and complexity that when brought to the level of consciousness, mature scholars often misanalyze them. This paradox was not very often alluded to, but of course it was always there whether it was alluded to or not. Now we can see that children can only learn language because, in effect, they already know a language.

Interestingly enough, a similar view was arrived at by Fodor (1975), arguing in a completely different way from a completely different starting point. According to Fodor, it is not just commonsense improbable, it is logically impossible for anyone to learn a language unless he already knows a language. "Learning a language (including, of course, a first language) involves learning what the predicates of the language mean. Learning what the predicates of a language mean involves learning a determination of the extension of these predicates. Learning a determination of the extensions of the predicates involves learning that they fall under certain rules (i.e., truth rules). But one cannot learn that (P)redicate falls under (R)ule unless one has a language in which P and R can be represented. So one cannot learn a language unless one has a language" (Fodor 1975:63-64).

Thus, to give a concrete example from the first case we looked at in this chapter, a child cannot know which members of the class *a NP* are specific and which are nonspecific unless he knows what specific and nonspecific mean, and he cannot know what they mean unless he has, in some sense, a language in which that meaning is somehow represented. As to how it might be represented, that must be reserved for the next chapter.

Marshall (1979) notes that "no-one has yet brought forth a convincing counter-argument" to Fodor's claim, although most people agree "that this conclusion is untenable." I find it bizarre that a strictly logical conclusion should be regarded as untenable, especially when neither Marshall nor anyone else has been able to suggest any cogent or coherent reason why it should be untenable. I find it doubly bizarre now that Fodor's claim can be supported by the large body of empirical evidence surveyed in the preceding chapters—evidence arrived at by methods totally different from Fodor's and, at the time of gathering, in total ignorance of his claims. When two such dissimilar approaches agree so completely in their results, neither coincidence nor *folie à deux* provides a convincing explanation.

However, there is tremendous emotional resistance to the idea that language is innate, some of the reasons for which I would like to glance at briefly in Chapter 5. In part, this emotional resistance is rationalized by some curious ideas about what is entailed in the making of innatist claims. Typical are the following:

> It is not very helpful, however, to stop with the conclusion that linguistic universals spring from innate predispositions (Clark and Clark 1977:517).

> ... to assume that deep structures are "innate" makes a postulate out of a problem and this in itself means that all further study can lead us nowhere (Luria 1975:383).

Similarly, I am quite certain that many students of acquisition who have read this far will at the moment of reaching this very paragraph be thinking something along the following lines: "Sure, he says that the problems of accounting for acquisition are much simpler if you assume an innate bioprogram. Of course they are; you can simply avoid them by making a completely untestable claim. Everybody knows that children learn; the real job is finding out how they do it, and he's just shirking that."

There are so many replies to this, one hardly knows where to start. Let me begin by saying that students of acquisition have shirked two tasks, not just one: the task of accounting for how creoles were learned, and the task of accounting for how the first human language, whatever that was, was learned. If they think that these two tasks are somehow different in kind from, or irrelevant to, the processes of "normal" language acquisition, the onus is now squarely on them to prove this.

Next, nobody is denying that children learn. Children learning English learn the difference between English and the bioprogram language, and I am sure that they use a whole battery of learning strategies, inductive processes, etc., in the course of doing this. Students of learning in the traditional sense need have no fears that the rug will be pulled out from under them; their field is still ample, and, if narrower, at least better defined than before.

All that is threatened is the assumption underlying their attitude: that language cannot be innate. This is in fact an a priori assumption for which the only evidence ever advanced is the ostrich-like pooh-poohing typified by Luria's comment. What is more, it is an inherently improbable assumption in view of the fact that the vast majority of behavior by animate creatures, especially behavior as crucial to a species as language is to ours, is biologically programmed. To suppose that language is not is against the balance of the evidence and a mere piece of species arrogance, as I am sure any Martian arbiter (if only there *were* Martians!) would quickly agree.

If indeed language is innate, then to continue looking for ways in which it could be learned from experience makes about as much sense as dropping your keys on the left-hand side of the road and then looking for them on the right-hand side because there aren't any streetlamps on the left-hand side. Further, the claim that the theory is untestable, like the claim that innateness represents a necessary terminus for research, is simply untrue.

In the course of the present chapter I have mentioned specifically a number of predictions which the theory makes about acquisition processes; these should be easily testable by reference to primary data. Moreover, acquisition has yet to be studied in the vast majority of human languages. All of them should show reflexes of the bioprogram features claimed in this chapter, although clearly those reflexes will differ from language to language since we cannot study the activity of the bioprogram directly, but only its interaction with particular target languages. Thus, the evidence available will not always be clear, and its interpretation will be more often than not a matter of legitimate controversy; but nobody can claim that such evidence is either scarce or hard to obtain. The fact that I have been able to derive so much evidence from works whose authors were not even looking for phenomena crucial to the present theory lends further support to the claim that evidence will be plentiful; if even the crude plow of the pioneer throws up nuggets, there can be little doubt that the trained prospector following on his heels will find many more.

Moreover, there are other ways in which the theory can be tested. One is by a study of the present-day acquisition of creole languages, a study which has yet to be carried out. Although creoles are nowadays acquired in just the same way as other languages, the nature of their origins ought to mean that they are acquired with far fewer mistakes on the part of the children, and in a far shorter period of time. Comparisons between acquisition in creole and noncreole cases can empirically test this hypothesis, and if differences in time span and/or quantity of error do indeed exist, they can give them a reasonably accurate statistical measurement. Of course, the results will be more meaningful the more that creoles relatively free of superstrate influence, which have remained relatively unchanged since their origin, are made the subject of study. Little value would be obtained from a study of HCE acquisition, for example, given the rising tide of English that is presently eroding it, and the fact that in its purest form it is spoken only by a minority of the population, few if any of whom are now under forty-five.

Eventually, of course, empirical testing of the theory will depend on advances in the field of neurology, since whatever is innate must have an objective physical foundation in the structure and/or mode of functioning of the human brain. Indeed, linguists are all too often woefully ignorant of this field. For example, Alleyne (1979) writes: "There is nothing *readily apparent* in the neurological and cognitive systems of humans that makes it natural or inevitable" that the categories I have proposed for TMA systems should be the appropriate ones (emphasis added). The expectation that the appropriateness of semantic categories should be "readily apparent" in our neurological and cognitive systems would appear to presuppose a human brain charted, labeled, and numbered like the old-time phrenologist's diagrams. We are nowhere near that stage yet; if we get there, it will be due in part to the linguist's telling the neurologist some things to look for, and the neurologist's telling the linguist whether what he has found confirms or disconfirms what the linguist predicted.

Remarks like those of Luria or Clark and Clark cited above seem to envision the linguist as some kind of bucolic sheriff, shaking his fist in impotence because the perpetrator has just fled across the county line. So what if we have to go learn neurology? So what if neurologists have to go learn linguistics? We are boring the same mountain from different sides, and the idea that innateness spells scholarly impotence reflects only the lack of imagination of those who entertain it.

We have not even yet exhausted the remedies available to us right here and now. There is a diachronic aspect to the whole issue which has not yet been appreciated. The bioprogram itself must have a history and an origin, and that history and origin cannot lie beyond all tracing. It is true that the attempt to trace them will lead us into what has proved a veritable Sargasso Sea of theories: glottogenesis, the origin of human language. But we will have at least one advantage over earlier voyagers. We will be equipped with a much more explicit theory, and one moreover that can draw on the many advances in evolutionary science which have taken place since the last time glottogenetic speculation was fashionable.

In the next chapter, accordingly, we will attempt to reconstruct the prehistory and early history of human language, in order to determine, if at all possible, what might be the origins of the language bioprogram whose consequences the first three chapters have explored. In particular, we will try to suggest specific bases for a least some of those semantic distinctions which, as the present chapter has suggested, must constitute an important, although far from the only, part of the structure of the bioprogram. For the convenience of the reader, I repeat the four major distinctions dealt with in this chapter, together with evidence for each:

1) *Specific-nonspecific.* Evidence: universality of creole zero versus indefinite article; errorless English acquisition of a_1 versus a_2.

2) *State-process.* Evidence: "skewing" of creole verbal systems; distribution of nonpunctuals in creoles; errorless acquisition of English *-ing* distribution; errorful acquisition of Turkish *-dI/-mIs* distinction.

3) *Punctual-nonpunctual.* Evidence: universality of nonpunctual marking in creoles; mode of acquisition of past tenses in French and Italian.

4) *Causative-noncausative.* Evidence: N_iV/NVN_i alternation in creoles and English acquisition; errorless acquisition of causative marking in Turkish and Kaluli; problems of English, Italian, and Serbo-Croat learners with "generative-semantics-type" causatives.

This list is by no means intended to be exhaustive. Its members are merely those distinctions best attested so far in both creoles and acquisition. In addition, we will look out for factors which might have influenced the more purely syntactic features we have surveyed, such as the order of auxiliaries, sentential complementation, verb serialization, etc.

So far, our flight has hugged the ground of empirical fact. Now, and quite unavoidably, we must take off for a more speculative realm. And yet in that realm, we must never lose sight of the fact that there is at least one thing there that is as certain as death or taxes. Even if it could be shown that natural languages are learned, even if it could be shown that creoles are learned, it cannot be shown that the original human language was learned—for it could not have been learned. Even if one believes that our ancestors were taught by spacemen, then the spacemen weren't taught, or whoever taught the spacemen wasn't taught. There is no escape in regress. Somewhere, sometime, somehow, human language began, and it could not have begun through acquisition strategies, or inductive processes, or hypothesis formation, or mother's home-cooked language lessons. It must have been "invented." And if there were already processes by which language could be invented, it goes against parsimony to suppose that the human species then had to acquire a whole lot of new processes in order to learn what it could already invent and therefore, presumably, reinvent, whenever occasion might arise. As we shall see in Chapter 4, it is much more plausible to suppose that each step slowly and painfully made in the direction of language was then—had to be—incorporated into the genotype so that it could serve as the take-off point for the next step.

Imagine a man ascending the face of a glacier. Painfully and laboriously he hacks out each step. Each step has to be hacked out to give him space so that he can stand and hack out the next step. But the steps remain behind him when he has moved on, and once they are complete, the merest novice can attain the summit with ease.

Chapter 4
ORIGINS

Ever since it has been anything you could even remotely call a science, linguistics has been set in a mold of static formalism. I do not make this remark in a spirit of reproach, as do so many who offer in exchange some form of quantitative, communication-oriented, or functionalist approach, equally static but a whole lot less rigorous. There are many points in the history of a science when developments that may not seem desirable from an ideal viewpoint may be strategically necessary if the discipline is to advance; such I believe were the idealizations initiated by de Saussure and refined by Chomsky. I would not even go so far as to say that such idealizations had outlived their usefulness. In particular, work by Chomsky and his associates over the last decade—which I understand is aimed principally at establishing, as it were, the outer limits of language—is I think extremely important and complementary, rather than opposed, to the present approach, as I shall try to show in the final chapter.

The only problem from my point of view with the generativist approach is that it tends to create a mind-set rather difficult to adapt to the kinds of problems we have to address in the present study. In acute cases, the mind-set may be so rigid that when problems can no longer be ignored, they are verbalized away, rather than grappled with; I am thinking, for instance, of Chomsky's response to a perfectly legitimate question by Harnad (Harnad et al. 1976:57).[1] Of course, if you believe that human language is always and everywhere the same, that all languages are equal in expressive power, and that how human language developed can have no conceivable relevance to what language is like today, if indeed it developed at all, if indeed it did not spring in its entirety from Jove's brow by some beneficent and unprecedented mutation—if you believe all of this, then you are ill-adapted to understand the dynamic processes which, as every man of sense since Heraclitus has realized, govern all that takes place in our universe. Those in whom the malady is less advanced are hereby requested to retune their receivers to a processual wavelength, if they wish to get the most out of the present chapter.

The fact that static formalism has prevented linguists from grappling with the origins of language has not, of course, prevented persons from other disciplines—with, unfortunately but inevitably, rather less understanding of all that language entails—from trying their hands at it. Their efforts—and those of earlier generations of linguists—have yielded a host of purely speculative theories which I shall not attempt to review here.[2] Suffice it to say that all of them suffer from the same defect: they concentrate, exclusively or almost so, on the moment when recognizable speech first emerged, when Ug first said to Og, "....." ("....." being some kind of meaningful, even if only monolexical, proposition, delivered in the vocal mode). This, which one can only characterize as the Flintstones approach to language origins, totally ignores the vast amount of preadaptation that was necessary before you could even get to that point, and equally ignores the vast amount of postadaptation that was necessary in order to get from that point to fully developed human language.

That the Flintstones approach lives is shown by the current hottest number in origins studies—the "gestural-origin" theory (Hewes 1973; 1976, etc.). Whether or not the theory that a gestural language preceded spoken language is a violation of parsimony (as suggested by

Hill and Most [1978]) is really beside the point. Either this gestural language was of a structure as complex and noniconic as modern sign—in which case the real question would be, how did this gestural language develop?—or it was some much simpler and more iconic system—in which case the real question would be, how did it get to be more abstract and complex? In fact, the "gestural-origins" theory is just as much focused on the supposed "critical point" of language development, and just as indifferent to any of the substantive questions about language origins as any of the other "Flintstone" theories.

The trouble with almost all previous attempts to look at origins is that they do not go back far enough. If we were to understand thoroughly all that language involved, we would probably have to go back to the birth of the lowliest animate creatures, for language depends crucially on a matrix of volition and primitive consciousness which must have begun to be laid down hundreds of millions of years ago. Such an approach lies far beyond the scope of the present volume, and will be addressed in a subsequent work, *Language and Species*. Here, I shall go back no further than, say, *Dryopithecus*, although a brief glance at the frog will not hurt us.

Again, as in previous chapters, a certain amount of ground-clearing work must be done if we are to avoid irrelevant distractions. At the very least, we will have to dispose of what I shall call the Paradox of Continuity.

The Paradox of Continuity is, at the present moment, perhaps the greatest obstacle to a proper understanding of language origins, as well as a powerful factor in keeping linguistics isolated from other human studies. It may be expressed as follows. On the one hand, all the species-specific adaptive developments that we know of have come about through regular evolutionary processes, and language, remarkable though it may be, is only one such development; therefore, language must have evolved out of prior mammalian communication systems. On the other hand, if one has anything like a complete understanding of what language is and does, one realizes that there is not simply a quantitative, but a qualitative and indeed unbridgeable, gulf between the abstractions and complexities of language and the most abstract and complex of known mammalian systems (which, indeed, seem pretty direct and simple); therefore, language cannot have evolved out of prior mammalian communication systems. Thus, there must have been evolutionary continuity in the development of language, yet there cannot have been evolutionary continuity in the development of language. This is the Paradox of Continuity, and debate on it has followed the approved political model of both sides hurling slogans at one another from their different and, as we shall see, mutually irrelevant positions.

All paradoxes that are resolvable are resolved by showing that one or more of the presuppositions on which they are based is incorrect or at best misleadingly stated. In the present case, both sides of the paradox have weak legs. The weak leg of the discontinuity side is a belief in the unitary nature of language; the weak leg of the continuity side is the belief that if language evolved out of anything, it must have evolved out of another communication system. Let us examine each of these in turn.

The belief that language is one and indissoluble has also taken its toll on the primate-experiment debate. In both areas, the central point of debate has been "When can X be said to have language?"— "language" being defined, by the discontinuity side, as something virtually indistinguishable from Modern English or Ancient (ancient!) Greek. Although the continuity side may have protested the definition, few have protested the gambit; instead of pointing out that the question "Has X got language or hasn't he?" is an intrinsically stupid, irrelevant, and actively misleading question, they have mostly contented themselves with trying to get linguists to lower the target (for a generally bracing and insightful, if overly soft on the continuity side, account of the ape debate, see Linden 1974).

In fact, we will get nowhere until we appreciate that anything as complex as language cannot possibly be an internally undifferentiated object, but rather must consist of a number of interacting systems, some of which may originally have developed for other purposes and many, perhaps all, of which must have developed at different times and under different circumstances. Once we accept this, we can perceive the development of language as a succession of stages and therefore amenable to reconstruction and study, rather than as a quantum leap, which then imposes on us, whether we will or no, some kind of catastrophe theory as the only possible origins story. It then becomes possible to replace "Has X got language or hasn't he?" with the more interesting, and more answerable question, "How far has X come along the road to language—specifically, which of the necessary prerequisites does he have, and which does he still lack?"

In the opposite camp, the belief that language must have evolved from some prior communicative system if it evolved at all is clearly connected with the belief that language is only, or originally, or primarily, a communicative system. Any doubt cast on this is enough to send the continuity side into a flurry of pooh-poohing. Typical is the attitude of Young (1978:175), who finds it "a further *problem*" that "a major use of language in each of us is internal—for thinking, that is *for speaking to ourselves*," but nevertheless concludes that it is "*rather perverse* not to consider human spoken or written language as primarily a functional system evolved for communication" (emphasis added). Perhaps a biologist may be forgiven for not realizing that language is not just "for communication" but is also that which is communicated. But in fact the belief is widespread that all language involved was giving labels to things and stringing the labels together. It is assumed as self-evident that when we were ready to talk, all the things in the universe stood there waiting—rock and river, dodo and elephant, storm and sunrise, thirst and evil, love and dishonor—all waiting patiently for their labels. That the world had to be recreated in the image of language before anyone could communicate about anything at all is an idea that seems simply not to have occurred on the continuity side. How that recreation was carried out will form an essential part of the analysis that follows.

Crucial to extant continuity models, even the most recent, is the belief, whether implicit or explicit, that you could get from a call system to modern language (with or without an intermediate stop at a gestural system) by a series of imperceptible stages. Thus, Stephenson (1979) proposes a "dialectical" evolutionary process by which, when our ancestors were more preyed upon than preying, they learned to control involuntary vocalizations and replace them with manual signs (how a four-foot hominid in five-foot grass informs his cohorts of the imminent approach of a sabertooth by gesture is left unclear); then when they got to be better predators and were less concerned with unobtrusiveness, they were able to return to voice, which was now under cortical control. "The dialectic consists in *an increase in the level of complexity of messages* coincident with a decrease in the limbic content of messages as one proceeds through calls, through gesture, to spoken language and into written language" (emphasis added). Steklis and Raleigh (1979) dismiss the gestural phase on principles of parsimony, but maintain call-language continuity by accepting the claim by Hockett and Ascher (1964) that progressive blending and differentiation of primate calls could have mediated the transition.[3]

All these views share the assumption that the only significant difference between call systems and language lies in "an increase in the level of complexity of messages." In fact, complexity is not the issue. A given alarm call could well receive the reading, "Look out, you guys, a large predator is already near and rapidly approaching, so get up the nearest tree as quick as you can," which is surely at least as complex as "the boy ran" or "John kicked Bill." Language depends crucially not on complexification but on the power to abstract, *as units,* classes of objects, classes of actions, classes of events, and classes of yet more abstract kinds (think, for example, for a moment of all the different kinds of relationships that can be conveyed by so simple a predication as *X has Y*). It is these classes, not the particular objects, actions, etc., of which they are composed, that constitute the units that language must represent; but in order to represent them it must first abstract them from the constant sensory bombardment to which all creatures are subject (we will see how in a moment). An alarm call abstracts nothing from that bombardment, but merely selects from it a set of stimuli (smells, colors, physical movement, etc.) to which some kind of immediate reaction is the only appropriate response. A call and a sentence may both constitute communication, but in the ways in which they work they are more at odds than chalk and cheese; for some chalks and some cheeses at least have the same color and texture, whereas language and call systems do not even have this superficial resemblance.

However, once we are prepared to consider the possibility that language could have developed in a regular evolutionary fashion without having sprung from some primitive repertoire of grunts, groans, and grimaces, all the objections to a continuity approach melt like snow in August. Once we have gotten over the "communicative" hang-up, we can see that where we must look for the distinctiveness of human language is not in what it shares with call systems—both communicate—but in how it differs from call systems—language communicates concepts, call systems communicate stimuli. If we don't understand conceptualization, we don't understand language, period.

However, if we are to write an evolutionary history of conceptualization, there is one more ghost to be exorcised—the ghost of Descartes. This particular specter is still haunting the behavioral sciences even though the naturalistic observations on which its man-animal dichotomy was based are now over three hundred years out of date. If you believe, as Descartes believed, that animal behavior can be explained by principles as simple as (and similar to) those hydraulic forces which activated the "living statuary" of 17th-century French gardens, then it does not seem so unreasonable to suppose that animals are automata but that we (with souls stashed in our pineal glands) are not. In light of all that has been learned about both the structure of the nervous system and the behavior of species since Descartes' day, it is merely absurd—possible to salvage only with the logical, if counterfactual, strategy of the hardcore behaviorist who would claim that animals are automata but that so too are we.

There are four possible answers to the question, "Who has consciousness, volition, etc.?" (all the so-called "nonphysical" attributes summed up under the illegitimate label *mind*): animals do, but we don't; animals don't, but we do; animals don't, and we don't; animals do, and we do. In all the history of human folly, I know of no one who has seriously asserted the first. The second is Descartes' answer. The third is the hardcore behaviorist's answer. The fourth, curiously enough, has seldom been made and has been scorned almost as often as it has been made, although in light of what we know now it would seem the most logical. Since it now appears that evolution has advanced not by leaps and bounds but by infinitesimal gradations, we either have to claim that with respect to a particular set of attributes (volition, consciousness, thought, language), evolution behaved in quite a different—and, incidentally, completely mysterious—way from that in which it behaved with regard to all other attributes, or we have to accept that at least some of, or some ingredients critical to, these attributes were and presumably still are shared by species other than our own. I know of no logical argument against the second move although the emotional arguments against it seem as numerous as they are strong. Let us therefore see how conceptualization—without which language would have been impossible—could have evolved.

Conceptualization is intimately linked to perception, if only in the sense that if there were no perception, conceptualization could not take place. But there is, I think, a great deal of difference between a concept and a percept, which tends to be obscured by loose ways of talking and thinking. We use "concept" for any kind of mental image. In fact, there are mental images of percepts and of concepts. We might say, loosely, that I have a concept of the glass that is presently standing on my table, meaning, I can close my eyes and present myself with a mental image of my glass. That is a mental image of a percept, i.e., my glass as I perceived it now—empty, but for a small slice of lemon. Of course, I could imagine it completely empty—which is a percept of how it was at another time; or full—which is the same. However, I can also have a mental image of the category *glass,* which embraces my glass and all other glasses, and which is not a percept, but a true concept.

In some species, percept and concept may not be so far apart. Consider the frog. The frog can discriminate "fly" and "not fly," at least as long as the fly is moving. It is unlikely that a frog can tell one fly from another or would preserve memory images of individual flies, even if it had a memory to preserve them in. In a sense, perception and conceptualization in the frog are one. Only in a sense, of course; for true conceptualization, you have to have volitional control of concepts, and the frog is as far from that as from flying. But in the sense that perception in the frog is generalized, it is like conceptualization.

Now, the fibers which connect a frog's retina with its brain are capable of passing only about four kinds of information, of which only two are relevant to the perception of flies. The first of these two kinds is supplied by a set of neurons specialized to detect small moving objects with curving edges; the second is another set specialized to detect sharp boundaries of light and shade (Burton 1970). There is then a rather tenuous and metaphorical sense in which we could say that the froggy concept of "fly" IS the firing of these two sets of neurons. Of course, we are several scores of millions of years away from true conceptualization; but the journey has certainly begun.

In the course of those years, it might have seemed that perception and conceptualization were moving apart, as perception became not only wider in range (most of the environment seems quite undifferentiated to the frog) but more particularized, with so many parameters recoverable that maybe even individuals could be recognizable to one sense or another, or a combination of several (when our dog recognizes us, smell is presumably dominant).[4] And yet the basic mechanics by means of which this enhanced perception was carried out were in fact no different from those of the frog. There might be many more sets of neurons programmed to respond to many more varied types of stimuli, but a percept would be still the particular firing pattern of the particular set of neurons activated by that set of stimuli which constituted the object perceived.

The problem of how a percept becomes a memory is still far from solved. Part of the problem may be that most studies of memory have really been studies of learning—that is, of forced situations in which given factors caused changes of behavior. Thus, if an octopus were trained to attack horizontal but not vertical rectangles, two sets of feature detectors, each of which could formerly initiate more than one program of action—advancement, withdrawal, indifference—can now only initiate one each, with corresponding changes in the neural connections involved (Bradley and Young 1975). Unfortunately, such findings do not seem to generalize to mammals, where "the search for the engram" remains as fruitless as it was thirty years ago (Lashley 1950). Furthermore, it would be unreasonable to expect them to generalize to the quite qualitatively different kinds of memory traces which concern us here. For the kinds of memory traces that modify behavior—those traditionally studied by psychologists—may be (although of course they are not necessarily) laid down in ways quite different from those of memories which may only modify behavior in the most indirect of ways, if indeed at all (e.g., my stored memory image of my neighbor's new car, accurate enough to enable me to distinguish it from others, but unlikely to prompt me to steal it, polish it, avoid it, etc., and hardly to be described as having been *learned* by me except under the vaguest and most vacuous reading of *learning*).

Therefore, I shall assume that long-term storage is achieved (precisely how need not concern us) by storing features of images rather than images themselves. Let us assume I can reliably identify several hundred human faces. Now, the mental representations of these faces that I need for matching purposes—I can think of no other way in which recognition could be carried out—are not stored separately in some analogue of a box in my head, not even in the form of macromolecules. Rather, each of the horizontal, vertical, slanted, curving, etc., lines that go to make up faces—as well as lots of other things, of course—is represented by a particular set of neurons. The superset composed by these sets is simply an analogue of the superset of feature-detecting neuron sets. The data recorded by the straight-vertical-line perceiving set of neurons (or however much of them are transferable) are simply transferred to the long-term storage set for straight vertical lines, and so on. The fact that a particular batch of data went into a particular batch of storage sets must also somehow be recorded, in terms of sensitized synaptic pathways or whatever, or I could never recover Aunt Emma's face from its component bits. But in some such general manner—and I apologize to neurologists for my rather Rube Goldberg picture—the processes of perception, storing, coding, and accessing must be carried out.

It follows that individual images would not be individually stored—members of the same class of images would not necessarily be stored together, while the storage of unlike objects might be strikingly similar. Let us consider the possible storage of the percept images of three objects, any one of which would have to be separately and individually recoverable: *Aunt Emma's latest hat, the Sugarloaf at Rio de Janeiro, the distribution curve for IQ in an average population.* These objects belong, respectively, to three quite distinct classes; the class of hats, the class of mountains, and the class of distribution curves. However, in their general shape they share some obvious similarities. Let A through G represent sets of storage neurons, each set representing storage of a particular parameter. Then *Aunt Emma's latest hat* might be represented by sets ABCDE, *the Sugarloaf at Rio de Janeiro* by sets BCDEFG, and *the distribution curve for IQ in an average population* by sets CDEF. If I wish to visualize an image of any one of the three, I activate just these sets.

(And what constitutes the "I" that activates? Analogy from observed conspecifics, use of mirrors and other reflecting substances, plus the higher-order "traffic-control" neurons which must exist to establish priorities in brain activity if the whole thing isn't to degenerate into electrochemical chaos.)

Some kind of memory storage of particular experiences must go pretty far down the mammalian phylum. So too, I suggest, must the power of playback—voluntary recall of images or sequences of images. At the very least, involuntary playback (another name for dreaming) does. Reptiles don't dream, mammals do. Moreover, dreaming (human dreaming, for sure; mammalian dreaming, very likely) consists not of just straight playback but of the recombination of stored imagery, something that would be difficult or impossible if memories were individually stored. Once playback, straight or crooked, came under cortical control, our ancestors were well on their way to the world map that is a prerequisite for language—without which there is hardly anything worth communicating to communicate.

The question evolutionists will ask at this point is: why? Why should mammals develop these capacities? Prehistory was not a dress rehearsal for *homo sapiens.* What selective advantage did the species gain? Some psychologists have attempted answers in very vague and general terms. For instance, Harlow (1958), discussing the fact that some apes and monkeys can solve in captivity problems far more complex than they would ever meet in nature, pins his faith on receptor system development, since more finely calibrated receptor systems entail an increase in the central nervous system: "As long as increasingly complex receptor systems provide the organism with slight survival advantages, one can be assured that increasingly complex nervous systems will develop; and as long as increasingly complex nervous systems develop, the organism will be endowed with greater potentialities which lead inevitably to learning." Similarly, Passingham (1979), who finds it "puzzling" that chimpanzees should have language capacities which "do not appear to be used in the wild," surmises either that "chimpanzees do in fact use their language capacities in the wild"— in ways which two decades of patient and trained observation have somehow still failed to reveal!—or that "their abilities . . . must be general ones, allowing them to do other things of importance to them in the wild."

The vagueness and timidity of these suggestions are, I am sure, due to the Cartesian hangover, although the class "Cartesian evolutionist" ought to constitute a logical contradiction. It should be pretty obvious that the power to review the past would provide its possessor with another power of the highest value in natural selection: the power to predict. Psychics aside, prediction is based on analysis of past events, and becomes of greater importance as creatures evolve and become more complex. Relatively simple creatures lead relatively simple lives; it is possible to program them, up to around the frog level, so that they will respond automatically to all or almost all the contingencies they are likely to encounter. With more complex creatures, in particular with predators who have to keep (literally!) one jump ahead of their prey, not only does the list of conceivable contingencies get too long to program, it would probably be dysfunctional for such creatures to be programmed down to the wire, so to speak. Such programming would leave them unable to respond appropriately, to vary the moment of attack in accordance with the wind, the light, the prey's motions, and countless other environmental factors, to determine which member of a herd to attack, and so on. The power to review past sequences of events, whether at a conscious or an unconscious level, and to abstract those factors which made for success or failure in particular cases, would confer a massive advantage on its possessor—or one that would have been massive had the prey not developed along similar lines. As shown in the excellent survey by Jerison (1973), brain size for both prey and predator has gradually but continuously increased throughout the mammalian era, with the predators always slightly ahead of the prey.

We do not of course know, and have as yet no way of determining, how far down the evolutionary scale such capacities might extend. But such capacities and more might have been needed to ensure the survival of the primates, creatures who were predators to some species and prey to others; and it is a reasonable assumption that *Dryopithecus*, the presumed common ancestor of ourselves and the chimpanzees, who lived between five and fifteen million years ago, had them and probably had more.

We have so far surveyed the capacity to form and store percepts and to review percepts and sequences of percepts under voluntary control. But we have not yet considered how percepts can become concepts. Until a percept—the image of a particular entity on a particular occasion—can be replaced at will by a concept—the image of a class of entities, divorced from all particular instantiations of that class—then the power to predict is limited. A creature concerned with prediction does not want to have to say, "The boar I wounded three years ago did such and such, and the boar I wounded a year ago did the same, but this wounded boar is a different boar so I suppose I'll just have to wait and see." It wants to be able to say, "Wounded boars do such and such, so I can anticipate what will happen and be ready to act appropriately." The prediction may be quite wrong, of course—with fatal results. But if it is right just that little bit more often than chance, the survival chances of the species are perceptibly enhanced.

Indeed, instantaneity would have rated above accuracy. The creature that could achieve 60 percent accuracy in one second would surely have outlasted the creature that could achieve 100 percent accuracy in ten seconds—because in those ten seconds, too many of the latter would have gotten themselves killed.

"To generalize is to be an idiot" (Blake 1808),[5] but for better or worse, the road to humanity was paved with generalizations. We assume our ancestors to have been primates not adapted for predation but driven by climatic change to adopt, in part, the habits of predators—or so most anthropologists have held for a good many years. Lacking the tiger's fang, the leopard's speed, the disciplined pack strategies of the canids, they had to compete with these and more in a dry epoch when pickings were scarce. Under such circumstances they would have selected very fast and very naturally for some kind of instant recognition-and-reaction device—one that would respond not merely to the briefest of glimpses of possible prey or rival predator, but to the most minimal clues in the environment: movement of a branch at a particular altitude, say, coupled with the appearance of a patch of brown slightly different in shade and texture from the fall leaves that surround it.

That modern hunters still have such a device, even though changing times have made it more dysfunctional, was illustrated a few years ago when a national magazine carried out an inquiry into shooting accidents during the deer season. Hunters were shooting one another instead of the deer. The vast majority of these incidents occurred in the half-light of dawn or dusk. The shooters, when interviewed, almost invariably said that they had seen a deer—not "thought" they had seen one, but actually seen it—and only seconds after they had pulled the trigger did this image resolve itself into a wounded or dying fellow-hunter. From a few half-perceived clues of color, shape, and texture, they had created phantom deer and reacted to their own creation before additional sensory input could replace the projected image with a real one.

The reader may easily demonstrate a similar if less lethal effect. Simply draw, on a piece of paper or a blackboard, the structure portrayed in Figure 4.1 below:

Figure 4.1
The minimal "flower"

If you then ask what this is, people will reply, nine times out of ten, "a flower." I have tried this many times on students; you can often see their jaws literally drop when you tell them, "No, it's a dot, nine short lines, and one long one."

The capacity to construct predictive images obviously entails the preexistence of class concepts. The misguided hunters did not project an image of some specific deer, but rather that of any member of the genus deer. To us, with the elaborate and labeled cognitive map which language provides for us, the genus deer seems self-evident. But try to imagine, if you can, the task of constructing the category *deer* from scratch, by inductive reasoning, without benefit of labels or of map. Deer come in a number of shapes, sizes, and species. Some are dark, some are light. Some have horns, some don't, some sometimes do, and some sometimes don't. Where do deer stop and other genera begin? The problems are endless.

Yet as work by Berlin (1972) and his associates has shown, generic names are the most richly represented in natural languages— more numerous than both the higher-order categories ("unique beginners," e.g., *plant, animal,* or "life forms," e.g., *tree, bush*) or the lower-order ones ("specific name," e.g., *Ponderosa pine, jack pine,* or "varietal name," e.g., *northern Ponderosa pine, western Ponderosa pine*); invariably monomorphemic (contrasted with specific or varietal names); subjectively perceived as primary; the first to be learned by children. It is a good bet they were among the first words of human language.

Why the genus and not the species? If your eyes are as sharp as I'm sure our ancestors' were, differences between species must often have been as salient as, or more salient than, differences between genera. But behavioral differences would have had greater significance for our ancestors than visual differences. All deer, whether large or small, plain or spotted, with or without horns, had a number of things in common: they were fleet of foot; nervous enough to make stalking them difficult but not impossible; often camouflaged by the light-and-shade effects of foliage; excellent eating if you could get them, and so on.

But the fact that classification of the genera would have been selectively advantageous for our ancestors does not in and of itself make such classification possible. A number of preadaptations would also have had to occur, perhaps the most obvious of which is cross-modal association—the importance of which for language has been stressed in a number of papers by Geschwind (1974). For the concepts of genera could not have been built on sight alone; each of the senses must have contributed in varying degrees. But the real key to the crucial developments must lie in the nature of the recognition device.

I have said that members of our species, and even dogs, if their behavior is anything to go by, must be able to distinguish individuals, and there is no reason to suppose that our capacity to summon up at will the visual images of individuals necessarily indicates any very recent evolutionary development. I suggested also that these images might be stored in a fractured manner, so that similar sets of bits, when put together in various ways, could constitute very distinct images. But why in that case do we not project genera that would include in the same category, say, *Aunt Emma's latest hat, the Sugarloaf at Rio de Janeiro,* and *the distribution curve for IQ in an average population?*

The utility, or lack of it, that such a category might have is beside the point. If we built category concepts on the basis of individual percepts, such would be the kinds of categories we would most likely wind up with. One of the main reasons that we do not is that concepts, as distinct from percepts, do not exist in isolation. We do not delimit percepts in terms of percepts. I do not distinguish Aunt Emma's face because it is bounded on one side by Aunt Mary's face, on another by Cousin Emily's face, and so on; nor (just to show that this fact has nothing to do with any heightened perception of conspecifics) do I distinguish my toothbrush because it is bounded on one side by my wife's toothbrush, on another by my son's toothbrush, etc. But I do distinguish deer because they are bounded by horses on one side, cattle on another side, and so on; I do distinguish toothbrushes in general because they are bounded by hairbrushes,

nailbrushes, bootbrushes, etc. Deer stop where horses begin. Toothbrushes stop where nailbrushes begin. But Aunt Emma's face does
not stop where Cousin Emily's begins, my toothbrush does not stop
where my wife's begins. That is the difference between percept and
concept, class member and class. Concepts are delimited in terms
of one another, percepts only in terms of themselves.

Concepts are like the counties on a state map, in several ways.
Where one stops, another starts. Although each is composed of so many
acres and contains so many individuals, none is merely the sum of
the acres that compose it or the people who inhabit those acres. Each
of them has its place with respect to the others. The same with concepts. Percepts inhabit concepts, but concepts are not the sum of
their percepts. *Aunt Emma's latest hat,* a percept, belongs to the
concept *hat* and not the concept *mountain; the Sugarloaf,* a percept,
belongs to the concept *mountain* and not the concept *distribution
curve.* It is not because of its individual characteristics that I do not
expect to find the Sugarloaf on Aunt Emma's head; it is because I
know that the Sugarloaf is a mountain and mountains do not belong
on people's heads. When I see the Sugarloaf for the first time, I do not
have to work out from scratch all the properties it has, including that
of not being on Aunt Emma's head; all those properties follow automatically once I have determined that it is a mountain. Mountains
have their place on the map, and so do hats; and those places are
different.

But how, on first seeing its picture, did I recognize that it was
a mountain (albeit a rather small one) at a distance, rather than a large
if rather eccentric hat, up close? Not by computing its peculiar properties. If I had, I could have gone wrong, because in outline it is less
like the archetypical mountain than it is like some hats. I did so by
putting two things together: the fact that it fulfilled at least some of
the qualifications for being a mountain together with its relations
to other objects: a harbor, clouds, a cable-car line to its summit. Of
course, it could still have been a hat in a Lilliputian model city; just
as the deer the hunter shot at could have been (and in fact was) a

fellow-hunter. The fact that our maps may occasionally let us down does not mean we could get along without them. We would be no-where without them.

If percepts could be filed fractured, so to speak, concepts must be filed as gestalts. I do not have the slightest idea how this is done, nor to the best of my knowledge has anyone else, although neurologists will quite likely find out in the next century or two. However, since speculation is useful if only to provide candidates for elimination, let us speculate. Having been stored one way as percepts, in a manner based on their immediate sensory images, phenomena would be copied and stored another way in accordance with their observed behavioral properties. Did they lie still or move? If they moved, did they soar, lope, or slither? These heterogeneous bundles of information would again, presumably, be stored in sets of neurons synaptically linked with, and as specialized in function as, those sets of perceptual neurons that distinguish movement from nonmovement, loping from slithering, and the smells characteristic of one set of phenomena from the smells characteristic of another set. However, instead of the same set of neurons representing similar aspects of the images of quite different things, as we supposed was the case in the storage of percepts, separate sets of sets, involving heavy duplication of function, would be required for each network of neurons that represented a concept.

If this were so, it would explain why, while percepts may be stored in literally infinite quantity, the list of concepts, or at least the list of primitive concepts, is certainly finite and probably quite short (of course, an infinite number of secondary concepts—*timber wolf, prairie dog*, etc.—can be constructed by combining two or more primitive concepts). It would also explain why the human recognition device works as it does. Each superset of concept-representing neurons would include representations of all features of a concept. If indeed the major genera constituted the first concepts (and there would seem to be no likelier candidates), this would mean in effect all features of a genus—sensory, behavioral, distributional, whatever. Then whenever any sufficient subset of features is detected by the perception neurons—

a patch of dappled light, motionless, at a certain height above ground
in a forest at dawn—the superset from which that subset is drawn would
immediately be activated in such a way as to yield the full concept—
deer, in this case. The subject has then "seen" a deer, or whatever,
and reacts accordingly.

This account is, again, necessarily crude, necessarily vague—
what constitutes a "sufficient subset of features" for concept triggering, for instance?—and quite possibly wrong in most or all of its
particulars. It is crude, vague, and possibly wrong because, as Blakemore (1977) observed, studies of memory (and allied human capacities)
have been "concerned with the *machinery* . . . not the *code*—the symbolic form in which the events are registered" (original emphasis); by
"machinery," Blakemore means "the manner in which events can cause
changes in physical structures," but the kinds of changes likely to be
caused by the mental processes we are considering, consisting as they
would consist of no more than the forging of additional links between
specialized neurons, would hardly be amenable to observation in the
state of today's technology (ten billion neurons with sixty thousand
connections each—where do you start to look?). It is crude, vague, and
possibly wrong because neurologists have considered the more "meta-
physical" implications of their task as somebody else's business, because "continuists" of the grunt-groan-or-gesture school have thought
that the nature of reality is self-evident and therefore didn't need to
be constructed, and because philosophers, who alone could be expected
to perceive the problems inherent in perceiving anything at all, have
resolutely refused to tie their ballooning speculations down to the nuts-
and-bolts of what we already know about what we have in our heads
and what we might be expected to be able to do with it. So the whole
area slipped between the cracks of the disciplines. But that area still
exists, and is crucial in the explanation of human capacities, so a bad
map is better than no map at all.

These last few pages may seem to have taken us a long way from
language, but I do not think that is the case. Unless we have some

notion of all that must have been involved in moving from moment-by-moment perceptions to class concepts—and it is class concepts that are named, not perceptions, percepts, or the extramental stimuli for these—then we simply do not know what it entailed for a species to get language. Moreover, until we appreciate just how difficult it must have been to name the major genera—the flora and fauna, successful interaction with which was our ancestors' very lifeline—we shall not even begin to conceive the role which is played by the perceiving mechanism, rather than the perceived data, as progressively more abstract phenomena are involved. We will come to that in a moment.

But before we do, we should note that if the foregoing account is correct even in its broadest outlines, we have already suggested an infrastructural motivation for one of the major semantic distinctions observed in the preceding chapters (the SNSD). We saw that both creole speakers and children were able to distinguish with great ease between specific and nonspecific (generic) reference. Now, if percepts—images of particular entities on particular occasions, therefore specific—and concepts—images of classes of entities, therefore nonspecific—are stored in different places and in different ways, this distinction would be built into the neural system. In consequence, something which seems highly abstract and far beyond the powers of two-year-olds, if we suppose it to be acquired in the traditional fashion, would apply automatically *provided that no alternative but incompatible distinctions* (such as those involved in Japanese case and topic marking, for example) were simultaneously being imposed on the child by the target language. Indeed, I shall later suggest that it was just those category distinctions based on sharply differing modes of cerebral coding and storage which were the first to be grammaticized, and which were thus to serve as a kind of scaffolding by which language was able to rise from an initial low plateau of short and relatively structureless utterances.

Now, from recent experimentation, we know that the power to abstract concepts from nature is something that we share with the great apes. As Mounin (1976), among others, has pointed out, the evidence of what chimps did voluntarily, after training, is much more impressive than what they were trained to do. The fact that they applied names to different-looking objects of the same class, as well as to pictures of such objects, and their frequent generalizations of names to broader classes, shows that to them, names were class names—concept labels—and not mechanical responses linked to particular, individual objects after the fashion of proper names. The fact that they invented names for classes of objects whose names they had not been taught—for refrigerators *(open-eat-drink)*, for ducks *(water-bird)*, for Brazil nuts *(rock-berry)*, for oranges *(orange-apple)*: Sarah knew only "apple" as a fruit descriptor but had orange separately as a color)—shows that they had far more concepts floating around in their heads than their caregivers had the time or patience to name for them, and also showed power of creativity on a lexical (nonsyntactic) level, a fact we will return to in due course.[6]

With regard to the independence of this power from anything you could call "training," it is worth citing a passage from Mounin (1976): "Sarah, all alone in her cage (outside any experimental situation) picked up objects or signs and composed utterances on the models of the structures she had just learned . . . . Can one discern the transition of the main and primary function of her code, social communication, to a secondary use of it, the possibility of developing for oneself the expression of one's own view of the world? *Or* does this expression *only* represent play?" (emphasis added).

This passage comes very close to blinding insight, yet it still manages to get things the wrong way around. Mounin is right, of course, in that the Premacks taught Sarah her code for strictly communicative purposes, so that if she turned it to private, computational purposes, that use would be secondary in a rather narrow sense. But in a much broader, evolutionary sense, things were the other way around. Possession of an elaborated world-view must precede, not follow, communication on even the lowest of linguistic levels. Sarah and Sarah's species must already have had an interior world of concepts, not of percepts, or they would have been unable to transfer names from one object to another, still less from one class to another.

Moreover, a name like Washoe's *rock-berry* (for Brazil nut) is a metaphor at a level appropriate for barroom joking, if not poetry; it shows awareness of a superclass of which both berries and nuts are members, and the sharing of an abstract quality—hardness, not normally associated with that superclass—by nuts and a member of another, nonvegetable superclass. The coiner of such expressions has a cognitive map of no mean quality.

A further telling, if oblique, bit of evidence for this claim comes from Gill and Rumbaugh (1974), who report that it took Lana 1,600 trials to learn the names for *banana* and *M&M,* but that the next five items were acquired in less than five trials each—two of them in two only. This stunning and instantaneous increment is inexplicable in terms of Lana's having "learned how to learn" in the course of those 1,600 trials; learning curves just don't jump like that. It is much more plausible to suppose that for a long time Lana simply couldn't figure out what her trainers were trying to do, and then suddenly it clicked: "My God, they're feeding me concept names—why couldn't they have *told* me, the dummies?" The concepts had been there all the while, and only the link between them and these mysterious new things that people were doing to her needed to be forged.

Finally, Mounin's use of *or* and *only* is a striking example of anthropocentric, or perhaps I should say Puritan business ethic, modes of thinking. On the one hand, you have "developing for oneself the expression of one's own view of the world," an activity automatically assumed to be solemn, to be heavy, to be *work,* in fact; therefore, on the other hand, something that is *play* couldn't possibly be "developing for oneself...," etc. Piaget (1962) came nearer the bone when he claimed that the symbolic function arises first in play, and anyone who has watched a young mammal exploring the environment for the first time knows that "play" and "building a cognitive map" are isomorphic activities (young lizards don't play because they don't have the spare brain cells). It may look like "mere play" to the supercilious human observer, and indeed it is play—the animal wouldn't do it if it weren't fun—but it is also the means by which lower creatures as well as human children set about constructing the mental representation of the world which gives them varying degrees of predictability and thus enables them to control to a greater extent their own chances of survival.

Now, if chimps can have concepts and label them just as we have concepts and label them, and if we know (or are reasonably sure) that we have a common ancestor in *Dryopithecus,* then we can begin to get some kind of evolutionary perspective on the development of linguistic infrastructure. When we find behavioral homologies in closely related species, we can reasonably assume that these homologies represent a common inheritance from a common ancestor (Campbell and Hodos 1970; Hodos 1976; Dingwall 1979:Figure 1.4). This would mean that the power to conceptualize and the potential for naming go back at least as far as *Dryopithecus* and maybe further back than that. In a moment I will try to answer the fascinating question that everyone must want to ask at this point: "Why, if language is so spectacularly adaptive, and if the basic infrastructure has been around for so long, didn't it develop millions of years sooner?" But first, there is more to be said about the problems of conceptualization and naming.

We began by tackling the infrastructure of language at just that point where the gap between language and the external world was most easily bridged; where the classes to be named were at least classes of discrete entities. Let us now turn from entities to their attributes, and in particular to color.

Color is not something that really exists in the external universe. We have all seen the landscape "change color" as the sun declines without thinking it at all odd or stopping to remember that the purpling of noon's green hills is due simply to the shortening of the wavelengths of light reflected from them. Color is simply created by the interaction between those wavelengths and sets of specialized perceptor neurons, longer wavelengths appearing as red, slightly shorter ones as orange, and so on across the spectrum. But color vision adds yet another set of parameters to those that are already sorting percepts into their appropriate classes. The boundary between two colors, for instance, is often a boundary and sometimes perhaps the only boundary between another entity and its background.

Useful though color vision is, it presents serious problems for language, problems of a kind quite different from those inherent in the naming of the species or genera. Creatures are discrete; the spectrum is one and continuous. We can perceive light at wavelengths of between roughly 380 and 800 millimicrons, and we can perceive it equally well at any wavelength within those limits. It is true that we can say of some colors, "that's a real green," or "a true yellow," but there are points in between where we cannot say whether green or yellow is involved.

If Og and Ug had sat down, as in some of the more simplistic Flintstone scenarios, with a bunch of different-colored pebbles to help them, maybe, and started out to "name the colors," they would have been stymied from the word go. Even more sophisticated accounts which would still assume some degree of arbitrariness and voluntary control in naming run up against the insuperable obstacle that words demand concepts, and concepts demand boundaries; but colors have no boundaries, so theoretically you should be free to cut up the spectrum into as many chunks as you fancy and draw the lines between them just where you feel like drawing them. In fact, as Berlin and Kay (1969) demonstrated in their pioneering study, nobody is free to do any such thing. Basic color terms (terms neither borrowed from names of pre-existing objects, e.g., *orange,* nor compounded, e.g., *dark green, yellowish brown,* etc.—that is to say, primitive concepts) are highly predictable across languages, and the semantic range of each term is determined by the number of terms in any given language system and by the ranges of pre-existing terms (if this sounds familiar, remember it was exactly the way I said TMA systems were structured, back in Chapter 3, and we will look at these, too, later in the present chapter). This is to say that if a given language has only two basic color terms, those terms must be "dark" and "light"; if it has three, they can be only "dark," "light," and "red"; and so on.

The neurological substrate of this structuring of color has been explained (McDaniel 1974; Kay and McDaniel 1978) in terms of Hering's "opponent" theory of color discrimination (Hering 1920; since experimentally confirmed for certain species of primates, cf. de Valois and Jacobs 1968). Primate brains, and those of some other orders, have various sets of perceptor neurons each adapted to different bands of the spectrum and activated only by stimuli that fall within those wavelengths. One pair of sets monitors the ranges corresponding to red and green. One member of the pair hits its maximal firing rate when stimulated by central red and its minimal firing rate when stimulated by central green. The other member of the pair hits its maximal firing rate when stimulated by central green and its minimal firing rate when stimulated by central red. Similar pairs deal in a similar way with yellow-blue and the light/bright versus dark/dull distinction.

The far-reaching implications of the Berlin and Kay discovery have yet to be absorbed by the scientific community. The conclusions reached in a summary by Clark and Clark (1977:527) are fairly typical in their unrevealing, indeed inaccurate, nature: "The very physiology of the human visual system makes some colors more salient than others. Children find these colors eye-catching and easy to remember . . . . There is more occasion to talk about salient colors, and listeners assume that speakers are more likely to be talking about them. Color terminology is universal because the human visual system is universal."

Quite apart from its chatty, wasn't-everything-simple-after-all tone, and its evident confusion of perception with lexicalization, this passage makes a grave factual error. The whole point of the Berlin and Kay thesis is that color terminology is NOT universal. If the color systems of languages reflected universalities of the human visual system, then color terminology would always be the same and always mean the same. But it is not and does not.

What happens in these languages that have only "dark" and "light"? Presumably speakers of these languages have the same visual system as everyone else, and presumably children learning these languages find red, yellow, blue, etc., as "eye-catching" as any other children. And if all the primary colors are equally salient, how is it that no language starts by distinguishing only green and blue, and then works its way back across to red in the opposite direction?

It is worth going into the structuring of color terms in some depth here as I believe this structuring is paradigmatic of a number of other semantic areas, some of them much more important than that of color.

First, and contra Clark and Clark, there is no simple one-to-one relationship between neurological equipment and semantic structure. Rather, the nature of neurological equipment enables semantic structure to be divided up in a number of possible ways. At the same time, it prohibits semantic structure from being divided in an infinitely greater number of ways, any of which might seem a priori no less logical or possible, and imposes rigid constraints on the sequence in which any given analysis of the semantic structure can be rendered more complex.

Let us look at some prohibited color terms. No language has the term *reen meaning 'red and/or green, but nothing in between', or the term *yellue meaning 'yellow and/or blue, but nothing in between'. There would seem to be no a priori reason for the absence of these terms, for it is easy to construct not only meanings but also possible neurological substrates for them. Thus, *reen would be the representation of activity in the red-green receptors (and no others), while *yellue would be the representation of activity in the blue-yellow receptors (and no others). However, we know that lexicalization does not simply represent outputs of particular neuronal sets, for two reasons. First, many languages have a term equivalent to grue 'green and/or blue', which represents partial outputs of two opponent sets, rather than the full output of one opponent set. Second, the factor that allows grue to exist, while blocking *reen, seems to be perceived spatial contiguity, which of course corresponds to wavelength contiguity. Green and blue are contiguous on the spectrum; red and green, or yellow and blue, are not.

It has often been noted that spatiotemporal contiguity is a condition on naming; no language has a word such as *larm meaning 'leg and/or arm', or *shee meaning 'shoulder and/or knee'; in no language can I say, *I teach on mwidays meaning 'I teach on Mondays, Wednesdays, and Fridays'. However, a further look at color terms will show that spatiotemporal contiguity, although a necessary condition on naming, is not a sufficient condition. If it were, some languages would have a word *yeen meaning 'yellow and/or green' instead of grue. Yellow and green are just as much contiguous as green and blue. Their conjunction would mean conjoining the outputs of two opponent sets, but the same is true of green and blue.

There would seem to be two possibilities. Grue conjoins the two short-wavelength outputs of two opponent sets: *yeen would conjoin the long-wavelength output of one opponent set (yellow) with the short-wavelength output of the other (green). Perhaps one kind of conjunction can be lexicalized and the other cannot; we simply do not know enough to say. But it is also possible that what can be lexicalized at any given stage of development may be constrained by the order in which lexicalization takes place.[7]

This brings us inevitably to the much deeper question: why were the basic color terms added to human language in just the order that Berlin and Kay showed them to be? The answer may lie in a suggestion of potentially immense explanatory power first made by Stephenson (1973) but not, to the best of my knowledge, subsequently developed: that the Berlin and Kay sequence of dark/light-red-green/yellow-blue may reflect the order in which color perception became established phylogenetically.

The argument, although hard to support from empirical studies—species representing the appropriate evolutionary stages may all be extinct—is nevertheless a highly plausible one. Stephenson points out that mammals were originally nocturnal and could probably only make lighter-darker distinctions; as they began to shift to diurnal habits, after the extinction of major reptilian predators, the perception of light-wavelength distinctions became selectively advantageous (it would permit a much sharper and finer differentiation of the environment). Stephenson argues that such perception would have begun with the longer wavelengths.

The transfer from the phylogeny of perception to the phylogeny of language would then have come about in the following manner. In any line of development, neurological structure is always incremental; no species sloughs off its neural inheritance in the act of adding new layers; the new layers are simply superimposed on the old ones.[8] It follows that older layers have a longer time in which to establish themselves, to multiply numbers of cells and cell connections. This process is likely to be halted or reversed only if the related capacity becomes dysfunctional to a species—which color perception is unlikely to do unless our species is forced back to a nocturnal pattern. Thus, other things being equal, the older of any two capacities should be the stronger. The greater neural strength of the oldest—the light-dark distinction—would then lead to its being first lexicalized; the neural strength of the next oldest—long-wavelength (red) perception—would lead to its being second lexicalized, and so on.

I shall therefore propose the following hypothesis: *those semantic distinctions whose neural infrastructure was laid down first in the course of mammalian development will be the first to be lexicalized and/or grammaticized in the course of human language development.* In the present state of our knowledge, such a hypothesis can have only a tentative status; yet we will see, when we consider the possible evolution of TMA systems, that it can still have considerable explanatory power.

After red, languages can lexicalize either yellow (next wavelength down from red, also the "high" member of the next color-opponent set) or green (the "low" member of the set already activated). It may be that herein lies the reason for the absence of *yeen. If one or the other member of *yeen must be individually lexicalized, then a larger category consisting of just those members cannot subsequently be constructed: lexicalization proceeds unidirectionally toward an ever finer dissection of the color area, so that while existing categories may be split, they can never be added to or collapsed. But again, research into the color vision capacities of more species of primates may clarify the situation by demonstrating a phylogenetic order of acquisition for the shorter wavelengths too.

We should also look at how the meaning of individual terms is affected by sequential development of semantic subsystems since there is good reason here also to suppose that similar phenomena will be found elsewhere. In their original (1969) treatment, Berlin and Kay referred to "dark" and "light" as "black" and "white." Indeed, "black" and "white" is what these terms shrink to in an eleven-term system like that of English where other terms have spread over most of the semantic ground. Yet it should surely be obvious that as lexicalization progressively dissects semantic areas, the meanings of the earliest lexical items must change: "black," which originally embraces half the spectrum, must gradually reduce in scope until it eventually occupies only a narrow band of it. Similarly, "red" in a three-term system must include much—orange, maybe the darker yellows—which it cannot possibly include in the eleven-term English system, which contains orange, yellow, and pink as units. Thus, the semantic range of terms in subsystems is determined by the number of terms in such subsystems and by the semantic ranges of the other terms.

Constraints such as these will loom ever larger as we continue to traverse semantic space away from representations of concrete entities and toward representations of ever more abstract relationships. So far, the semantic infrastructure we have dealt with is in all probability shared by *Homo sapiens, Pan troglodytes,* and *Dryopithecus.* I doubt whether similar sharing extends to much or even any of the areas we are about to enter. Indeed, if we were reconstructing to a strict chronological timetable, we should probably drop semantics here and start talking about syntax, since from here on out, syntactic and semantic developments were almost certainly intercalated and their interaction served to drive language up along a beneficial spiral. However, in the interests of clarity of presentation, and to counteract the obsession with "communication" that has so far vitiated any understanding of how language must have evolved, I shall continue to deal with semantic infrastructure (or rather with such small patches of it as there is space to deal with) in order to show just how much conceptual preadaptation was necessary before a "communicative system" as simple as the simplest of early creoles could be made to function communicatively. Later on, we will retrace our steps to the present point and deal with the early development of syntax, relating the latter, wherever possible, to concomitant developments in semantics already touched on.

The first of the semantic areas I shall touch on concerns predications which may be felt to be central in any structured language system: *There is an X, X is at Y, Z has X, X is Z's.* I shall refer to the relationships expressed by these predications as Existence, Location, Possession, and Ownership. I should emphasize that these labels are chosen only for convenience of reference and are not meant to have any particular semantic significance: "possession," for instance, is grossly inadequate for the semantics of *has,* which might better, though still inadequately, be defined as "stands in a close and superordinate relationship to."

In an original and insightful study, Eve Clark (1970) reviewed the ways in which these four relationships are represented across a sample of fifty-odd languages. She found a high degree of similarity in the syntactic structures involved, but a good deal less similarity in lexicalization. Some languages (indeed, almost half the sample) used only a single morpheme to lexicalize the entire area; others used four different items, i.e., lexicalized each of the four relationships differently. Between these extremes there were several different patterns, with two or three of the relationships being jointly lexicalized, but seldom the same two or the same three from one language to the next. Not surprisingly, Clark concluded that, in this area, the lexicon was without internal structure.

At first sight, an area such as this might seem to be affected by constraints far different from those which would affect the area of body parts or even the more abstract area of color terms. One would not expect to find, for example, contiguity constraints of the type that bar items like *yeen* and *shee,* since the relationships we are now talking about do not seem to have any discernible concrete correlatives of which contiguity or noncontiguity could reasonably be predicated. And yet, contiguity constraints exist here too.

Consider Figure 4.2 below:

Ownership	Location
Possession	Existence

Figure 4.2
Semantic space for four relationships

If the four relationships are arranged spatially as in Figure 4.2, and if we consider only the primary (shortest, simplest, most frequently used) morphemes in each language—e.g., not allowing *exist* to substitute for *there IS,* or *possess* for *have*—the following constraint on lexicalization seems to apply: no language can use the same morpheme to express any two noncontiguous relationships (i.e., location and possession, or existence and ownership) unless that same morpheme is also used to express one of the intervening relationships (i.e., existence or ownership in the first case, location or possession in the second). In other words, the semantic space mapped in Figure 4.2 is as structured as real space, and, as with real space, only contiguous sectors can be jointly lexicalized. This constraint operates on all the languages in Clark's sample, on all creoles for which adequate data are available, and for at least thirty other languages checked so far, or at least one hundred languages in total; I have not yet met with any counterexamples.

The reasons for the existence of such a constraint in this particular case are far from obvious. The categories involved are not only highly abstract, but seem to be mutually inclusive. Species and color terms are mutually exclusive: if something is a cat, it is not a dog; if something is red, it is not yellow or blue, and so on. If the semantic space associated with species, color, and certain other areas is sharply divided, then such divisions can be regarded as no more than analogues of divisions which exist in the material universe. But it is hard to see what real-world divisions would be correlates of the constraint governing the location-existence-possession-ownership area, since existence and possession (in the relational sense given above) can be predicated of all entities whether abstract or concrete, while location and ownership can be predicated of all concrete (and perhaps some abstract) entities. So why should it not be possible to conjointly express location and possession, or existence and ownership, given that any other pairs, any triples, or all four together may be conjointly expressed?

I can think of two possible explanations, not necessarily mutually exclusive. Both explanations involve principles of broad, indeed universal, application. As yet, I know of no way in which these alternatives could be tested.

The first explanation involves semantic primes. The term *semantic prime* is normally used in reference to unanalyzable concepts; here I use it in a rather different sense, to refer to a very limited set of binary oppositions; any concept can then be defined in terms of plus and minus (and perhaps null) values for these oppositions, in much the same way as phonological units can be defined in terms of plus and minus values for Jakobsonian distinctive features.[9]

Semantic change would then proceed in a manner analogous to phonological change. A phonological change cannot spread from voiceless velar or bilabial environments (____ −voi, −cor) to voiced apical environments (____ +voi, +cor) without first occurring in voiceless apical environments (____ −voi, +cor), or in voiced velar or bilabial environments (____ +voi, −cor), or both. In the same way, semantic change could not spread from an environment which had minus values for two semantic primes to an environment which had plus values for those same primes without first affecting at least one environment which had a minus value for one prime and a plus value for the other prime.

An example can be found if we compare the article system of Modern English with the article system of Guyanese Creole, which is probably not much different from the article system of Middle English (the theory predicts that when an article system arises, it will be governed by similar constraints irrespective of whether it arises in a creole system or elsewhere). The Guyanese system is shown in Figure 4.3 below:

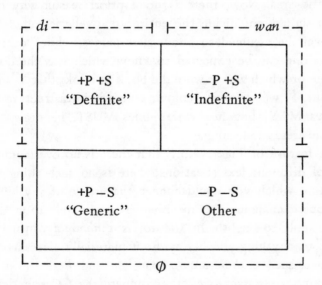

(P = presupposed; S = specific)

Figure 4.3
Semantic space for Guyanese articles

In Figure 4.3, "definite" and "indefinite" have their traditional meanings; "generic" refers to the subject NP in *The dog/A dog/Dogs is/are (a) mammal(s),* and "other" includes NP in the scope of negation, "a book or books," and similar cases (see Chapters 1 and 2 for a more detailed analysis of the creole system). It was claimed earlier in this chapter that the specific-nonspecific distinction had as its cerebral foundation the differential storage of percepts and concepts; if this is so, then the SNSD must represent one of the oldest (phylogenetically speaking) of semantic primes. If it is old, it must (by the infrastructural hypothesis proposed in our discussion of color terms) be strong, and this superior strength may account for the configuration of Figure 4.3. Although the SNSD divides the entire semantic area, with "zero" on one side and "some marker or other" on the other, the presupposed-nonpresupposed distinction (*presupposed* in this context refers to "information presumed shared by speaker and listener") divides only the +specific area. Now, there is no a priori reason why the latter distinction should not divide the entire area; generics are +P because everyone can be assumed to know class names, while "other" is −P because no one can be expected to know which was the dog that X DIDN'T see or which was or were the book or books that Y might have bought. But, as we saw with colors, semantic infrastructure tells you where lines MAY, but not where lines MUST, be drawn between lexicalizable areas of meaning.

One feature of Figure 4.3 is that there is no overlapping of the territory of different lexicalizations; there is no such thing in GC as a sentence in which you could change the article of any NP without simultaneously changing the meaning. This generalization does not, of course, apply to English. In *The dog is a mammal* you may change the article to anything you like without materially affecting meaning, and sentences such as *there are no cows here* and *there isn't a cow here* are synonymous. In fact, we may compare the GC situation shown in Figure 4.3 with the English situation shown in Figure 4.4 on the following page:

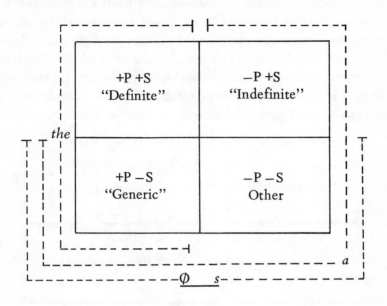

Figure 4.4
Semantic space for English articles

Here, *the* has spread from +P +S to +P −S, on the basis of both "definite" and "generic" being +P, while *a* has spread from −P +S to +P −S,
but only by virtue of having first spread to −P −S, on the basis of both
"indefinite" and "other" being −P; of course, once *a* has reached
"other," it can then spread to "generic" on the basis of their both
being −S. In other words, a contiguity constraint similar to that governing Figure 4.2 obtains, preventing "definite" and "other," or "indefinite" and "generic," from being jointly lexicalized unless intermediate categories are also jointly lexicalized.

A similar spreading process of individual lexicalizations across
semantic space could account for the variable ranges of lexical items

in the location-existence-possession-ownership area. Let us make the
same assumption for that area as we made for articles: that the configuration that emerges in creoles is the primary configuration whenever
articles appear (including, of course, in the original development of
human language as well as in the development of every existing natural
language). Then the primary configuration for the location, etc., area
will be as shown in Figure 4.5 below:

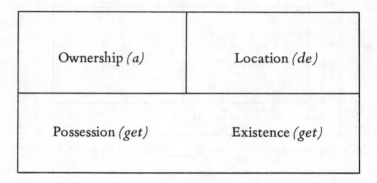

Figure 4.5
Semantic space for location, etc., in GC

The resemblance to the configuration of Figure 4.3 is obvious.
Again, two semantic areas are jointly lexicalized, while the remaining
two are separately lexicalized. Again, as with Figure 4.3, we know that
the pattern illustrated is one that is followed by most, perhaps all,
creole languages, and one that cannot be explained by appeal to the
structures of the languages that were in contact at the time the creoles
came into existence. If this represents the primordial pattern, then
those languages which separately lexicalize all four relationships would
have reached that state by dividing and separately lexicalizing the two
lower quadrants, while those that jointly lexicalize three or even four
quadrants would have reached that state by procedures similar to those

which spread *the* and *a* to the second and third quadrants, respectively, but without at any stage of the process jointly lexicalizing noncontiguous quadrants.

However, it remains to identify the semantic primes by virtue of which the contiguity constraint is maintained in the domain of Figures 4.2 and 4.5. Clearly, the specificity prime, dominant in article systems, cannot be involved, for any entity must be marked as +specific before it can have existence, location, possession, or ownership predicated of it. However, there is evidence that presupposedness, the next prime down, so to speak, may be crucially involved. Entities of which location and ownership can be predicated must be assumed known to the listener: compare *the desk is in a corner* with **a desk is in a corner,* or compare *the briefcase is mine* with **a briefcase is mine.* On the other hand, entities of which existence and possession can be predicated must be assumed unknown to the listener; thus, we have *there is an answer* versus **there is the answer,*[10] and *I have a cold* versus **I have the cold* (the fact that the latter sentence is grammatical under contrastive stress, as in *(It's) I (that) have the cold, not Mary,* is, of course, completely beside the point).

Perhaps less clear here is exactly what the second prime involved is. I shall suggest, very tentatively and provisionally, something I shall call "relatedness." A claim that something exists entails no claim that that something is significantly related to anything else; similarly, a claim that something is located somewhere entails no claim that there is any significant connection between that something and its location. However, claims of possession and ownership involve a substantive link of some kind, whether genetic *(Bill has children, those children are Bill's),* creative *(Mary had an idea, that idea was Mary's),* or of some other nature. We could then illustrate semantic primes and their interrelationship as in Figure 4.6 on the following page:

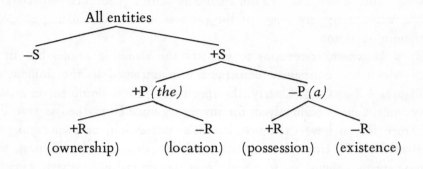

Figure 4.6
Hypothetical tree structure for semantic primes

This would enable us to define ownership as +P +R, location as +P −R, possession as −P +R, and existence as −P −R. If this were the case, no lexicalization could spread directly from ownership to existence (or vice versa) or from location to possession (or vice versa), since in either case the process would involve simultaneously reversing the polarity of two semantic primes. The observed facts for this area would thus be fully accounted for.

However, doubts about the status of "relatedness"—which does not appear to figure crucially in any other semantic area, unlike presupposedness—may make it worthwhile to consider an alternative explanation for these facts.

A slightly different kind of contiguity constraint has recently been claimed by Keil (1979, 1981). The constraint envisaged by Keil derives from a structure which he terms a "Predicability Tree." A predicability tree defines the range of different predication types over various semantic classes of NP (see Figure 4.7 on p. 253). Each predication type ranges only over those classes of NP which it dominates in the structure. Thus, predications such as X *is interesting* and X *is thought about* can be made of any class of NP, while at the

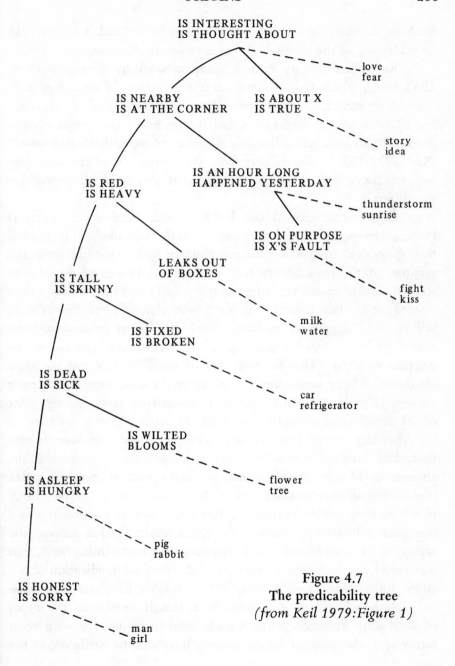

Figure 4.7
The predicability tree
(from Keil 1979:Figure 1)

furthest extreme, predications such as *X is honest* and *X is sorry* can be made only of the class of NP that is +animate, +human.

Keil's predicability tree is based on work by Sommers (1959, 1963, etc.), which first pointed out the existence of what Keil calls "the M constraint." The M constraint prevents any pair of predicates (A, B) from intersecting, i.e., A and B "can never span terms in common and also have terms that just A spans and terms that just B spans" (Keil 1979:16). It also follows from this that no predicate can span two noncontiguous sets of terms unless it also spans all intervening sets of terms.

Experiments carried out by Keil with children as young as kindergarten age suggest that the M constraint is unlikely to be learned by experience. Even the youngest children had somewhat truncated versions of the predicability tree, and such violations of the M constraint as were found tended to support Keil's hypothesis rather than disconfirm it. For example, children who claimed that dreams were tall (thereby apparently violating the hierarchy of predicability) revealed under further questioning that they believed dreams to be physical objects: "They're made out of rock," "They just got grass on them," "They turn white and go up in the sky" were among their answers (Keil 1979:110). Thus, the violations arose through assignment of "dreams" to an inappropriate category, rather than a violation of the hierarchy per se. Since children's output, as we have seen, is anything but isomorphic with their input, it cannot be claimed that the absence of M-constraint violations in their speech is merely a reflex of a similar absence in adult speech. There would appear to be no way in which they could negatively define the scope of predications as a result of inductive processes; thus, Keil's results further support the argument of Fodor (1975), referred to at the end of Chapter 3, that one could not learn the extensions of the predicates of a natural language unless one already knew the extensions of those predicates.

Although the M constraint is strikingly similar to the types of contiguity constraints that we observed in connection with color terms and the area of location, etc., it relates to predication (the establishment of a relationship between two lexicalizations) rather than delimiting the scope of lexicalization itself. Still, since *have, be,* etc., and their cross-linguistic equivalents are indeed predications, it may be that the predicability hierarchy affects permissible lexicalizations within that semantic area. We noted above that existence and possession could be predicated of all things, and thus would include the entire tree in their scope; location, however, could only be predicated of classes dominated by the second node down *(is nearby/at the corner)*, while ownership could only be predicated of classes dominated by the third node down *(is red/heavy)*. Joint scope of existence and possession could therefore have favored their joint lexicalization, while the disjoint scopes of location and ownership would have favored disjoint lexicalization.

In the present state of our knowledge, there is no principled way to choose between the two explanations. Those explanations, however, have served to show us other ways in which semantic space is structured, and suggest that the contiguity-constraint approach may yield a rich store of insights into the massive conceptual infrastructure that underlies, and that alone could make possible, the simplest "communicative" uses of language.

Before turning back to survey the growth of the syntactic structures that were based upon that infrastructure, we should look at one last area of semantic space where contiguity constraints arising from semantic primes, rather than from the predicability hierarchy, appear to be operative. At the same time, problems that were deferred to the present chapter when we encountered them in Chapter 2 (in connection with creole variability in the treatment of iteratives) and again in Chapter 3 (in connection with variable treatment of iteratives by children) may now be dealt with.

This area can best be understood if we start from those problems. Readers will recall that although a majority of creoles (including Guyanese Creole, which here as elsewhere will be taken as representative) merge iteratives with duratives in a single nonpunctual category,

Jamaican Creole (and perhaps one or two others) treats iteratives the same way as past punctuals, while São Tomense (and perhaps one or two others) treats iteratives the same way as futures (and perhaps other members of the irrealis category—existing descriptions are too inadequate for one to tell).

As was seen in the discussion of Bronckart and Sinclair (1973) in Chapter 3, there is more than one way of looking at iteratives. From one viewpoint, an iterative predication such as *John walks to work* ranges over an ill-defined series of instances in which John already has walked (and may be expected to continue to walk) to work. Since it does not represent a single event perceived as a unit (such an event as might be represented by *John walked to work last Thursday*, say), it can be regarded as falling into the nonpunctual category along with events perceived as extended and uncompleted processes *(John is/was walking to work)*.

But, from another viewpoint, each of the series of actions over which *John walks to work* ranges is itself an isolated event seen as a unit. If one regards the nature of the units in the series as primary, rather than the fact that those units constitute a series, then iteratives can be perceived as falling into the punctual category.

From yet a third viewpoint, one can point to the fact that while sentences like *John worked yesterday* or *John is working today* refer to specific occasions on which John worked or is working, sentences like *John works* do not. A sentence such as *John works* may be true even if John is not working now and even if John works considerably less than the average person. The key to the difference here lies in what it takes to establish the truth value of an iterative predication. Let us look a little more closely at the problem of how we would assign truth value to the sentence *John walks to work on Thursdays.*

We cannot falsify this sentence by pointing to a particular Thursday on which John did not walk to work. But we would be wrong if we assumed that the sentence means "John walks to work on most Thursdays." Not only does it not mean this, but it is also the case that the sentence could be falsified for any individual member of any set of Thursdays or for any combination of Thursdays (provided that such a combination did not equal the sum of all Thursdays) and still be true. Let us suppose that John drives to work every Monday, Tuesday, Wednesday, and Friday, and also on a majority of Thursdays, but on the remaining Thursdays, he walks to work. Then it is true that *John walks to work on Thursdays* (but not on Tuesdays, Fridays, etc.). Moreover, let us suppose that John has only ever walked to work on one Thursday. In that case, the sentence *John does not walk to work on Thursdays* is false and can be shown to be false by instancing the solitary occasion on which he did walk to work on a Thursday. If that sentence is false, its converse, *John walks to work on Thursdays*, must be true, no matter how uninformative or misleading it might appear to be.

It should be obvious then that predications of the iterative class do not refer to events in the same kind of way that other types of predication refer to them. *John walked to work last Thursday* is true if and only if John walked to work last Thursday, and *John is walking to work today* is true if and only if John is walking to work today. In fact, we could claim that *John walks to work on Thursdays* does not refer at all to any specific events, but rather to a generalized concept which may be based on one or more such events. Since the realis category embraces real events in real time, it could be concluded that iterative "really" belongs in the irrealis category.

The foregoing paragraphs constitute an informal account of the relationship between iterative and the nonpunctual, punctual, and irrealis categories. The question is now whether, in terms of well-motivated semantic primes, we can show formally how those categories would interact in an analogue of the relevant area of semantic space.

The status of punctual-nonpunctual and realis-irrealis as semantic primes will be dealt with a little later on in this chapter, when we try to see whether the ordering of TMA markers can be accounted for in evolutionary terms. For the present analysis we need only these and one other primary distinction which has already been independently established, i.e., specific-nonspecific. Predications like *John works* or

John walks to work may be regarded as having the same relationship
to predications like *John worked yesterday* or *John is walking today*
as generic NPs have to particular-reference NPs, or as concepts do to
percepts. In other words, habituals are −specific, while nonhabituals
are +specific.

The SNSD thus crosscuts the area of semantic space which
includes the punctual-nonpunctual and realis-irrealis distinctions. In
order to adequately represent this situation, we would require a three-
dimensional model, but for convenience we will represent the SNSD as
a square boundary within a larger square, as shown in Figure 4.8 on
p. 259. Since, as has been stated already, semantic infrastructure
determines where conceptual boundaries MAY, but not where they
MUST, be drawn, the configuration of Figure 4.8 leaves the three
analyses of Figures 4.9(a), (b), and (c) (p. 260) as further possibilities.

Analysis (a) of Figure 4.9 corresponds to the Guyanese (majority creole) analysis; analysis (b), to the Jamaican Creole analysis;
and analysis (c), to the São Tomense analysis. It leaves open, of course,
a fourth analysis: that of English, Yoruba, and a number of other
languages which would correspond to Figure 4.8. In this analysis,
habituals are separately grammaticized *(John works)* from continua-
tives *(John is working)*, punctuals *(John worked)*, and various kinds
of irrealis *(John will work, John would work)*. It should be noted,
however, that the Romance languages in general follow the analysis
of Figure 4.9(a), the majority creole analysis, merely superimposing
upon it the past-nonpast distinction: Spanish *yo trabajo* means 'I am
working' or 'I work', while *yo trabajaba* means 'I was working' or 'I
worked (habitually)', and in consequence, *yo trabajé* is limited to
'I worked (punctually, on a particular occasion)'.

We now have a vague inkling (probably little more than that,
as it may turn out) of the complexities of semantic space: a space that
had to come into existence before language as we know it could be
born. Some of that space was required for the very first, earliest,
and simplest stages of language. Other parts, although they were not

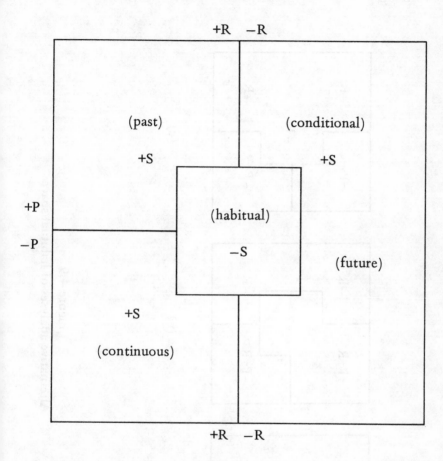

(R = realis, P = punctual, S = specific)

Figure 4.8
Semantic space around habituals

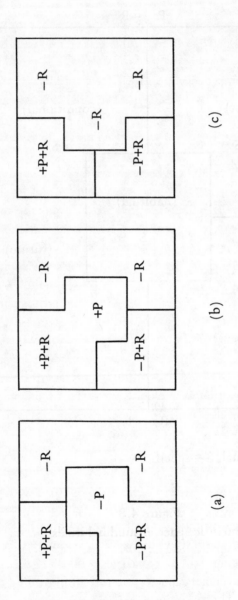

Figure 4.9
Alternative analyses of habitual space

immediately required, probably came into existence prior to the emergence of language, as we shall see, but were only incorporated into language as language grew. Yet other parts may only have come into existence subsequent to the initial stages of language development. However, I suspect that such parts, if they exist, will prove to be minor, and that the common notion, more often implicit than explicit (if made explicit, it is hard to defend), that language bootstrapped its way upward, creating the conceptual categories it needed as it grew, producing thought, consciousness, and volition as mere epiphenomena, is simply false.

As I try to develop the scenario of how a language based on the conceptual categories we have surveyed could have developed, I shall incur a heavy debt to a seminal work in glottogenesis, Lamendella (1976). This paper represents the first systematic attempt to use the development of language in the child as a possible model for the development of language in the species. Lamendella claims that "ontogeny manifests a repetition of several phylogenetic stages in the neurofunctional system that allows human infants to learn languages." In his case, as in mine, "it strains credulity to pretend that language as we know it *suddenly sprang up intact as a cultural invention* in the absence of *extensive cognitive and communicative preadaptations*" (emphasis added); he envisages, accordingly, a series of hominid species, each developing a particular element or stage of language and then transmitting that development to the next species via the genetic code.

Lamendella defends the foregoing model against accusations of Lamarckism by pointing out that in all species, individual members show differences in their capacities. Thus, at any given stage of the development toward full language, relatively slight differences in the associated capacities would have conferred a selective advantage on their possessors, so that there would have developed "a concentration of genotypes producing [these capacities] in the gene pool of the species." Thus, the average capacity of the hominid line at stage $n+1$ would have equaled the maximum capacity at stage n, and the biological foundations of language would have been laid down, not in a single cataclysmic event, but in an ordered series of steps.

This series would then necessarily repeat itself in the course of child acquisition since, as Lamendella points out, "more recently encoded genetic information generally tends to unfold later in ontogeny so as to preserve the temporal sequence in which the new components of the genetic information code were laid down." Lamendella is careful to show that his claims do not fall under the two main criticisms to which early recapitulationist theories in biology were subject. First, he points out that "embryonic" stages of language may reproduce not the developmental stages of *adult* language but the language of children at corresponding stages. At any stage, adults using general-purpose strategies might have developed language beyond the range of contemporary children, although without being able to transmit such developments via the genotype. Second, he is aware that embryological features do not always or necessarily occur in the same order as their corresponding evolutionary features, so that the developmental stages of child language do not necessarily occur in the same order as corresponding stages in the original development of language.

With regard to this latter point I think that Lamendella is too cautious. Recapitulationist theory in general biology had to cover a very wide range of phenomena, many of which were only very remotely connected. Consider any pair of such phenomena, say, dentition and the structure of the foot in a given species. Clearly, these two things are not wholly unconnected since we do not normally find herbivores with claws or carnivores with hooves. However, within both herbivorous and carnivorous species there is quite a wide range of tooth and foot structures, detailed development of each of which must have proceeded with a good deal of independence from the other. It should therefore be unsurprising that on occasion the precise sequence of developments should have been shuffled somewhat between phylogeny and ontogeny—that, for example, in a given phylum, a certain type of tooth might have developed earlier than a certain type of foot, but that, in the embryonic forms of some contemporary species, that type of foot might develop earlier than that type of tooth. However, when we are dealing with the development of language, we are dealing with a very tight subsystem of neural structures rather than with a wide range of quite dissimilar physical features; and within such a subsystem, a high degree of mutual interdependence might be expected to obtain. We would expect, therefore, that reversals of phylogenetic ordering in the ontogeny of language would be quite rare, if indeed any exist at all.

I shall not examine in detail the stages that Lamendella proposes, which differ in some respects from those to be suggested here; his work was carried out from a slightly different perspective and his conclusions are worthy of study in their own right. I shall return to the last of our speechless ancestors, whose cognitive equipment need not have differed in any material respect from that of the contemporary great apes.

Earlier in this chapter reference was made to the question why, if there was such massive preadaptation for language, it did not arise earlier. Attempts to account for this fact often take the form of simply pointing to the parlous state of hominids expelled from an arboreal Eden and forced to compete with fitter predators; the compensatory advantage offered by language then seems self-evident. But evolution does not behave like the U.S. Cavalry; if it did, it would surely have ridden to the rescue of the gorilla, now threatened more seriously by our species than our species was ever threatened by others. Need does not create function unless that function is already within a species' grasp.

This view might seem to directly contradict the view expressed earlier that intense interspecific competition may have rapidly expanded the cognitive capacities of our species. In fact, there is no contradiction. Cognitive growth—the increase in the capacity of creatures to analyze the environment and predict outcomes—has always been the major thrust of evolution, and to claim this is in no sense to be guilty of teleology, since the more cognitively developed any species

becomes, the greater would be its chances of survival. Thus, the hominid line may have been capable of a relatively rapid growth of cognitive
capacity precisely because there was already a broad evolutionary base
to build on. But there could be no basis to build on with regard to
language, since the kind of cognitive capacity hominids were only now
building—the conceptual capstone, so to speak, on the vast arch of
perception that had been building ever since the first microorganism
responded to light or to the touch of another—was the necessary
prerequisite for the most rudimentary form of language.

Yet the question remains. If apes have adequate prerequisites
for at least a fraction of what we have in the way of language, then the
probability is that *Dryopithecus* had similar prerequisites, and that
gives a period of at least five million years in the pongid line, and *x*
million years in the hominid line, in which the capacity for language
existed, and the need for language existed, but there was no language.

Here we must consider the channel problem. However refined
the conceptual schemata, however detailed and accurate the cognitive
map that a species can construct, it will profit that species little (except
in terms of individual survival) unless there is also a mode of expression.
The only two modes of expression that seem to have even a chance of
being viable for primates are the vocal and the manual. Without full
cortical (consequently voluntary) control over one or another of these
channels, language as communication would not have been possible.

However, the channel problem has quite another dimension, a
dimension seldom referred to but equally critical. This dimension is,
in fact, twofold. We will take the second half and then the first half.
The second half is: when A, the first hominid ever to use either a sound
sequence or a gesture referentially, made such sequence or gesture to B,
another hominid, how did B know that A was communicating referentially, and not merely coughing, clearing his throat, scratching himself,
or brushing a fly away? The first half is: given the same situation, how
did A, totally ab ovo, conceive the idea of representing some object or
event in the environment in terms of a sound sequence or gesture—an
act unprecedented since the Big Bang?

These problems cannot be dismissed by hand-waving. Either language began as a consciously intended performance, in which case we have to show both how the intent could have been formed and how a conspecific could have grasped both the fact that there was an intent and the reference that was intended, or it began accidentally. Although it is no aim of this chapter to add to the already overlong list of Flint- stone scenarios, one of the (possibly numerous) ways in which language could have arisen accidentally is the following: Mrs. Og, breast-feeding a lusty one-year-old with one hand, is trying to feed herself with the other. Young Og, ready for a change of diet, makes a grab for the meat. Mrs. Og pushes him away. He tries harder, babbling in his frustra- tion: *gaga*. His stubbornness amuses Mrs. Ug, sitting nearby, and she imitates *gaga* and maybe makes a playful grab for the meat. For a while after that, the favorite joke in the tribe is to creep up on somebody, shout *gaga,* and try and grab his or her meat. Perhaps it dies out, as jokes do. Perhaps words were found and lost and found again a score of times before they took root, or perhaps the slightly older kids picked it up and began to use it seriously when they got hungry or when they thought the grown-ups were dividing the food unfairly.

Or a slight variant on this: Ig, young Og's uncle, is pretending to be a tiger, an avuncular activity still widespread today and presumably of no very recent evolutionary history. Young Og withdraws in real or simulated fear, shouting *wawa!* Uncle Ig imitates him, and again everyone laughs, but tigers are not everyday occurrences, so the thing is quickly forgotten. But a couple of days later Ig sees a real tiger about to pounce on Og. By a sheer fluke he yells out *wawa!* instead of the regular alarm call, and Og saves himself in the nick of time. Maybe they and the rest of the band are able to kill the tiger, and dance and em- brace around its carcass like European soccer players after a goal, shouting *wawa!* And the word, perhaps soon followed by others of a similar nature, gets incorporated into the earliest of human rituals; for, as Marshack (1976) insightfully observed, "Language, in fact, may have been as useful, or more useful, in this cultural realm than in the comparatively self-evident strategies utilized in hunting, butchering and gathering."

Many such scenarios could be elaborated, all equally probable (or improbable). How the Rubicon was crossed is of minor concern; what matters is how it was reached and what happened after it was crossed. But origin stories like these which feature ludic and jocular components do have some advantages. First, they do not require intent on anybody's part, and since they do not require intent, they do not require understanding, at least in the everyday sense of that term. Thus, they neatly avoid both halves of the understanding-intentionality problem referred to a few paragraphs earlier. Secondly, they are based on behaviors—imitative and joking behaviors—which are independently attested for other members of the primate family and which therefore must have been common to all our immediate ancestors. Thirdly, they provide an element which may be essential in the acquisition of language anywhere in the universe: external modeling.

It is not, I think, accidental that chimps did not acquire language until we taught them. It cannot be the case that they lacked the intelligence to invent it, since they can use it creatively (within, admittedly, quite narrow limits) once their pump has been primed, so to speak. It could be that the conceptual leap is too great to be made in a single stride by any species—that some kind of external model is needed, whether that model is intentional (as was the case with human teaching of apes) or unintentional (by young human children, as in the stories above); otherwise, the whole idea of referential communication would have been just too radical to work out (in either sense of *work out*). But if this is so, there is a channel block for the pongid line that did not exist for the hominid line.

In other primates, vocal outputs have not come under sufficient cortical control for the vocal channel to be viable for linguistic use; the great apes cannot suppress spontaneous vocalizations, have very little if any capacity for voluntary vocalization, and "show little or no ability to imitate sounds" (Dingwall 1979). But if hominids could have imitated and assigned meaning to the spontaneous vocalizations of children, why could not chimps or other primates have done the same with their own infants' spontaneous gestures?

If we replay the two scenarios given above with an ape cast, the reason will become obvious. Instead of *gaga* for 'meat' or more probably some more general 'food', you would have had some kind of grabbing motion. Instead of *wawa* for 'tiger' you would have had some kind of fear behavior. Paradoxically, infant gestures could not have served as proto-words *because they were not arbitrary enough.* For the first signs to have had a narrow enough range to fit individual concepts, they must have had NO RANGE, have been quite empty, communicatively speaking, so that they could be filled by the particular reference of the immediate context, by "food" or "tiger," as the case might be. You could not use a grabbing motion as a symbol for food because there were so many other things you might grab for. You could not use a fear gesture as a symbol for a tiger because there were so many other things you might be afraid of. But something that had no clear meaning for the parent, such as a child's pre-speech utterance, could be hooked to any of the hominid's preexisting concepts precisely because it lacked any such general associations.

There would be little point in spending so much time on the actual emergence point of language if the suggestions just given were not a logical outgrowth of all that we have already discussed. The major point of this chapter has been that language grew out of the cognitive system used for individual orientation, prediction, etc., rather than out of prior communicative systems. It would follow from this that the most likely means of expression, when this cognitive infrastructure finally emerged as a communicative system in its own right, would have been one which was quite separate from, and unlikely to be confused with, the prior system. True, both hominid calls and hominid proto-words would have been in the vocal channel, but the acoustic ranges of the modern "call system"—shrieks, laughter, etc.— and those of speech sounds do not overlap and very likely have never overlapped.

Once the Rubicon was crossed, progress may well have been rapid, a matter of a few generations, since the necessary infrastructure for a fairly rudimentary level of language would have already been in place. Chimps have progressed (with training, granted) from one-word to several-word utterances in a matter of months, so I suspect that the one-word, two-word, etc., stages of early child development do not necessarily reflect stages in adult language development, but rather rehearse cognitive growth stages in the hominid line that PRECEDED the emergence of language. Not a lot turns on this, either way, and even how we would decide between the two alternatives is at present very far from being clear. But somehow the idea of our ancestors communicating via one-word utterances for several millennia while awaiting the growth of the requisite neurological infrastructure (whatever that might have been!) that would permit them to add word two to word one falls short of being wholly persuasive. In the absence of any evidence to the contrary (but bearing in mind the possibility that such evidence might appear at any time) we will conclude that in the first flush of language, our ancestors were able to get about as far as chimps have; that is, they could:

a) Lexicalize concepts corresponding to classes of sensorily perceptible entities and sensorily perceptible attributes of entities (things like *color* and *size* as opposed to things like *courage* and *justice*).
b) Lexicalize secondary concepts by conjuncts of primary concept names.
c) Organize brief (up to 3-5 word) utterances on a predominantly topic-comment basis (i.e., proceeding from the proximal to the distal, the old to the new, more or less irrespective of case-role relations).
d) Despite (c), distinguish in a pinch between X-Vs-Y and Y-Vs-X sequences (e.g., form appropriately, and react appropriately to, the difference between *Roger tickle Lucy* and *Lucy tickle Roger,* in at least a majority of cases).

On the other hand, it is likely that they, in common with modern primates, were not able to:

e) Produce utterances of more than one clause.

f) Grammaticize even the most basic semantic distinctions, such
   as those of tense, plurality, possession, etc.

These two capacities are, as I shall try to show, phylogenetically
linked. Together they constitute minimal requirements for anything
even approaching the kind of language we have today, and the reluc-
tance of many linguists and psychologists to accept that, lacking them,
modern apes could be capable of language, is very understandable.
However, such linguists and psychologists feel under no obligation to
give an account of how language was initially acquired, which makes
things easier for them, but does not do anything toward helping us to
understand ourselves. What apes have, what our ancestors had, you may
or may not call language, but it seems to me simply bizarre to suppose
that it wasn't something that you had to have in order eventually to
have languages like those of today. Those who disagree have no right to
do so unless they can provide a more plausible route to our present
situation.

Seidenberg and Petitto (1979), in reviewing (pessimistically) the
linguistic achievements of apes, make the point that no convincing
evidence has yet been provided that an ape can use a sign for any object
that is not in its immediate environment. This is equally true of children's language in the first few months of acquisition, of course; and
indeed, with only (a)-(d) as one's resources, it is hard to see how
reference could escape from the prison of the here-and-now. But being
able to talk, if only about the here-and-now, is an immense advantage
for children, and was presumably at least an equal advantage for our
forefathers, over not being able to talk about anything at all. You
could convey highly specific warnings, bring about cooperative behavior, settle disputes, even construct primitive rituals. In rituals, displacement begins; the head of the cave-bear on a pole stands for all
the cave-bears who control the warm caves you will need in order to
get through the next Ice Age. But it is one thing to be able to think
displacement, and quite another to be able to talk it.

Consider the following situation. You are Og. Your band has just severely wounded a cave-bear. The cave-bear has withdrawn into its cave. Ug wants to go in after it. "Look blood. Bear plenty blood. Bear weak. Ug go in. Ug kill bear. Ug plenty strong." You want to be able to say something along the lines of *the bear we tried to kill last winter had bled at least as much as this one, but when Ig went in after it to finish it, it killed him instead so don't be such an idiot.* Since in order to think this all you had to be able to do was to replay the memory of events you yourself had witnessed, I can see no reason to believe that you could not have thought it because you didn't have the words to think it in. But saying it is another story. Let's suppose you try. Since you have nothing approaching embedding, there is no way you can use a relative clause to let the others know which bear you are thinking about. Since you have no articles or any comparable device, there is no way you can let the others know that you are talking about a bear that they know about too. Since you have no way of marking relative time by automatic tense assignment or even adverbs, there is no way you can let the others know that the bear you want to talk about is one that is not here anymore. Since you have no verbs of psychological action (we'll see why in a moment), there is no way you can use the verb form itself to inform the others that you are speaking of a past time (*remind, recall, remember,* etc.). You can try "Og see other bear." Everybody panics. "Where? Bear where?" "Bear not here." Some laugh, some get angry; Og's up to his practical joking again. "Bear kill Ig," you try. Now even the ones who are laughing are sneering. "Ig! Ig dead! Og crazy!" If you have any sense, you shut up, or someone will get the idea to push you into the cave instead of Ug.

It was mentioned earlier in the chapter that the power to predict the course of future events was what gave a selective advantage to those species which developed their cognitive capacities, and that this power depended crucially on the power to categorize and analyze past events. Both powers in turn depend upon the quality of the cognitive map—

its accuracy, degree of detail, and universality or lack of it. A language that could advance beyond the initial plateau of the here-and-now could potentially do two things which would lead to an exponential increment in the survival power of the species possessing it.

First, it could code the cognitive map in such a way that processing time would be drastically reduced. One can think nonverbally, by processing images, or one can think verbally, using lexical items instead of images; in order to utter, or comprehend, or merely mentally construct the sentence *John drove the tan Oldsmobile from Arkansas to Texas,* it is not necessary to frame mental images of John, or driving, or Oldsmobiles, or Arkansas, or Texas. A number of psychological experiments (several referenced in Hamilton [1974]) have shown that where labels for objects are available, human subjects perform more effectively and much more rapidly; for instance, Glucksberg and Weisberg (1966) showed that solution times for label-aided as against label-free versions of a problem differed by a factor of fifteen to one. The mere fact that processing time is reduced automatically makes possible many analyses that could not previously have been attempted. For instance, where previously there might have been only time to model a single hypothetical solution to a practical problem (such as that of dealing with an angry cave-bear in its cave without getting killed in the process), there is now time not only to model several hypothetical solutions but also to compare them and make a choice on the basis of that comparison.

Second, it could make solutions available to other members of the species. Cognitive development without the power to communicate the results achieved by it may serve the survival of the individual but cannot serve the survival of the group. You could remember about the bear that killed Ig, but if there is no way in which you can convey your thinking to Ug, then the odds are that although you won't get killed, Ug will, and so will lots of Ug's children and grandchildren. True, your smart genes will multiply, while their dumb ones won't, but all that will do is bring a little bit nearer the time when the species will break through the here-and-now barrier and achieve, not just predictability, but the dissemination of predictability—the unique capacity that launched a single primate species on its unprecedented career.

Let us consider some fairly minimal requirements that language must have satisfied before it could emancipate itself from the here-and-now.

First, the structure of one-clause sentences must have been stabilized. It must have been stabilized because freely variable word-order minus case-marking devices equals growing ambiguity as two- and three-clause sentences develop. In fact, word-order cannot have stabilized *so that* longer sentences should be unambiguous; there must have been some motivation at the single-clause level. Let us consider what such motivation might have been.

To begin with, we need to look at something apparently quite unconnected with sentence-order—that is, word-formation. Although there is an extensive and controversial literature on the range of distinctive speech sounds that early species (in particular, Neanderthal man) could have produced—see Spuhler (1977) for references—there can be little doubt that that range was considerably smaller than the range of our own species. Let us assume a capacity for five consonants and three vowels (not much less than the range of modern Hawaiian, with eight consonants and five vowels) together with CV syllable structure; this would give a maximum capacity of only 15 monosyllabic words and 225 disyllabic words. Moreover, all languages we know of under-utilize their inventories, leaving numerous lexical gaps, so that the practically attainable total would be lower still. Factors such as these would encourage use of the same lexical item in causative and non-causative senses. In that case, as we saw in Chapters 2 and 3, only the frames $N_{ii}V$ and N_iVN_{ii} (where N_{ii} is nonagentive and N_i, agentive) would distinguish causative from noncausative senses of V.

Let us now consider a hypothetical word, *keke,* which means 'die' in the context N *keke,* but 'kill' in the context N *keke* N. We have assumed that the first word-order in early language was topic-comment, with shared, old information first (or zeroed) and nonshared information second. There is now a potential conflict. Let X be old information and Y new information, and let it be the case that Y killed X. Topic-comment order would then call for *X keke Y*, equivalent to 'X was killed by Y'. However, *X keke Y* would also correspond to the structure $N_i VN_{ii}$, in which V has its causative sense and N_i is agentive—yielding an alternative reading, 'X killed Y'. In theory the conflict might be resolved by adopting either strict topic-comment or strict SVO order, but since the latter holds less chance of ambiguity than the former, and is therefore fractionally more economical in processing time, we can assume either that it was universally adopted or that those languages that failed to adopt it died without issue. In fact, languages that did fail to adopt SVO must surely have died out when the strict-order languages achieved embedding and complex structure; it is tempting, although quite futile, to speculate that what caused the large size of the Neanderthal cranium was the apparatus needed to process (and store in short-term memory) multiply-ambiguous parsings of multiclause sentences in which the constituents were not systematically ordered.

If we accept Lamendella's hypothesis, there is support for the foregoing picture from acquisition processes. Bever (1970) has demonstrated the existence of what he terms "Strategy C"—"Constituents are functionally related internally according to semantic constraints"—and "Strategy D"—"Any Noun-Verb-Noun (NVN) sequence within a potential internal unit in the surface structure corresponds to actor-action-object." Experiments carried out by Bever and his associates indicate that children between two and three rely on Strategy C to comprehend sentences but that a little later they switch to Strategy D. This serves to explain the otherwise quite baffling fact that children's performance with regard to sentence types which involve nonagentive initial NPs (passives, clefts) actually deteriorates rather than improves between three and four.

The acquisitional sequence Strategy C-Strategy D would then replicate stages in the early development of language. Strategy C would have had to be developed in order to interpret case roles in the stage in which topic-comment ordering was dominant. Strategy D would have succeeded it as soon as sentence-order stabilized and became the primary marker of case relations. Note that, originally, adoption of Strategy D would have had none of the dysfunctional side effects that it does nowadays with children acquiring English since, at that time, there were no passives and no clefts; Strategy D would have given the right answer every time.

We can assume that neural modifications accompanied the change. What these may have been is still beyond anyone's power to determine; what they would have had to be able to accomplish is slightly less opaque. There is no evidence that SVO ever got hardwired into the system, but assignment of case roles must have become automatic, and underlying this must have been a hierarchy of cases with the rank-order, *agent-experiencer-patient*—subjecthood in any given sentence being assigned to the highest-ranking case in that sentence. Also, if the ape experiments are anything to go by, speech would have had to be speeded up considerably (Rumbaugh and Gill [1976] report a human-chimp conversation of only twenty-one sentences which took nine minutes): more rapid processing would presumably have required qualitative as well as quantitative increases in neurons and neuron connections.

So far we have assumed a limit of two case roles per sentence. However, this does not mean that there were only two case roles in the hominid repertoire. Insofar as apes can use tools and give things to one another, one must assume that cases such as instrumental and dative are potentially within their grasp. But problems arise once a third case role is added.

Any two case roles can be ordered around V so that the higher of the two precedes V and the lower follows. But presence of a third means that two NPs must be conjoined. This creates parsing problems. If you want to say something like *Ug gave Ig's meat to Og,* there are three possible ways in which you can overcome these problems.

You can indicate the oblique cases with prepositions, or postpositions, or some other purely grammatical case-marking device.

In *Ug gave Ig's meat to Og,* *'s* marks the genitive and *to,* the dative case. It is perhaps possible, but highly unlikely, that our predecessors could have invented grammatical case marking ab ovo; even in many synchronic languages, case markers can be traced back to original content words which have been bleached of their original semantics and downgraded from their original syntactic roles.

In the absence of grammatical marking, you can simply string case roles together and hope that Strategy C—which must simply be overridden, not erased, by Strategy D—will suffice to parse the result. In most cases it may, but in many it will not. The sentence introduced above, for example, would come out as *Ug give Ig meat Og,* which might be parsed as 'Ug gave Ig's meat to Og' but could also be parsed as 'Ug gave Ig the meat of Og'. Note that parsing mistakes in discourse must be cumulative; the listener who thought Ig got Og's meat and the listener who thought Og got Ig's meat would put quite different constructions on the sentences that followed.

The third alternative would be to preserve the two-case-roles-per-sentence restriction and conjoin sentences: *Ig have meat, Ug take meat, Ug give Og.* This is cumbersome but unambiguous. But note that if the second occurrence of *Ug* is omitted, you get *Ug take meat give Og*— the same serial structuring of dative-incorporating sentences that we found as a frequent feature of creoles in Chapter 2.

In fact, verb serialization, probably arising out of paratactic conjunction plus equi-deletion, represents the only plausible means by which early language could have broken out of single-clause structure. It is difficult for us now to appreciate the magnitude of the advance that was involved. The single-clause apelike proto-language was, as we have said, almost certainly limited to dealing with physical activities in the here and now. Sentences representing mental activities almost always demand more than one clause. If we say that something happened *when* something else happened, or will happen *if* something else happens, or happened *because* something else happened, we are representing not something that we have perceived directly through the senses, but the result of some kind of mental computation performed on sensory inputs (or, to be more precise, on things that originated as sensory inputs but that have already had a lot of processing done to them, along lines suggested earlier in this chapter). Still more clearly, if we *remember,* or *believe,* or *think,* or *hope,* or *expect* that something happened or will happen, or if we *want* or *hope* or *decide* to do something, we are again directly representing a mental operation on the product of past inputs or the projected product of possible future ones, and in either case, one that cannot be expressed in a single clause. The gap between monopropositional sentences and multipropositional sentences is the gap between talking only about observables in the external world and communicating the contents of one's mind. And the bridging of that gap must have constituted the greatest single step in what anthropologists mean by the ugly terms "hominization" or "sapienization"—the process of becoming the kind of species that we now are.

Verb serialization helped to bridge this gap, and the way in which it accomplished this is worth looking at a little more closely. At first glance, the results of verb serialization may look a little like those underlying structures that were once proposed by generative semanticists in which verbs were distintegrated into what were supposedly primitive concepts; perhaps the most widely discussed of these was the proposed derivation of *kill* from *cause to become not alive.* Similarly, if one found a language that expressed the meaning of *bring the book to me* as the equivalent of *carry the book come give me,* it might seem that sentences of the latter type reflected the absence of a means for generating derived lexical forms. Such a view might lead to the conclusion that there were two types of action, a type that was "semantically complex" (capable of being broken down into primes) like *kill* or *bring,* and a type that was "semantically simple" (its members being themselves primes) like *cause* or *carry.*

Such a view is, I think, incorrect. There is probably no action verb which is either intrinsically simple or intrinsically complex in the ways suggested above. How actions came to be lexicalized is something which, like so many other things of equal or greater importance, we have had to skim over or ignore altogether in an account as compressed as this one. However, we need to note that verbs are abstractions from sensory input in a way that nouns are not. At first glance, one might think that the referent of a verb like *hit* was as unambiguously unitary as the referent of a noun like *dog*, although in fact *John hit Bill* could be rendered more accurately (if more circumlocutiously) as *John clenched fist John drew-back arm John thrust-forward arm fist met Bill*. In fact, there are perhaps no "semantically simple" verbs that could not be represented in a "semantically complex" way, and vice versa. What determines whether a particular referent action is represented by one verb or more than one is nothing to do with semantic complexity, but has a lot to do with the number of case roles the action involves. It is precisely those actions which involve a number of case roles that are singly lexicalized in prepositional languages, and multiply lexicalized in verb-serializing languages.

The aid supplied by verb serialization in bridging the gap between monopropositional and multipropositional sentences had nothing to do with semantics. Verb serialization simply made available structures more complex than had existed hitherto—structures that added the possibility of NVNVN to the previous NV and NVN structures.

Now we need to consider how the representation of mental activities could have commenced. We have a syntactic bridge, but we also need a semantic bridge. I shall propose that the semantic bridge was provided by two classes of verbs: verbs of reporting and verbs of perception. Both represent actions that are in some sense "more physical" than the true psychological verbs of thinking, hoping, remembering, etc. Both entail dual-propositional sentences. Both are likely to be of high utility in hunting-and-gathering communities where members frequently split up in their search for food and need to convey to the others information about their degree of success in that search. I shall not attempt to determine priority as between these two classes.

Verb-class membership would now become critical in parsing.

The developing grammar would generate NVNVN sequences, but these would be ambiguous between two interpretations, e.g., NV[NVN] or NVN[(N)VN] (where the constituent in parentheses had been equideleted). However, if the first V was one of perception or reporting, the second N would be subject of the second V; if the first V belonged to some other class, the second N would be the object of the first V, and the sentence would be parsed as a serialization. When the "true" psychological verbs came to be added, they too would follow the first of these patterns.

The development of reporting verbs would have begun at the same time as the development of displacement. If I report what another person said and that other person is not present, then obviously the saying must have occurred on a previous occasion. If I tell you *Ug say honey here*, it requires no Socratic intellect to figure out that the honey may be here now (although of course it need not be) but that the saying of *honey here* by Ug must have occurred at a previous time (and perhaps in another place, although my capacity to translate Ug's actual utterance of *honey here* is something else that cannot simply be assumed). However, as sentences become more complex, the need to distinguish observation from computation, earlier from later, and general from specific statements must increase. Failure to make such distinctions, preferably in some quite rigorous and automatic way, leads to parsing problems which could compound even more rapidly than parsing problems arising from case assignment. Some scaffolding is required that will accurately fix the place of sentences in the world of time and reality; TMA systems supply this scaffolding.

Quine (1960:170) expressed frustration and puzzlement with the fact that all sentences of all human languages must obligatorily express tense, but then, from Reichenbach on, philosophers have glaringly failed to make any kind of sense out of TMA systems. Their recipe has always been, "Take the distinctions that are said by traditional grammarians to be made in modern English and reduce them to some kind of a formal schema." Since the advantages, if any, of this approach are totally opaque to me, I shall discuss it no further. From an evolutionary viewpoint, it appears plausible that the only distinctions the first TMA system could grammaticize must have been distinctions which were somehow already implicit in the ways in which the brain processed and stored information. If certain types of information were already stored in different places or in different ways, then attaching some kind of grammatical index to the products of different stores would not have presented too much difficulty. On the other hand, the only possible alternative—that the species invented categories for which there was no such preexisting infrastructure, and then either built a redundant set of infrastructures to reprocess it, or somehow assigned marking with 100 percent efficiency in the absence of such infrastructure—is at best an improbable one.

People find this hard to comprehend because categories such as "past," "present," and "future" seem quite natural and transparent. In fact, the so-called "moment of speech" which marks the elusive "point present" which is the linchpin of Reichenbachian analysis is an abstraction which can never be experienced but can only be inferred by beings who already have produced some kind of time-marking device. People talk about "present" as if it were somehow on a par with "past" and "future"; but while any single point action can be in the "past" or the "future," no such action can be in the "present," simply because it must already be in the "past" before you can get time to open your mouth to talk about it. As for "future" and "past," the former is of dubious status in that events assigned to it, however probable or plausible, are artifacts of the imagination ontologically indistinguishable from wants and wishes, however unlikely or even counterfactual, while the latter, although the most tangible of the three, suffers in utility from being internally undifferentiated.

In fact, time presents itself in experience as an unchanging state—it always was, is, and will be "now," as far as the experiencing individual is concerned—and, with an assist from memory and prediction, as a constant and unbroken flow pouring against us. No remotely plausible mechanisms of perception or neural processing would seem to yield the neat bisection of time into two equal portions divided by a constantly moving point which constitutes the "commonsense" analysis of time-imprisoned Western man.[11] Far different is the case for the distinctions to be argued here.

I shall propose that if the distinctions of ±anterior, ±irrealis, and ±nonpunctual are the TMA distinctions consistently made in creole languages, and if these distinctions struggle to emerge, as they seem to, in the course of natural language acquisition, then they represent the primary TMA distinctions made in the earliest human language(s), and appear in all three places because of their naturalness. Since the word "naturalness" has been subjected to so many abuses, I had better make very plain what I mean by it in this context. The naturalness of a distinction is assumed to be an all-or-nothing characteristic and not a matter of degree. A distinction is natural just in case it corresponds to a difference in the mode of perceiving, processing, storing, or accessing data in the brain, such difference in turn depending on specific features of the brain's physical structure. It is assumed that only distinctions of this kind can be candidates for primary grammaticization.

Quite obviously, in the present state of our knowledge, any claims about brain structure can have no more than hypothetical status. This fact is no excuse for imitating the ostrich, as does Muysken when he claims (1981a) that an earlier and much sketchier account of this area[12] "will remain arbitrary until we know a lot more about the functioning of the brain." We will not know a lot more about the functioning of the brain until we have made and compared and evaluated a lot more models of the brain along the lines of the one I have tried to construct in this chapter. The idea that scientists "increase knowledge" simply by "finding out facts" in the absence of any kind of theoretical model-building is an illusion which, remarkably enough, flourishes only among those who themselves deal with mainly theoretical issues, while it simply does not exist among workers in the physical sciences, who so much take for granted the interaction of speculative models and empirical findings that they never even see the need to defend their methods. In fact, it is quite conceivable that we could track every dendrite to its synapse and still not have the faintest idea how the brain worked, just because we had no adequate model of what all its electrical and molecular activity might be designed to accomplish. Therefore, to try to rebut the claims made here with the mere cry of "You can't prove it!" is as irrelevant as it is redundant. Those who disagree with the model presented here, which may indeed be wrong in detail or even in totality, have no recourse other than to construct better ones.

Muysken was right, however, in pointing out that my earlier account had failed to explain the syntactic ordering of TMA markers, and accordingly, the present account will remedy that deficiency. Let us review some relevant evidence. We know that the ordering of markers in creoles is always TMA, anterior-irrealis-nonpunctual. We know that in VO languages, as we are assuming the primordial language(s) to have been, free verbal elements which modify the meaning of the main verb usually precede the main verb. We know that the commonest source for TMA markers in creoles (and in other languages) is that of former full lexical verbs.[13] We will assume that whatever distinctions the original markers may have made, the markers themselves were derived from full lexical verbs. We will further assume that the markers must have been added in some order, that is to say, they were not added all at the same time. These two assumptions seem to me to be unexceptionable.

Almost as unexceptionable is the assumption that when the first marker was added, it became an immediate constituent of the verb, and hence any markers added subsequently would have to be positioned externally to the unit formed by the verb and the first marker. Certainly, it is hard to think of any motivation there could have been for inserting a new marker BETWEEN the original marker and the verb. Granted, we cannot prove that this did not happen. But there are ways in which the assumption can be tested.

Earlier in this chapter it was claimed that between any pair of distinctions, the distinction whose neural infrastructure had been laid down earliest in phylogeny would be the first to be realized in language.

Also, by Lamendella's hypothesis, the distinction first realized in language should be the first to be realized in the acquisition of language. Thus, in principle, we have two different ways of testing the assumption made above about adding order, two ways that are completely independent of one another: if both yield the same answer, then this constitutes mutual support for the two hypotheses, and if the answer yielded by both is the answer yielded by our (independently motivated) assumption, then further support is provided for the assumption.

According to that assumption, the nonpunctual marker, being always closest to the verb, represents the first of the three distinctions to be grammaticized. Therefore, punctual-nonpunctual should be the first of the three distinctions to acquire the appropriate neural infrastructure, and it should also be the first to be acquired by children.

In Chapter 3, we surveyed a considerable body of evidence which suggested that whatever children might be thought to be learning (and sometimes they might be thought to be learning past-nonpast before other distinctions), what they really learned first was punctual-nonpunctual. Our second criterion is thus satisfied. With respect to the first, let us consider possible neural infrastructures for punctual-nonpunctual. One of the earliest neural structures known to us is that which underlies the phenomenon known as *habituation*. In *Aplysia*, a sluglike marine mollusk whose nervous system contains only a handful of ganglia with a few hundred neurons each, the sensitive organs are extruded from a mantled cavity and consist of a gill for breathing, a siphon for eating, and a purple gland. The last two serve as primitive organs of perception. If anything touches the siphon or the gland, the gill retracts into the cavity. However, if you touch either gland or siphon at regular, brief intervals, the withdrawal response will diminish in both speed and intensity until eventually it is extinguished. *Aplysia* has done its equivalent of deciding that your actions are nonthreatening and thus it is wasteful to respond to them.

Aplysia's actions are of course entirely automatic and represent the workings of a mechanism which has evolved in the vast majority of animate creatures to prevent them from being wholly at the mercy of every external stimulus. It enables them to disregard irrelevant stimuli and reserve their energies to react to imminent danger or to seize feeding opportunities. If mechanisms such as this go back as far as mollusks, they antedate by some hundreds of millions of years any mechanisms that might underlie the other two TMA distinctions.

Clearly, habituation mechanisms have grown considerably more sophisticated since *Aplysia* emerged. Each of our senses has mechanisms that filter abrupt and sudden outside stimuli, which require immediate action on our part, from ongoing or persistently repeated stimuli, which do not. Driving down a crowded street, we are not at all perturbed by the constant movement of countless pedestrians, but let a ball bounce off the edge of the pavement, and (hopefully) we instantly slam on the brakes in anticipation of the child that may follow it. Working alone in an empty house, we pay no attention to sporadic noises in the street outside or the background murmur from the freeway a block or two off; we probably do not even consciously hear these things if we are engrossed in what we are doing; but let the slightest sound come from the rooms around us, and we stop whatever we are doing and become instantly alert. After the event we may tell the story as if we DECIDED to brake or DECIDED to attend to the strange sound, but these are post hoc rationalizations of our neuronal watchdogs' purely autonomous activities. In other words, the sorting of punctual from nonpunctual actions is done for us automatically, and it seems reasonable to suppose (although it is still far from provable) that percepts in the memory store are somehow coded with reference to whether they originated from sets of neurons specialized for perception of punctual events or from sets specialized for nonpunctual ones.

This capacity to make the punctual-nonpunctual distinction in real life, so to speak, must have been crucial to our ancestors, intermediate as they were between those who might prey on them and those on whom they might prey. It is hard to think of any distinction which could have been more important for them to make as they began to build up the store of communal experience that would become the traditional wisdom of human groups. The interrelation of punctual and nonpunctual, foreground and background, provided basic ways of analyzing and classifying the diverse experiences with natural forces and with other species which could now be handed on from generation to generation, growing as it spread through time, yielding knowledge of a wide range of phenomena and the actions appropriate in the presence of those phenomena.

Alone of the three TMA distinctions, punctual-nonpunctual correlated with observable phenomena. The realis-irrealis distinction contrasts observed events with events that are unobservable, at least at the time of speech; the anterior-nonanterior contrasts, not events at all, but the relative timing of events, a highly abstract feature. Punctual-nonpunctual, however, can be directly observed whenever a single action interrupts a more protracted or a repeated one. It could therefore have been grammaticized at a stage when only physical objects or events were capable of being grammaticized or lexicalized. Whether or not grammaticization took place this early, all the evidence suggests that punctual-nonpunctual was the first TMA distinction to be grammaticized, and accordingly, the form that marked the distinction would have been juxtaposed to the main verb.

To find the evolutionary ancestry of the second distinction, realis-irrealis, we need to know the earliest source for items in the memory store that did not originate in the organs of perception. In all probability that source was dreaming. Dreaming began with mammals—reptiles, as far as we are aware, do not dream—and its origins and evolutionary function remain mysterious. One explanation treats dreams as "providing for better building of the memory model by continued operation of the mechanism for memorizing during the night, even when no further information from external sources is available" (Young 1978:209). Certainly, dreams appear to permute actual experiences in ways that produce novel constructs. However, we have hypothesized that items in the memory store are coded in ways that reveal the source of each item. If this is so, all items in the store must have (at least) coding which will indicate whether they originated from perceptions of the external world or whether they lacked any such origin.

At whatever point our ancestors achieved the power to consciously manipulate the memory store in order to generate hypothetical future events or "might-have-beens," a new dimension would have been added to irrealis, but the essential coding difference would not have been affected; whatever was internally generated would be coded differently from whatever was externally generated. Nowadays, of course, most of us can consciously and quite explicitly distinguish, if required to do so, between events that really happened and events that are the product of dreams, desires, wishes, and expectations; if we cannot, we are separated from the remainder of the species and maintained in institutions specializing in this and similar conditions until such time as we recover the capacity. To be able to tell realis from irrealis is a crucial part of being fully human. But the foundation of this capacity and of our capacity to mark verbs in a way appropriate to the status of their referents must be the same: some kind of neural coding of memory items that reflects internal as opposed to external source.

Unfortunately, in the case of realis-irrealis and anterior-nonanterior, we cannot draw the evidence that we drew from child acquisition in the case of punctual-nonpunctual. While it is highly possible that children make irrealis distinctions before they make anterior distinctions, the point is not easy to prove since the lack of correspondence between the bioprogram TMA system and the systems of most target languages is such that it is by no means easy to tell when children have acquired whatever forms may correspond to irrealis and whatever forms may correspond to anterior. It is true, for instance, that children learning English acquire futures long before they acquire pluperfects, but since future does not correspond one-to-one with irrealis and pluperfect does not correspond one-to-one with anterior, it would be unfair and unrealistic to base any claims on this fact alone. Hopefully, studies of acquisition of those creole languages which preserve the original distinctions fairly intact, as well as more sophisticated studies of the acquisition of other types of language, may be able to provide the needed evidence.

However, even in the absence of such evidence, it seems likely that anterior was the last of the TMA distinctions to be added. In order to make the distinction, the order of past events has to be accessible. Perhaps all creatures that have memories have mechanisms, as we must, by which the order in which memories are laid down corresponds with the order in which the relevant experiences occurred. However, recoverability of that order is another matter, for any kind of recoverability entails volitional manipulation of the memory store, and there is no reason to suppose that volitional manipulation preceded nonvolitional manipulation (i.e., dreaming). Thus, the antecedents of anterior are almost certainly more recent than the antecedents of irrealis.

Furthermore, the utility of anterior as a category would be unlikely to arise until discourse had become fairly complex. Anterior marking is primarily a device which alerts the listener to backward shifts of time in a narrative or a conversation, thus enabling him to preserve the correct sequence of reported events—a must if features such as causality are to be extracted from it—even when the reporting diverges from that sequence. Thus, not only are the mechanisms underlying anterior probably more recent than the mechanisms underlying irrealis, but the functional need for anterior is almost certainly more recent than the functional need for irrealis.

If this is the case, we can claim that according to four sets of criteria—age of infrastructure, age of functional utility, time of child acquisitions, and sequence within Aux—the three basic TMA distinctions are ranked in the order: nonpunctual first, irrealis second, and anterior third.[14] Note that the surface order of tense-modality-aspect which this yields is not only the order of creoles but also what has been assumed from Chomsky (1957) on to be the underlying order for English, and perhaps other languages too.

Although considerations of space have prevented us from surveying a number of other features—such as the development of pronouns, pluralization, movement rules, etc.—which must have accompanied or closely followed the developments actually described, we have carried our account of the early history of language to a point at which, in its degree of complexity, it can have fallen but little short of an early creole language. In other words, we have brought language close to a point at which, for all practical purposes, the biological development of language ceased, and the cultural development of language began. I have not even attempted to provide a time scale for these developments, either absolute or relative; they may have been spread out over two or three million years or they may have come in a series of bursts or even (though this is intrinsically less likely) in a single explosion of creativity.

Although at present we can do little more than guess, the suggestion by Hockett (1973) that there might be some connection between the emergence of fully-developed language and the sudden and extremely rapid series of cultural changes that were initiated some ten thousand years ago is quite an appealing one. There is something inherently implausible in the idea that an evolutionary line which had existed for countless centuries within the hunting-and-gathering framework in which some members of our species still exist should suddenly begin to grow crops, herd animals, build permanent settlements, construct complex belief systems, and evince countless other behaviors typical of our species, and highly atypical of all others, merely because certain small areas had exceeded their carrying capacity (if indeed they had). With all species, areas exceed their carrying capacity from time to time, and the result is always the same—the species moves, if there is anywhere to move to, and if it is not an unduly territorial species; otherwise, individual members of the species die off until the balance of nature is restored. Similar experiences must have happened to our ancestors countless times and in countless places during the Pleistocene, with its sudden and extreme changes of climate, but the responses must always have been the same: migration or population loss.

It seems likely that agriculture commenced not as a reaction to climatic change, population imbalance, or any other external cause, but rather as a result of vast changes in the computational and communicative power of the species. Dearth was feared rather than experienced, and plans were made to prevent it. The shift from taking what nature provided, an attitude characterizing all previous species, to attempting to control nature was a vast one involving the power to construct an imaginary future and then communicate that construct to others so that concerted efforts could be made to realize it. Such attempts could hardly have been carried out without the aid of a language developed at least to the extent that we have envisaged here; but if such a language long antedated the birth of agriculture, how was it that that and all the other arts and sciences were not born far earlier than in fact they were?

At present, no adequate answer can be attempted. In any case, the precise dating of the events detailed in this account is really irrelevant. Some series of events such as have been described must have happened at some time during the last couple of million years or so for our ancestors to have passed from a state of no language to a state in which there existed languages recognizably similar to those of today. When those events occurred is a matter of legitimate interest, but not one that can affect either positively or negatively the validity of the foregoing account.

No one can be more acutely aware than I that the account given here is provisional, hypothetical, and can at best serve as no more than a rickety bridge between our present condition of almost total ignorance and some future state in which we may have at least a handful of relative certainties to build upon. However, the purpose of this chapter never was to write a definite prehistory and early history of language, but rather to show that, first, a series of capacities that might be plausibly held to have been latent in our last speechless ancestors, plus some capacities that could plausibly have evolved in the course of constructing a linear vocal language, could have yielded something recognizably similar to an early creole language, and second, that on the basis of what we at present know about our own species, such an outcome—a creole-like language—would have been intrinsically likelier than any other kind of possible language. The test of such an account lies not in whether this detail or that detail of it may be proven true or false, but in whether or not it proves possible to build better (more plausible, more detailed, more explanatory) models.

If the present model is in essence correct, and if a creole-like language was the end product of a long period of biological evolution, then the overall capacity to produce languages of this type (itself a composite of neural capacities that preexisted any kind of language and neural capacities that were added as language evolved)[15] must at that point (and for the rest of the life of the species, it should go without saying) have formed a part of the genetic inheritance of every individual member of the species. It would then unfold, as we have claimed, as part of the normal growth development of every child—in most cases, being quickly overlaid by the local cultural language, but in a few, emerging in something not too different from its original form. It would merely require triggering by SOME form of linguistic activity from others—how much, and of what kind, remains one of the most interesting questions we can ask about language—which is why wolf children, who share our biological inheritance, cannot speak, and why the interesting experiments of Psammetichus, James IV, Frederick II, and Akbar the Great all failed.

It is not without some interest that the account given here resembles, in some respects, the Biblical account of language. The Bible claims that language is a divine gift. This account can offer no objection to such a belief, assuming that God has chosen to work through evolutionary process; certainly, both accounts firmly reject the suggestion that language was in any sense a conscious or deliberate human invention. The Bible claims that our species originally spoke a single language. This account claims the same, with a slight qualification: the issue of whether language first arose in one group or in several independently is entirely irrelevant since, assuming the latter, all groups would have had the same neurological equipment, and thus their languages, although perhaps differing in lexical choices (as modern creoles do, for that matter) would have been structurally identical or almost so. The Bible claims that human language diversified coincidentally with a sudden surge of technological capacity, symbolized by the erection of the Tower of Babel (a tower aimed at reaching heaven, i.e., usurping powers over nature which were properly part of the divine prerogative). This account would also claim (and I will develop the claim a little further in the next paragraph) that human language diversified as a direct result of rapid cultural and technological diversification, aiming, consciously or not (and in our time it has become a conscious goal) at "The Conquest of Nature." I would be the last person to adduce Scriptural authority in support of a scientific theory, but the resemblances are intriguing, to say the least.

The question most frequently asked about the theory presented in this volume is: "If our biological inheritance provides for us a ready-made language, so to speak, how is it that we ever abandoned that language in favor of the diverse and far more complex languages of today?" The answer is that, in a sense, the biological language self-destructed. It had made possible the construction of cognitive maps more detailed and complete than those available to any previous species, maps which enabled their users to enter what was in effect a wholly new cognitive domain, a domain in which events could be predicted and forestalled and even altered rather than passively endured as all previous species had endured them. It had conferred on our species the power to LIVE DIFFERENTLY—differently from the past, and differently from one another.

So, differently was how they lived. Previously, as in all other species, our ancestors had all lived roughly the same kind of life; if they happened to live near a mud flat, they would include shellfish in their diet; if they didn't, they wouldn't; and that was about the extent of the difference. Now, some went on hunting and gathering and some became pastoralists and some became cultivators and some founded cities and lived by farming other people. New needs arose. New categories were established to take care of those needs. Some groups found it convenient to code verbs in such a way that the evidential status of any remark was immediately apparent. Some groups found it convenient to code nouns in such a way that the major semantic classes to which they belonged were immediately apparent. These new categories were superimposed on the old ones, but a language is a system or it is nothing, so that this superimposition shifted and distorted the older, more "natural" categories and in some cases, perhaps, overlaid them completely. This, too, was natural, in its way. No biological language could have been designed to suit the needs of all humans under all the different circumstances in which humans could live; indeed, if any such language could have been designed, it would either have been itself subject to change (since cultural evolution is not a closed process) or if not so subject would have been positively dysfunctional, since it could not have adapted to our changing needs and priorities. Thus, one hundred centuries of cultural change and development have produced the world of diverse, yet underlyingly similar, languages which we know today.

But not only cultural factors served to change the bioprogram language. Factors concerned with language processing are also operative. I will illustrate just two different types of such factors here.

The first involves relative clauses. As we saw in Chapter 1, HCE has no surface marker of relativization, even where English obligatorily requires one, provided that there is a head noun. If there is not a head noun, then an English relative pronoun is supplied. Thus, we get headed relatives like *da gai gon lei da vainil fo mi bin kwot mi prais* 'The guy WHO was going to lay the vinyl for me had quoted me a price', with no marking, but headless relatives like *hu go daun frs iz luza* '(THE ONE) who goes down first is the loser', with an English relative pronoun. Obviously, the difficulty of incorporating English relatives per se cannot be what is responsible for sentences of the first type. Rather, the cause must be, first, that all HCE sentences require some kind of overt subject (except imperatives, of course), and, second, that as we hypothesized in earlier chapters, HCE lacks—"used to lack" might be more accurate—a rule that would rewrite NP as N S, but possesses a rule that would rewrite NP simply as S, thus yielding the structure NP[NP V X] VP for both the above sentences.

However, as was shown in Bever and Langendoen (1971), zero relative pronouns in sentences where the head noun is subject of the relative clause can cause serious ambiguities in a minority of sentences. Practically all creoles now have some kind of relative marking, presumably as a consequence of such processing problems. Thus, change away from the bioprogram pattern can set in very quickly even where it is not triggered by language contact, if the functional pressure is sufficient.

The second factor involves word order. It has been claimed here that the original language order was SVO with serialization but that this order was not necessarily hard-wired. This directly contradicts a claim by Givón (1979:Chapter 7) that the original language order was SOV. Givón's evidence is that a majority of the world's language families are either synchronically SOV or reconstruct back to SOV, while change in the reverse direction is rare. But in fact, serial SVO often forms an intermediate stage between SVO and SOV in Austronesian languages which are changing under the influence of Papuan languages (Bradshaw 1979). In our original language, a similar change could have come about in the following manner: first, there occur a number of NVNVN sequences in which the final N is realized as a pronoun; second, object pronouns become cliticized; third, the first V is reanalyzed as a preposition. In this way, a structure that was originally analyzed as Subject-Verb-Object-Verb-Object changes until it can be reanalyzed as Subject-Preposition-Oblique Case-Verb—SXV, in fact. This is then interpreted as the canonical order, and any full-NP objects left behind the verb are moved in front of it in order to remove what now appears to be an anomaly. It is, of course, not necessarily implied that all early languages followed this course; but if a number of them did, then the data which Givón took as proof of original SOV could easily be accounted for.

There is not space here to discuss in detail how the bioprogram theory would affect the theory of linguistic change. It should be apparent that an entire volume could easily be written on this topic.

The study of linguistic change has been effectively paralyzed for many decades by the empirically groundless belief that all the world's current languages are at a similar level of development. Even the study of Greenbergian universals led only to suggestions of a kind of ceaseless seesawing between OV and VO orders. I would predict that, right or wrong, the present theory would at least give something tangible for diachronic linguistics to chew on.

However, it should at least be pointed out that the present theory does not claim a steady progression away from the bioprogrammed base. Quite apart from the drastic recyclings which pidginization precipitates, there are likely to be partial reemergences of bioprogram features in a number of linguistic situations, prominent among these being, first, the constant surfacing of so-called "substandard" varieties in classes where prescriptive monitoring is minimal, and second, contacts between typologically different languages (such as the Austronesian-Papuan clash mentioned above) which set in motion extreme change processes in one party or the other. Thus, despite a very rightly skeptical survey by Polomé (1980) which concludes that creolization may hardly ever or never have been responsible for historical changes, there may still be some truth in the persistent claims that Germanic, or Egyptian, or Old Japanese may owe some of their features to "creolization." In fact, Polomé would still be correct in claiming that true creolization had not taken place; the creole-like features would be derived from the same bioprogram that is responsible for creoles and for many acquisitional features, but surfacing under rather different and somewhat less radical circumstances than those which give rise to creoles.

We have now completed our survey of creoles, acquisition, and origins, showing the wide range of similarities that unite the first two and that could derive in both cases from the reenactment of the third. In the fifth and final chapter I shall briefly summarize the theory which these findings support, and place it in the context of existing linguistic theories, and I shall also glance at a few of the more obvious arguments that may be brought against it.

Chapter 5
CONCLUSIONS

The foregoing chapters have surveyed the three major areas of language development: development in the individual, development of new languages, and original development of language. Parsimony alone would suggest that these developmental processes might have much in common with one another, and the common pattern that emerges has an independent support that no other linguistic theory that I know of could claim: it is in accord with all we have so far learned about evolutionary processes and it is in accord with all we have so far learned about how processes in the brain determine the behavior of animate creatures. During the sixties and seventies, we heard a good deal about something called "psychological reality," although what it was was never well defined; I would suggest that whatever the fate of the theory argued here, any future linguistic theory will have to be able to claim "biological reality" if it is to be taken seriously.

The theory argued here has claimed that many of the prerequisites for human language were laid down in the course of mammalian evolution, and that the most critical of those prerequisites—for even things like vocal tract development were necessary, but in no sense sufficient, requirements[1]—was the capacity to construct quite elaborate mental representations of the external world in terms of concepts rather than percepts. In other words, something recognizable as thought (though clearly far more primitive than developed human thought) necessarily preceded the earliest forms of anything recognizable as language.

Circumstances still obscure enabled our (fairly remote) ancestors —perhaps *Homo erectus,* perhaps some other species—to lexicalize concepts and construct a primitive form of language probably not too dissimilar to that achievable, under training, by modern apes. Language even at so primitive a level conferred a sharp, selective advantage to its users. Over a long period, language developed biologically in the following manner. In any group of any species, there is a certain amount of random variation which allows for variation in individual skill. Those individuals who had higher skills in the manipulation of language had those skills as a direct result of the fact that such random variation had produced, in their brains, mechanisms better adapted for converting preexisting mental representations into linguistic form by lexicalizing and grammaticizing the categories into which those representations were already sorted by neurological processes. Since language-skilled individuals possessed a higher potential for survival, they would produce more offspring than other individuals, and the capacities that had arisen in them by random variation would be preserved and transmitted intact to their descendants.

Note that there is nothing particularly novel about all of this; most people nowadays would agree without any hesitation that the giraffe's neck, the hummingbird's bill, and all other adaptive developments ON A PHYSICAL LEVEL have originated in precisely this manner. It is merely the superstitious persistence of Cartesian dualism that makes people reluctant to admit that since mental characteristics have just as firm a physical foundation in neurological structures, the same processes of biological evolution must apply to them also.

If language arose in the way I have indicated, then what was passed on from generation to generation was not some vague, abstract "general learning capacity," or even some highly-specified "language learning capacity." Biological evolution does not trade in nebulous concepts like these; it hands out concrete features, concrete capacities for specific operations. What was passed on was precisely the capacity to produce a particular, highly-specified language, given only some (perhaps quite minimal) triggering in the form of communal language use. This capacity had attained the level of contemporary creoles when the computational power it bestowed on its owners triggered the cultural explosion of the last ten millennia;[2] and since cultural evolution works far faster than biological evolution, and since it operates at a far more abstract level, the effects of cultural evolution on language could not be transferred to the gene pool. Therefore, biological language remained right where it was, while cultural language rode off in all directions. However, it was always there, under the surface, waiting to emerge whenever cultural language hit a bad patch, so to speak; and the worst patch that cultural language ever hit was the unprecedented, culture-shattering act of the European colonialists who set up the slave trade. But it is true that out of evil, good may come, and if they had not done this, we might never have found the one crucial clue to the history of our species.

However, even without such setbacks, cultural language could not expand away from the biological base indefinitely. Just as biology produced a floor below which human language could not fall, so it produced a ceiling above which human language could not rise. The realm of variability of any species has upper limits consisting of capacities from which it is barred genetically from ever having. There can be little doubt that what we genetically have determines how far (and in what directions) we can go culturally in ways which, hopefully, will be major focal points of linguistics, philosophy, psychology, and anthropology in the decades to come. Thus, though languages may diversify and complexify, they can never become unlearnable—or if they do, children will soon pull them back to earth again.

The child does not, initially, "learn language." As he develops, the genetic program for language which is his hominid inheritance unrolls exactly as does the genetic program that determines his increase in size, muscular control, etc. "Learning" consists of adapting this program, revising it, adjusting it to fit the realities of the cultural language he happens to encounter. Without such a program, the simplest of cultural languages would presumably be quite unlearnable. But the learning process is not without its tensions—the child tends to hang on to his innate grammar for as long as possible—so that the "learning trajectory" of any human child will show traces of the bioprogram, and bioprogram rules and structures may make their way into adult speech whenever the model of the cultural language is weakened.

This, then, in outline is the unified theory of language acquisition, creole language origins, and general language origins for which the present volume has amassed numerous and diverse types of evidence. The question must now arise: how does this theory relate to existing linguistic theories, and what modifications in such theories does it appear to demand?

Generative theory has now survived for more than two decades as the leading theory in modern linguistics, despite attacks from diverse quarters. Although in the course of this book I have said some harsh words about some current generative stances, it should have been apparent, first, that the theory expressed here would probably have been impossible to frame if generative grammar had never existed, and second, that there is no hostility between the two theories on major issues. The present theory complements and amplifies generative theory. The latter has, in fact, ceded most of the former's territory. The leading figures in generative grammar have simply ignored creoles and shown a positive antipathy to the mere idea of language origins; as for acquisition, while they have theorized about it, they have not deigned to get their hands dirty by actually examining it.

In fact, bioprogram theory and Chomskyan formal universals fit rather well together, as illustrated in Figure 5.1 on the following page. The bioprogram language would constitute a core structure for human language. Natural languages would be free to vary within the space between the outer limit of the bioprogram and the overall limit imposed by formal universals, which represent neural limits—species-specific limits—on human capacity to process language.

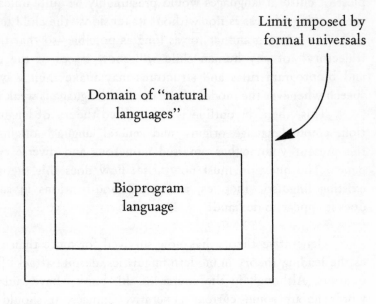

Limit imposed by
formal universals

Domain of "natural
languages"

Bioprogram
language

Figure 5.1
Relationship of bioprogram to formal universals

Note, however, that the bioprogram does not correspond directly to superficially similar concepts such as "substantive universals" or (in one of its several senses) "universal grammar." That is, it does not constitute a body of categories, rules, and structures that are necessarily shared by all languages. Indeed, above the trivial level on which all languages have nouns, verbs, oral vowels, etc., I would argue that such a body could not exist. Language systems are wholes, and earlier parts necessarily get mutated to accommodate later parts. Such a statement would be wholly uncontroversial save for the hostility to process that is shown, quite gratuitously, by generative grammar.

In fact, what linguistics will have to change is not generative theory, in its essential rather than accidental aspects, but a set of much more widely held beliefs, central to which is the belief that all existing languages are at the same level of development. Beliefs that have no empirical foundation generally stem from some kind of political commitment, and I am sure that this one, often expressed as "there are no primitive languages," arose as a natural and indeed laudable reaction to the claim that thick lips and subhuman minds underlie the characteristics of both creole and tribal languages. According to 19th-century racists, languages and people alike were ranged along a scale of being from the primitive Bushman with his clicks, grunts, and shortage of artifacts, to the modern Western European with his high pale brow and plethora of gadgets. That was when everyone, racist or anti-racist, did believe that Western Man was superior; the only argument was about how nasty this superiority permitted him to be toward "lesser" breeds. Now that we are rapidly disabusing ourselves of this kind of mental garbage, it becomes possible to uncouple language from "level of cultural attainment" and look at it developmentally without any pejorative implications.

That there is indeed no simple connection between language development and cultural development should be obvious from just two facts. First, many peoples with hunting-and-gathering cultures have languages of horrendous complexity which seem to be a lot further from the bioprogram than "rich cultural" languages like English or Chinese.[3] Second, creole languages originated in the most advanced cultures of their day. I do not mean that the strains of Mozart nightly pervaded the barracoons; I mean that it was in the slave colonies that the Western powers developed the industrial technology and systems of disciplined mass labor which later, with the aid of the capital amassed by so doing, they generously bestowed upon their own citizens. While creole speakers were working in organized bodies of hundreds or even thousands and operating complex mechanical processes, the leading technocrats of Western Europe were sitting in their own kitchens with their handlooms. So much for simplistic "culture-and-language" equations.

However, old beliefs die hard, and assuredly, no matter what I say, racists will pounce on the phrase "developmental differences" and use it to suggest that in some never-to-be-precisely-specified fashion my work "proves" that creoles, or their speakers, or both, are inferior to those who *s* their third person singulars and cross their *as*, *thes*, and zeros when they come to generics. Assuredly, too, progressives, rallying indiscriminately to the struggle, will feel obliged to include this theory in their denunciations, and to accuse me of having called creoles "primitive languages" and of having revived the despised "baby-talk theory" of creole origins. There is no prophylactic against ignorance. But to anyone who has read this book with even a minimum of care, it should be apparent that the theory presented here is at an opposite pole to those which sought to derive creoles from the babyish imitations of Europeans' condescending simplifications, and that creoles, far from being "primitive" in anything but the sense of "primary," give us access to the essential bedrock on which our humanity is founded; their re-creation, in the face of what the French sociologist Roger Bastide aptly termed the "Cartesian savagery" of colonialism, represents a triumph of the human spirit, and if it were necessary to justify them in such a fashion, I could show a dozen ways in which they are more lucid, more elegant, more logical, and less easy to lie in than English or other European languages. But I will let the dedication of this volume speak for itself.

The idea of language development is not, I would suspect, the only aspect of the present theory that is likely to arouse ideological rather than logical opposition. A great deal of human self-esteem is vested in the belief that there is a qualitative difference between ours and other species, and there is much in this volume that might be thought to weaken such a belief. Weakening such a belief, it is often claimed, may destroy "the Dignity of Man" and lead members of our species to treat other members as if they were no more than beasts.

One could ask a Tasmanian what he thought of this claim, if the advanced techniques of transplanted English foxhunters had left any Tasmanians to be asked. Anyone who casts a candid eye down the perspective of human history must find it hard to explain how the idea that "people are no more than animals" could get people any worse treatment than they have gotten already. Moreover, as the discussion of Cartesian dualism at the beginning of Chapter 4 made clear, the position of this theory is not "Animals don't have souls, and we don't either"; rather, it is "We have souls, and animals do too." The result, I should have thought, would have been to upgrade animals rather than downgrade ourselves.

Further hostility may arise from fears that the theory threatens free will and human perfectibility. If we speak what we are biologically programmed to speak, and if what we are biologically programmed to speak directly reflects the structure of our central nervous system, then the thoughts we think must be biologically programmed too.

If other reactions to the theory can be dismissed as knee-jerk alarmism, this one cannot. It is, I think, pretty likely that our thinking is species-specific, and therefore, almost by definition, incapable of providing adequate solutions to the problems we see ourselves facing or of answering the questions about the nature of the universe which we find so easy to ask. If this is so, it is so. If it is even possible that it could be so, then the appropriate reaction is not to hide behind a smokescreen of rhetoric, but to determine whether or not it is so. If it is not so, we have a green light to go ahead with human perfectibility, despite the unpromising auguries of our previous efforts in that direction. If it is so, then we have to learn either to live within our limits or to change those limits, if we can. For one thing is certain: if they exist, they cannot be talked away.

Although I am convinced that future research will show the scope of human freedom to be narrower than we had believed, and although there is no value that I personally rate above human freedom, I do not find myself in the least depressed by the prospect. Evolution has maintained a steady increase in the autonomy of its creatures without, so far as I am aware, a single retrogressive step. We as a species may lack the infinite capacities which some members of it have thought, and continue to think, that we possess, but the range of options open to us is still infinitely greater than that available to any other species, and the peculiar powers we have inherited allow the possibility that we may one day transcend the limits of species. But we will not do this by laying claim to capacities that we do not possess. We will do it only by determining what the limits of our species are, and then deciding what we want to do about that knowledge.

We may decide that less is more, small is beautiful, and that we must live within our cognitive means, even if so living entails perpetuating the cycle of injustice, revolt, and more injustice which constitutes the major part of our history to date. But somehow I do not think that this will be our choice.

One recalls the TV game show in which the quizmaster asks, "Will you take the money or open the box?" "Open the box, open the box!" the studio audience roars. I think we would try to open the box of species that encloses us, even if we knew that it was an inside-out Pandora's Box, and that once we had broken free of it, all the terrors of the universe would rain down upon our heads.

Notes

CHAPTER 1

1. I have not found any evidence for rule-ordering in either Hawaiian Creole English or Guyanese Creole. It would seem that rules apply wherever their structural description is met. It may be that below a certain level of linguistic complexity, rule-ordering is not required. The topic merits further study.

2. The appropriate response in Hawaiian would have been *ka ilio* 'THE dog'; *ilio* alone is quite ungrammatical.

3. In fact, it is very difficult to answer substratomaniac arguments because of the profound vagueness in which they are invariably couched. For instance, Alleyne (1979) states: "In dealing with the [substratal] input source, we have *to make allowances for plausible processes of change* analogous to what in anthropology are called reinterpretations . . . . It is the *failure to make such allowances* that reduces the merit of those statements that seek to refute the derivation by 'substratomaniacs' of Atlantic creole verbal systems from *generalized West African verbal systems,* because the two do not match up exactly point by point" (emphasis added). Since nowhere are we told what kind of allowances to make or what is or is not plausible, this simply amounts to a plea to swallow anything that fits the substrato-

maniac case—even such an absurdity as the existence of "generalized West African verbal systems" (if you want to flavor the condescension implicit in that concept, substitute "generalized European verbal systems"), or the greater absurdity that real-world speakers could derive anything from such a chimera. In the case under discussion, if we took the semantic range of the Japanese form, half the syntax of the English form, and the HPE indifference to tense, we MIGHT wind up with something approximating HCE *stei V*—but would anyone seriously propose that you can construct a language in this way? Moreover, if anyone did, the burden would be on that person to show why that particular mix of features from those particular languages, rather than dozens of other possible mixes from the dozen or so languages in contact, happened to get chosen. Until substratomaniacs are prepared to deal with problems of this nature, there is really nothing to argue against.

4. I am aware, of course, of the research that shows that English does make realized-unrealized distinctions, although in a much more oblique and clumsy fashion: e.g., the contrast between *I believed that John was guilty, but he wasn't* and **I realized that John was guilty, but he wasn't*. But (a) this distinction is made in *that*-complement sentences rather than *for-to* complement sentences; and (b) it is not surface-marked in the form of complementizer differences, but rather has to be inferred from the semantics of individual verbs. Again, it is true that *-ing* complementation is in general "more factive" than *for-to* complementation, but many cases go the opposite way, e.g., *Bill managed to see Mary* (entails *Bill saw Mary*) versus *Bill dreaded seeing Mary* (does not entail *Bill saw Mary*). For more relevant examples, see Chapter 2, examples /31/-/34/.

5. Alleyne (1979) uses this fact to argue that there never were antecedent pidgins—if there had been, he claims, they should have left traces in contemporary creoles, but he denies the existence of such traces. This argument will be dealt with further in Chapter 2. Meanwhile, the reader may well wonder how much pidgin structure one could legitimately expect to be left in creoles, given the relationship between the rules of HPE and HCE illustrated in /86/-/111/ above.

CHAPTER 2

1. Very few writers on creoles seem to have much background
or experience in variation study, and on all the numerous occasions
on which writers have used historical citations to make claims about
earlier stages of creoles, I cannot recall a single one where the possibility of codeswitching was even mentioned. It may well be that the
average fieldhand was monolectal, but the slaves whose speech was
most likely to be cited by Europeans were precisely the domestics
and artisans who had the most access to superstrate models and who
would therefore be the likeliest to be able and willing to adapt their
speech in a superstrate direction when interacting with superstrate
speakers. Historical citations should therefore be handled with great
care, especially when they suggest earlier stages of a creole which
would show a heavier superstrate influence than is found in the contemporary basilect of that creole.

2. It is at least highly questionable whether even an absolute
majority of speakers of a single substrate language can influence the
formation of a creole. Just after the turn of the century, when creolization must have been actively in progress, the Japanese constituted
50 percent of the population of Hawaii, yet there is virtually no trace
of Japanese influence on HCE. It would be interesting to hear the
substratomaniac explanation for this fact, but dealing with counterevidence has never been the strong point of that particular approach.

3. "It is clear that R(éunion) C(reole) is, to quite a large degree,
a different animal from M(auritian) C(reole), Ro(drigues) C(reole), and
S(eychelles) C(reole) . . . . There can be no doubt that RC shares many
features in common with MC, RoC and SC . . . . The usual explanation
. . . is that RC is a 'decreolized' version of proto-I(ndian) O(cean)
C(reole) . . . . Another, and perhaps more plausible explanation, is
that RC is, on the contrary, a modified version of a variety of *French*
(original emphasis) . . . . The modification of this *lete ki* French may
be seen in terms of convergence . . ." Corne is led to conclude that
Bourbonnais (the conventional term for proto-IOC) did not originate
on the Ile de Bourbon (the old name for Réunion), but he is unable

to say where it did originate, or to commit himself as to whether there was or was not a true proto-IOC. In fact, only an analysis along the lines of Bickerton (1975) can hope to make sense of RC history; but so far, no such analysis has been attempted.

4. Note that *fakter* 'postman' also lacks an article, although the definite article is required in English. But in fact, the NP here is as nonspecific as *let*. 'THE postman', 'THE doctor', 'THE cashier', etc., are really role titles. Postmen often change routes and schedules, and there is no indication in the sentence that one particular postman might have brought the letter, that either the speaker or the listener could have answered the question "WHICH postman?" or that the identity of the postman had the slightest relevance to the topic.

5. The anterior-nonanterior distinction is not an easy one for the naive speaker (i.e., anyone who does not speak a creole) to understand, as I have found in trying to teach it to several classes of graduate students. The reader who wishes to understand this is strongly recommended to read the account in Bickerton (1975:Chapter 2).

6. Jansen et al. have a different (and much more complex) explanation involving logical form, propositional islands, truth values, etc. Although they cite Roberts (1975) in another context, they appear to be unaware of the JC examples in that paper, cited above as /27/ and /28/, as well as of the other parallels cited here.

7. There is the possibility that an African source may also be involved. Yoruba, for instance, has both *fi* and *fún* (final nasals in Yoruba orthography mean that the preceding vowel is nasalized, and do not indicate the presence of a nasal consonant). Both verbs have a number of functions, but perhaps the most relevant for creoles are those found in sentences like *ó fi owó náà fún mi*, lit. 'He take money the give me', or 'He gave me the money'. The similarity to creole instrumentals is obvious, but if Yoruba *fi* is the source for JC *fi*, the shift in meaning is baffling. *Fún* is puzzling in a slightly different way. Rowlands (1969) notes that "Bilingual Yorubas tend to use *fún* rather indiscriminately to translate 'for'," making a joint source for GC *fu*, SR *foe* (phonetically /fu/) sound very plausible. Also many creoles use

verbs meaning 'give' to introduce dative and/or benefactive cases (e.g., HC *bay,* ST *da,* etc.). But if SR *foe* is derived from Yoruba *fún,* why did SR select *gi* (from Eng. *give*) to mark oblique cases and use *foe* as a complementizer? Moreover, HCE uses *fo* as a complementizer without the benefit of any Yoruba model, and French and Portuguese creoles turn Fr. *pour* 'for' and Pg. *para* 'for' into complementizers even though no one, to my knowledge, has suggested any verb with the form *pu* or *pa* in Yoruba or any West African language that could have served as a model. The question is by no means closed, however; it merely underlines the fact that we need to know a lot more both about different West African grammars and about what African languages were spoken in which creole areas.

8. Both Christie (1976) for LAC and Corne (1981) for SC propose a tripartite division of verbs into Action, State, and Process. As far as I can tell (neither treatment is particularly rigorous), this proposal arises from a confusion of syntactic rules with semantic interpretation. For instance, it is not syntactic rules that (normally) bar co-occurrence between stative verbs and nonpunctual markers, as is shown in the discussion of the sentence *i bina waan fu no* in Bickerton (1975:38), which shows that pragmatic factors can also be involved.

9. A problem not faced by those who call for the examination of non-European creoles is that it is far from clear that there are any. The only languages without a European superstrate which might qualify under the conditions specified in Chapter 1, above, are Ki-Nubi and Juba Arabic. Although the data that have emerged on these languages so far are scanty and unclear (and for this reason I have refrained from citing them in the present volume), most of what is available suggests that they follow the creole pattern described here. But even these languages do not have a third condition which may be necessary to qualify for true creolehood: their populations were not, in general, displaced from their native homelands. It is a historical fact that it was only Europeans who uprooted people from their cultures and carried them across thousands of miles of ocean in order to exploit them;

therefore, it is only in European colonies that one would expect to find the massive disruption of normal language continuity which would permit the emergence of innate faculties.

10. However, anyone wishing to use Quow as a historical source should be warned that the above remarks apply only to his rendering of basilectal speakers. Like many whites, he did not feel threatened by illiterate blacks, and could therefore treat them objectively; but he did feel threatened by literate blacks, and in consequence, his renderings of *their* speech are spoiled by facetiousness and condescension.

11. There have been some nonserious nonchallenges, of course. Christie (1976) produced an analysis of LAC which showed it to be not far short of identity with GC but insisted on preserving traditional terms, obvious though it was that these did not fit (getting the distribution of anterior correct and then calling it past is, to me at least, a quite incomprehensible maneuver). Seuren (1980) endorsed the analysis of Voorhoeve (1957), shown in Bickerton (1975) to be internally incoherent, and neatly avoided having to consider the latter analysis by calling it "sociolinguistic" [sic!]. But no one has systematically attempted to criticize my analyses of GC, SR, HC, and HCE, for the obvious reasons.

12. It is perhaps worth observing that no account of Papiamentu that I know of translates *I had worked,* so that the PP TMA system may not, in fact, differ as much from the classic system as those accounts might suggest. In general, not only are most analyses of TMA systems incorrect, nine out of ten of them are simply incomplete, lacking the critical information which would make it possible to determine how they work. Yet, since these defective analyses buttress Eurocentric prejudices, they are hardly ever questioned, let alone criticized.

13. When I wrote this paragraph, I was quite unaware that Baker had produced an extremely interesting account of the historical development of MC, based in part on an analysis of all currently known historical citations (Baker 1976), which provides a striking piece of independent support for this analysis. While *fini* is recorded as a preverbal marker in 1780, *ti* is not recorded until 1818; but the *ti va*

combination is recorded in 1828, while the *ti fin* combination is not recorded until 1867! Granted that these dates are probably all late—nonstandard speech phenomena tend to have a long and lively life before they tickle the bourgeoisie, cf. *olelo pa'i'ai* (see Chapter 1) which blushed unseen in Hawaii for nearly a century—there is no need to doubt that their order and spacing are substantially correct. Baker seems not to realize, however, that the 1780 source derives, on both internal and external evidence, from a pidgin and not a creole speaker.

14. Corne (1981) observes that "with state 'Verbals' *fin* does not occur, since a state has by definition already been attained." Thus, the failure of *fin* to take over anterior marking in statives is a principled one, and not some inexplicable accident.

15. Here Corne falls victim to the First Law of Creole Studies, since he himself stated five pages earlier (1977:103) that *ti* is omitted from subordinate clauses. But I suspect that he was mostly right on this occasion and that he had not made allowances for the nonhomogeneity of SC. I would be prepared to bet that /110/ came from a higher-class, more decreolized consultant.

16. If you believe in raising. If you don't, substitute "whatever rule marks the second NP as object of the first V."

17. As mentioned earlier in this chapter, it seems likely that in reality GC does not have VP as a constituent at the basilectal level. The contrary is assumed here merely in order to simplify the comparison between the English and GC *processes,* and is not meant to imply any substantive claim about GC structure.

18. It is interesting to note that while *fi*-clauses in complement position can refer to one-time actions (as in /210/), and in consequence the higher verb can take punctual marking, preposed *fi*-clauses can refer only to habitual actions, and in consequence the higher verb must take nonpunctual marking. At the moment I have no idea why this is so.

19. Washabaugh's analysis of *fi* differs radically from that made in the present chapter, although there is no reason to suppose that the facts of PIC differ significantly from those of GC. However, since I

have dealt with that analysis in Bickerton (1980), I will not repeat my criticisms of it here.

20. It would seem highly likely, indeed, that the inadequacies of existing creole descriptions, often referred to in this volume, have served to diminish, rather than exaggerate, the degree of creole similarity. To give just one very recent instance, it was long held that the verb-focusing rule discussed earlier in this chapter was not found in the grammars of any of the Indian Ocean creoles. Substratomaniacs could point to the nature of the substratum—Eastern Bantu, Malagasy, and Indian languages—as an explanation of this. Now Corne (p.c.) reports the finding of verb-focusing structures with a copied verb identical to those discussed in this chapter. Substratomaniacs will now doubtless seize on the claim by Baker (1976) that in 1735, 60 percent of the nonwhite population of Mauritius was from West Africa. However, this finding is strongly challenged by Chaudenson (1979) on the basis of historical documents which he claims Baker did not examine; according to Chaudenson, the percentage of West Africans never rose much above 33.

In fact, the outcome of the disagreement is rather irrelevant to the real issue. Baker's "60 percent" contained 66 percent of speakers from Guinea, and Guinean languages differ markedly in structure from the Kwa languages which are usually claimed as the source of creole structures. On Baker's own figures, the Kwa speakers in Mauritius in 1735 must have amounted to about 130! Within a few years, the population of Mauritius topped the 10,000 mark, swelled by recruits from India and Madagascar (Baker admits that hardly any Kwa speakers arrived after 1735). The question that substratomaniacs have to answer is: how did 130 people manage to impose their grammar (assuming they had a common one, which is a big assumption) upon a population in which they were outnumbered 100 to 1?

21. I am only too well aware that Piaget draws conclusions from his studies quite contrary to those drawn here. That he does so, however, has always seemed to me baffling in light of the fact that the developmental stages he posits bear a nativistic explanation much more

easily than they do an experiential one. But there is not space here to attempt a reinterpretation of Piagetian findings, desirable though such an activity might seem. We will see in the next chapter, however, that some linguistic findings of Piaget's disciples can very easily (and very fruitfully) be reinterpreted in a nativistic manner (see especially the discussion of Bronckart and Sinclair [1973]).

CHAPTER 3

1. Even today, I know of no study of child language acquisition in any language which follows the simple and obvious procedure of noting the very first emergence of a given form or structure in a child's speech, then following the development of that feature until Brown's "criterion" is reached—meanwhile noting what that form or structure alternated with in those contexts where it was inappropriate, as well as those where it was appropriate, with the aim of figuring out why variation occurred and what the form or structure might mean to the child. Normally, second-language acquisition trots along obediently in the footsteps of first-language acquisition, but here roles are reversed, as my student, Tom Huebner, is about to complete a dissertation which applies the above approach to the acquisition of English by an immigrant Hmong speaker (see also Huebner 1979). The field is wide open for similar first-language studies, which should help to revolutionize our understanding of acquisition.

2. In fact, rather than such a conflict, the present theory entails a division of labor. The innate component is necessary in order to get the child into a position where he can learn any human language, for as Fodor (1975) argues (see below), it is impossible to learn a language unless you already know a language. Some other kind of component is necessary to get the child from the innate creole-like grammar to the idiosyncratic grammars of Italian, Yoruba, Akawaio, Walbiri, or whatever language that particular child is going to have to learn as part of his socialization. Because I have not discussed this second component in the present volume, the reader should not conclude that I deny its

importance. My failure to say anything about it is, as I said, strategic; until we know where the innate component stops, we cannot know where any other devices start.

3. Or at least it is implausible to suppose that he could utilize them if he did not have some overall conceptual framework in which past tense (punctual, in our treatment) was associated with unique events and present tense (nonpunctual, in our treatment) was associated with generic events. How such an arbitrary framework could be derived from experience is totally opaque to me. But it might be derivable from species-specific or even genus-specific neural wiring, along the lines suggested in Chapter 4.

4. Students of the acquisition of Turkish please note: it would be most revealing to analyze 43 hours of a single child's speech (one hour at three-week intervals from 2:0 to 4:6) in order to determine exactly how he moves from a state-process to a direct-indirect analysis, along the lines indicated in Note 1 above.

5. One of these exceptions is Miller (1978). In a brilliant flash of insight, Miller suggests that "perhaps the difference between *go* and *went* is used to mark something else, like momentary happenings as opposed to persisting states"; and, in discussing forms like *wented,* adds that "if they did not understand *went* as incorporating a concept of pastness, then adding pastness with *-ed* would not seem redundant." However, a stiff dose of Reichenbach and formal logic enables him to climb back into the sheepfold of the conventional wisdom. It should be noted, however, that one of his presuppositions— that forms like *wented* are quite uncommon in child speech—fails to take into account forms like *did he went?, he didn't went,* etc., which are semantically identical and much more common. These forms are discussed in Hurford (1975), Kuczaj (1976), Fay (1978), Maratsos and Kuczaj (1978), and Erreich et al. (1980); but unfortunately, it seems not to have occurred to any of these writers to look at the sentences with "double pasts" and the sentences with "single pasts" in their appropriate contexts and see whether, semantically or pragmatically, there are any differences between them. This is the first thing that

an investigator should do, as a matter of simple routine, whenever he is confronted by variable data of this kind.

6. The question is the more interesting in that the form auxiliary + past participle—the first to be acquired by French and Italian learners —is among the last to be acquired by English learners. Maratsos (1979) observes of the latter that "its late acquisition, coming after children hear it used around them for years, probably stems from its subtle meaning," and indeed it is surely the case that the meaning of the "composite past" in French or Italian (a punctual meaning) is easier for the child to grasp than the meaning of the English perfect (a completive meaning). But this only opens up a host of other issues. For instance, if the meaning of English perfect is "relevance to present state," and if, as Antinucci and Miller suggest, the child assigns his early past marking on the basis of "relevance to present state," why should the meaning of perfect be so "subtle" in the child's view, and why should it not be the first, rather than the last, verb form to be acquired? Further, is it a matter of mere coincidence that perfect should be the last form to be acquired by both children learning English and speakers of an English creole in the course of decreolization (see Bickerton [1975:126ff.] for details on the latter process)? If, as suggested later in this chapter, decreolization and the later stages of acquisition are processes which show a principled relationship, then there is no coincidence, but rather a joint reflection of one of the difficulties involved in getting from the bioprogram to English.

7. For instance, "double pasts" of the kind discussed in Note 5 above are assumed in orthodox generative accounts (e.g., Hurford 1975) to stem from a process which copies the past-tense marker in Aux onto the verb-stem, as in the familiar "Aux-Hopping" rules, but then fails to delete the original occurrence of past tense under the Aux node (but see Maratsos and Kuczaj [1978] for criticism of this proposal). The fact that "double pasts" occur so frequently while "double-WHs" don't occur at all casts strong doubt on the assumption that children's mistakes stem from incomplete applications of standard transformational processes.

8. In other words, creolization and decreolization correspond to the two (overlapping) halves of the acquisition process proposed at the beginning of this chapter. The first half, dominated by the bioprogram, corresponds to creolization, but the second half, dominated by other components, in which the child bridges the gap between bioprogram and target language, corresponds to decreolization. The only significant difference would seem to be that creolization and decreolization cannot overlap, while the evolution of the bioprogram and the pressure from the target language can, do, and indeed must overlap. However, since this difference stems directly from purely pragmatic differences between the circumstances of the "normal" child and the circumstances of the creole-creating child, it can in no way invalidate the correspondence.

9. See also the theoretical discussion of this process in Bickerton (1980).

10. Why children don't do what they don't is often even more mysterious (for the conventional wisdom) than why they do what they do, so that questions such as the one at the beginning of this paragraph are studiously avoided. However, there is no need to avoid such questions with the present model; why they don't do what they don't is in fact loaded with clues as to why they do do what they do.

11. It should not need to be emphasized that, first, there is no evidence for "hyperstrategic" devices as such, beyond the problems whose solution might seem to call for them, and second, that if they did exist, they would constitute an innate component no less surely (although with far less justification) than does the bioprogram proposed here.

CHAPTER 4

1. The exchange, which took place at the New York Academy of Sciences Conference on Language Origins in 1975, should be quoted at length; it demonstrates the orthogonal approaches and seemingly invincible mutual incomprehensibility that have bedeviled glottogenetic

studies better than could countless pages of exegesis:

> *Harnad:* Let me just ask a question which everyone else who has been faithfully attending these sessions is surely burning to ask. If some rules you have described constitute universal constraints on all languages, yet they are not learned, nor are they somehow logically necessary *a priori,* how did language get that way?
> *Chomsky:* Well, it seems to me that would be like asking the question how does the heart get that way? I mean, we don't learn to have a heart, we don't learn to have arms rather than wings. What is interesting to me is that the question should be asked. It seems to be a natural question; everyone asks it. And I think we should ask why people ask it.

The question "Why do you ask that question?" is of course a stalling ploy familiar to psychoanalysts; indeed, it was programmed into the "robot psychiatrist" with which some ingenious psychologists were able to simulate, with surprising plausibility, a therapeutic session. The present writer believes, as firmly as Chomsky, that we get language like we get a heart and arms, yet I entirely fail to see why Harnad's question was an illegitimate one or why it does not deserve, or rather demand, an answer. How we first got arms or a heart are questions so phylo-genetically remote and so unrelated to the mental life of our species that Chomsky is right to dismiss them as not worth asking (except, presumably, for those whose professional specialism they are). But the evolution of language is so recent that we may reasonably suppose that its present nature is still conditioned by those origins, and its crucial role in distinguishing between us and other species (while any number of other species have arms and hearts) is such that it must strongly influence, even if it does not wholly determine, all that we think and do. Thus, to put the determination of its origins on a par with the determination of the origins of physical organs seems to me a piece of evasive perversity.

2. Hewes (1975) provides a fairly exhaustive account of these theories.

3. In the Hockett and Ascher "Flintstone," the key development is a hominid who, in encountering food and danger at the same time, gives half the call for food and half the call for danger. Not one shred of even the most oblique evidence from ethological or other studies, or even the authors' own ratiocinations, is adduced in support of this inherently unlikely development, beyond their admission that they can't think of any other way language could have begun.

4. However, I have some (admittedly anecdotal) evidence that dogs use cognitive mapping in recognition. Our dog, Rufus, will rush from the opposite end of the apartment to greet my wife when she comes home, but on meeting her on campus he ignores or even recoils from her until she is just a couple of feet from him, whereupon he performs his usual acts of greeting. It is not easy to account for such behavior unless (as is the case with us) part of the way he recognizes people has to do with a network of particular associations. He recognizes her where he expects her to be, and fails to recognize her elsewhere, in the same way (and why not for the same reason?) that we fail to recognize, on the beach or in a restaurant, the clerk or cashier we may have met dozens of times in a work setting.

5. Nothing Blake ever wrote should be taken lightly. In the broad brush-strokes with which we have to draw our cognitive maps, infinite details are lost, and what is worse, we get locked into stereotypic reactions to stereotypes (*kike, freak, faggot* are some pernicious examples) which lead us to deny one another's individuality. A creature that could compute from percepts rather than concepts would outshine us as the sun outshines the moon (more on this in *Language and Species*).

6. Some scholars remain unimpressed by the evidence that apes have concepts. For instance, Seidenberg and Petitto (1979) seem to need reassurance that before and after Washoe signed *water-bird* he did not also sign *banana-bird, water-berry, banana-berry*—in other words, they at least envisage the possibility that signing apes proceed like

demented computers, throwing off random strings of signs (they have, after all, been reinforced for signing) from which biased experimenters simply pick out the rare one which happens, by pure chance, to be contextually appropriate. Leaving aside the unmerited slur which this casts on the morals and/or wide-awakeness of many dedicated researchers, the approach adds a Cartesian twist to the old behaviorist-nativist controversy: scholars who are behaviorists with regard to animals and nativists with regard to people. It is more parsimonious as well as more fruitful to suppose that when animals similar to ourselves evince behavior like ours, similar mechanisms underlie both sets of phenomena.

7. That the nature of linguistic facts can be determined by the order in which they necessarily occur and/or originally occurred has already been suggested in the contrast between the development of tense that takes place in learners of English and that which takes place in learners of Italian. Those who continue to believe (see Note 1, this chapter) that there is nothing to be learned from learning how language developed should read and compare these two cases and then ask themselves whether their attitude is not one of simple obscurantism.

8. This is not, of course, to say that older structures do not undergo changes, adaptations, and linkages. The neural dysfunction known as Gilles de la Tourette's syndrome is one that affects the limbic area, yet its victims shout lexical obscenities as well as more animal-like cries. In general, lexical utterances are under cortical control, but in the case of those which express strong emotion, like nonverbal vocal utterances, linkage between the speech areas of the neocortex and the limbic area must have been forged at some stage subsequent to the former's development.

9. In fact, discussion of semantics would be clearer if *semantic prime* were reserved exclusively for category distinctions of potentially universal application (like the SNSD, the PNPD, etc.) and if what are sometimes referred to as "semantic primes" were referred to as *primitive concepts*. However, note that primitive concepts are not necessarily constructed out of semantic primes.

10. The reading "The answer is *there!*" is of course not intended.

11. It is an open question whether any language could make the past-present-future distinction before the culture that used it produced any kind of time-measuring device. The fact that time-enslaved linguists may have analyzed preliterate languages as having such a distinction is, of course, no proof of anything—they have consistently done the same for creoles and they have been consistently wrong in so doing. In fact, there already exist more careful studies of such languages (e.g., Arnott 1970, Welmers 1973) which explicitly recognize the absence of the characteristic Western temporal framework. Analysis of TMA systems is too subtle to be left to logicians.

12. In Bickerton 1974.

13. Another common source is (phonologically salient) auxiliary verb forms in the superstrate. However, since there could not have been auxiliaries before there were auxiliaries, the situations of creole and primordial languages will differ in at least this respect.

14. Order in terms of distance from the verb is of course intended, and not the left-to-right ordering of surface constituents.

15. It was observed in Chapter 2 that the similarities between creole languages were in many cases closer and more consistent in the semantic component than they were in the syntactic component. This result would issue very naturally if the semantics of language depended on relatively old neural structures while syntax depended partly on relatively new neural structures but also partly on extraneural factors intrinsic to the task of building a linear vocal language. These latter factors might in a number of cases permit more than one possible solution to a given structural problem, whereas with semantic structures, single solutions would be imposed in almost all cases.

CHAPTER 5

1. Indeed, one objection to the hypothetical history of language given in the preceding chapter might be that many essential prerequisites of language, such as the development of the neural and physio-

logical mechanisms required for vocalization, the lateralization of the brain, and the growth of auditory processing mechanisms· or "templates" which, as suggested in some fascinating work by Marler and associates (Marler 1977, 1980; Marler and Peters 1979, etc.), show striking parallels to those of avian species, have simply been ignored. However, these omissions in no way reflect my estimate of the importance of such developments. The reasons for them are threefold. First, reasons of space (and the overall purpose of this volume) prevented me from describing everything that went into the makeup of language; second, these other developments have been excellently treated elsewhere; and third, I wanted to deal precisely with those aspects of language development which have been most systematically ignored or misunderstood. Certainly, such omissions were not for the purpose of strengthening my case since all the omitted developments are much more obviously the product of the genetic code than the developments discussed in this volume.

2. I certainly do not wish to suggest by this that no sooner had language reached the creole level than agriculture began. There may well have been an interval of tens of thousands of years between these two events, years during which cognitive maps became only gradually more complex; or the interval may have been quite short. There is no way, at present, that we can choose between these alternatives—or even prove that language in its present form did not exist two million years ago, although the latter possibility seems intrinsically unlikely.

3. I write "seem to be" because only empirical investigation will reveal whether such languages are indeed as far from the bioprogram as our intuitions would suggest. One test will be the time taken by children to acquire the main grammatical structures of given languages. It was often claimed (at a time when acquisition had hardly been studied!) that all languages were equally easy for children to learn. This belief was, of course, simply deduced from the "all-languages-are-developmentally-equal" dogma. Work by Slobin and his associates already suggests this may be quite far from the truth.

Bibliography

Aaronson, D. and R. W. Rieber, eds. 1979. *Psycholinguistic Research: Implications and Applications.* Hillsdale, NJ: Erlbaum Associates.

Alleyne, M. C. 1971. Acculturation and the Cultural Matrix of Creolization. In Hymes 1971, 169-86.

———. 1979. On the Genesis of Languages. In Hill 1979, 89-107.

———. 1980. *Comparative Afro-American.* Ann Arbor: Karoma.

Antinucci, F. and R. Miller. 1976. How Children Talk About What Happened. *Journal of Child Language* 3.167-89.

Arnott, D. W. 1970. *The Nominal and Verbal System of Fula.* Oxford: Clarendon.

Bailey, B. 1966. *Jamaican Creole Syntax.* Cambridge: Cambridge University Press.

———. 1971. Jamaican Creole: Can Dialect Boundaries Be Defined? In Hymes 1971, 341-48.

Bailey, C.-J. N. 1973. *Variation and Linguistic Theory.* Washington, DC: Georgetown University Press.

Baker, P. 1972. *Kreol: A Description of Mauritian Creole.* London: Hurst.

———. 1976. Towards a Social History of Mauritian Creole. Unpublished B.Phil. dissertation, University of York.

Berlin, B. 1972. Speculations on the Growth of Ethnobotanical Nomenclature. *Language and Society* 1.51-86.

Berlin, B. and P. Kay. 1969. *Basic Color Terms.* Berkeley: University of California Press.

Bever, T. G. 1970. The Cognitive Basis for Linguistic Structures. In *Cognition and the Development of Language.* Ed. by J. R. Hayes, pp. 279-352. New York: Wiley.

Bever, T. G. and D. T. Langendoen. 1971. A Dynamic Model of the Evolution of Language. *Linguistic Inquiry* 2.433-63.

Bickerton, D. 1971. Inherent Variability and Variable rules. *Foundations of Language* 7.457-92.

———. 1973a. On the Nature of a Creole Continuum. *Language* 49. 640-69.

———. 1973b. The Structure of Polylectal Grammars. In *Proceedings of the 23rd Annual Round Table.* Ed. by R. Shuy, pp. 23-43. Washington, DC: Georgetown University Press.

———. 1974. Creolization, Linguistic Universals, Natural Semantax and the Brain. *Working Papers in Linguistics* (University of Hawaii) 6(3).124-41.

———. 1975. *Dynamics of a Creole System.* Cambridge: Cambridge University Press.

———. 1976. Pidgin and Creole Studies. *Annual Review of Anthropology* 5.169-93.

———. 1977. *Creole Syntax.* Vol. 2 of Final Report on NSF Grant No. GS-39748. University of Hawaii, mimeo.

———. 1980. Decreolization and the Creole Continuum. In Valdman and Highfield 1980, 109-28.

Bickerton, D. and T. Givón. 1976. Pidginization and Language Change: From SXV and VSX to SVX. In *Papers from the Parasession on Diachronic Syntax.* Chicago: Chicago Linguistic Society.

Bickerton, D. and C. Odo. 1976. *General Phonology and Pidgin Syntax.* Vol. 1 of Final Report on NSF Grant No. GS-39748. University of Hawaii, mimeo.

Blake, W. 1808. Annotations to Sir Joshua Reynolds' *Discourses.*

Reprinted in *The Portable Blake*. Ed. by A. Kazin. New York: Viking.

Blakemore, C. 1977. *Mechanics of the Mind*. Cambridge: Cambridge University Press.

Bollée, A. 1977. *Le créole français des Seychelles*. Tübingen: Niemeyer Verlag.

Bowerman, M. 1973. *Early Syntactic Development*. Cambridge: Cambridge University Press.

———. 1974. Learning the Structure of Causative Verbs: A Study in the Relationship of Cognitive, Semantic and Syntactic Development. *Stanford Papers and Reports on Child Language Development* 8.142-78.

———. 1979. The Acquisition of Complex Sentences. In Fletcher and Garman 1979, 285-306.

Bradley, E. A. and J. Z. Young. 1975. Comparison of Visual and Tactile Learning in Octopus after Lesions to One of the Two Memory Systems. *Journal of Neuroscience Research* 1.185-205.

Bradshaw, J. 1979. Causative Serial Constructions and Word Order Change in Papua New Guinea. Paper presented at the Annual Meeting of the Linguistic Society of America, Los Angeles, December 1979.

Bronckart, J. and H. Sinclair. 1973. Time, Tense and Aspect. *Cognition* 2.107-30.

Brown, R. 1973. *A First Language*. Cambridge, MA: Harvard University Press.

Brown, R. and C. Hanlon. 1970. Derivational Complexity and Order of Acquisition in Child Speech. In *Cognition and the Development of Language*. Ed. by J. R. Hayes. New York: Wiley.

Bruner, J. S. 1979. Learning How To Do Things with Words. In Aaronson and Rieber 1979, 265-84.

Burton, R. 1970. *Animal Senses*. New York: Taplinger.

Campbell, C. B. and W. Hodos. 1970. The Concept of Homology and the Evolution of the Nervous System. *Brain Behavior and Evolution* 3.353-67.

Carayol, M. and R. Chaudenson. 1977. A Study in the Implicational

Analysis of a Linguistic Continuum. *Journal of Creole Studies* 1.179-218.

Cazden, C. 1968. The Acquisition of Noun and Verb Inflections. *Child Development* 39.433-48.

Chaudenson, R. 1974. *Le lexique du parler créole de la Réunion.* Paris: Librairie Honoré Champion.

———. 1979. A propos de la genèse du créole mauricien; le peuplement de l'île de France de 1721 à 1735. *Etudes Créoles* 2.43-57.

Chomsky, N. 1957. *Syntactic Structures.* The Hague: Mouton.

———. 1962. Explanatory Models in Linguistics. In *Logic, Methodology and the Philosophy of Science.* Ed. by E. Nagel et al. Stanford, CA: Stanford University Press.

———. 1964. *Current Issues in Linguistic Theory.* The Hague: Mouton.

———. 1973. Conditions on Transformations. In *A Festschrift for Morris Halle.* Ed. by S. R. Anderson and P. Kiparsky. New York: Holt, Rinehart and Winston.

———. 1977. On WH-movement. In *Formal Syntax.* Ed. by P. W. Culicover et al., pp. 71-132. New York: Academic Press.

Chomsky, N. and M. Halle. 1968. *The Sound Patterns of English.* New York: Harper and Row.

Christie, P. 1976. A Re-Examination of Predicate Marking in Dominican Creole. Paper presented at the Conference on New Directions in Creole Studies, Georgetown, Guyana, August 1976.

Clark, E. V. 1970. Locativeness: A Study of "Existential," "Locative" and "Possessive" Sentences. *Working Papers in Language Universals* (Stanford University) 3.L1-L36.

Clark, H. H. and E. V. Clark. 1977. *Psychology and Language.* New York: Harcourt Brace Jovanovich, Inc.

Clark, R. 1977. What's the Use of Imitation? *Journal of Child Language* 4.341-58.

Comrie, B. 1976. *Aspect.* Cambridge: Cambridge University Press.

Corne, C. 1973. Tense and Aspect in Mauritian Creole. *Te Reo* 16.45-59.

———. 1974-75. Tense, Apsect and the Mysterious *i* in Seychelles and Réunion Creole. *Te Reo* 17-18.53-59.

―――. 1977. *Seychelles Creole Grammar.* Tübingen: Narr.

―――. 1981. A Re-Evaluation of the Predicate in Ile-de-France Créole. In Muysken 1981b, 103-24.

Cromer, R. F. 1976. Developmental Strategies for Learning. In *Talking to Children: Language Input and Acquisition.* Ed. by V. Hamilton and M. D. Vernon. Cambridge: Cambridge University Press.

Daeleman, J. 1972. Kongo Elements in Saramacca Tongo. *Journal of African Languages* 11.1-44.

DeCamp, D. 1971. Toward a Generative Analysis of a Post-Creole Continuum. In Hymes 1971, 349-70.

de Valois, P. L. and G. H. Jacobs. 1968. Primate Color Vision. *Science* 162.533-40.

Dillard, J. L. 1970. Principles in the History of American English— Paradox, Virginity and Cafeteria. *Florida FL Reporter* 8(1-2).32-33.

Dingwall, W. O. 1979. The Evolution of Human Communication Systems. In *Studies in Neurolinguistics* (Vol. 4). Ed. by H. Whittaker and H. A. Whittaker, pp. 1-95. New York: Academic Press.

Erreich, A., V. Valian and J. Winzemer. 1980. Aspects of a Theory of Language Acquisition. *Journal of Child Language* 7.157-79.

Fay, D. 1978. Transformations as Mental Operations: A Reply to Kuczaj 1976. *Journal of Child Language* 5.143-49.

Ferraz, L. 1979. *The Creole of São Tomé.* Johannesburg: Witwatersrand University Press.

Fletcher, P. 1979. The Development of the Verb Phrase. In Fletcher and Garman 1979.

Fletcher, P. and M. Garman. 1979. *Language Acquisition.* Cambridge: Cambridge University Press.

Fodor, J. A. 1975. *The Language of Thought.* New York: Crowell.

Forman, M. 1972. Zamboangueño Texts with Grammatical Analysis: A Study of Philippine Creole Spanish. Unpublished Ph.D. dissertation, Cornell University.

Geschwind, N. 1974. *Selected Papers on Language and the Brain.* Dordrecht: Reidel.

Gill, T. and D. Rumbaugh. 1974. Mastery of Naming Skills in a Chimpanzee. *Journal of Human Evolution* 3.482-92.

Givón, T. 1971. Historical Syntax and Synchronic Morphology : An Archeologist's Field Trip. In *Papers from the 7th Regional Meeting*. Chicago: Chicago Linguistic Society.

———. 1974. Serial Verbs and Syntactic Change. In Li 1974, 47-112.

———. 1979. *On Understanding Grammar*. New York: Academic Press.

Glock, N. 1972. Role Structure in Saramaccan Verbs. In *Languages of the Guianas*. Ed. by J. E. Grimes, pp. 28-34. Norman, OK: Summer Institute of Linguistics.

Glucksberg, S. and R. W. Weisberg. 1966. Verbal Behavior and Problem Solving: Some Effects of Labeling in a Functional Fixedness Problem. *Journal of Experimental Psychology* 71.659-64.

Goilo, E. R. 1953. *Grammatica Papiamentu*. Curaçao: Hollandsche Boekhandel.

Goodman, M. 1964. *A Comparative Study of French Creole Dialects*. The Hague: Mouton.

Grimes, J. E. and N. Glock. 1970. A Saramaccan Narrative Pattern. *Language* 46.408-25.

Hall, R. A., Jr. 1953. *Haitian Creole*. American Anthropological Association Memoir No. 74, Washington, D.C.

Halliday, M. A. K. 1975. *Learning How to Mean*. London: Arnold.

Hamilton, J. 1974. Hominid Divergence and Speech Evolution. *Journal of Human Evolution* 3.417-24.

Hancock, I. F. 1970. A Provisional Comparison of the English-Derived Atlantic Creoles. *African Language Review* 8.7-12.

Harlow, H. F. 1958. The Evolution of Learning. In *Behavior and Evolution*. Ed. by A. Roe and G. C. Simpson, pp. 269-90. New Haven: Yale University Press.

Harnad, S. R., H. D. Steklis and J. Lancaster. 1976. *Origins and Evolution of Language and Speech*. Annals of the New York Academy of Science, Vol. 280, New York.

Hering, E. 1920. *Outline of a Theory of the Light Sense*. Cambridge, MA: Harvard University Press.

Hewes, G. 1973. Primate Communication and the Gestural Origin of Language. *Current Anthropology* 14.5-24.

———. 1975. *Language Origins: A Bibliography.* The Hague: Mouton.

———. 1976. The Current Status of the Gestural Theory of Language Origins. In Harnad et al. 1976, 482-504.

Hill, J. and L. Most. 1978. Review of Harnad et al. 1976. *Language* 54.647-60.

Hill, K. C., ed. 1979. *The Genesis of Language.* Ann Arbor: Karoma.

Hockett, C. F. 1973. *Man's Place in Nature.* New York: McGraw-Hill.

Hockett, C. F. and R. Ascher. 1964. The Human Revolution. *Current Anthropology* 5.135-68.

Hodos, W. 1976. The Concept of Homology and the Evolution of Behavior. In *Evolution, Brain and Behavior: Persistent Problems.* Ed. by R. B. Masterton et al. New York: Wiley.

Huebner, T. 1979. Order of Acquisition versus Dynamic Paradigm: A Comparison of Method in Interlanguage Research. *TESOL Quarterly* 13.21-29.

Hurford, J. 1975. A Child and the English Question Formation Rule. *Journal of Child Language* 2.299-301.

Huttar, G. L. 1975. Some Kwa-like Features of Djuka Syntax. Paper presented at the International Conference on Pidgins and Creoles, Honolulu, January 1975.

Hyman, L. H. 1974. On the Change from SOV to SVO: Evidence from Niger-Congo. In Li 1974, 113-48.

Hymes, D., ed. 1971. *Pidginization and Creolization of Languages.* Cambridge: Cambridge University Press.

Jansen, B., H. Koopman and P. Muysken. 1978. Serial Verbs in the Creole Languages. *Amsterdam Creole Studies* II.133-59.

Jerison, H. J. 1973. *Evolution of the Brain and Intelligence.* New York: Academic Press.

Joos, M. 1964. *The English Verb: Forms and Meanings.* Madison: University of Wisconsin Press.

Karmiloff-Smith, A. 1979. *A Functional Approach to Child Language.* Cambridge: Cambridge University Press.

Kay, P. and C. K. McDaniel. 1978. The Linguistic Significance of the

Meanings of Basic Color Terms. *Language* 54.610-46.

Keil, F. 1979. *Semantic and Conceptual Development.* Cambridge, MA: Harvard University Press.

———. 1981. Constraints on Knowledge and Cognitive Development. *Psychological Review* (to appear).

Klima, E. and U. Bellugi. 1966. Syntactic Regularities in the Speech of Children. In *Psycholinguistics Papers.* Ed. by J. Lyons and R. J. Wales, pp. 183-208. Edinburgh: Edinburgh University Press.

Koopman, H. and C. Lefebvre. 1981. Haitian Creole *pu.* In Muysken 1981b, 201-21.

Kuczaj, S. A. 1976. Argument Against Hurford's "Aux Copying Rule." *Journal of Child Language* 3.423-27.

———. 1978. Why Do Children Fail To Generalize the Progressive Inflection? *Journal of Child Language* 5.167-71.

Labov, W. 1971. On the Adequacy of Natural Languages. MS.

Lamendella, J. 1976. Relations between the Ontogeny and Phylogeny of Language: A Neo-Recapitulationist View. In Harnad et al. 1976, 396-412.

Larimore, N. F. 1976. A Comparison of Predicate Complementation in Krio and English. Unpublished Ph.D. dissertation, Northwestern University.

Lashley, K. S. 1950. In Search of the Engram. In *Physiological Mechanisms in Animal Behavior* (Society of Experimental Biology Symposium No. 4). Cambridge: Cambridge University Press.

Le Page, R. B. and D. DeCamp. 1960. *Jamaican Creole: An Historical Introduction.* London: Macmillan.

Li, C. N., ed. 1974. *Word Order and Word Order Change.* Austin: University of Texas Press.

Li, C. N. and S. A. Thompson. 1974. An Explanation of Word Order Change SVO-SOV. *Foundations of Language* 12.201-14.

Limber, J. 1973. The Genesis of Complex Sentences. In *Cognitive Development and the Acquisition of Language.* Ed. by T. E. Moore. New York: Academic Press.

Linden, E. 1974. *Apes, Men and Language.* New York: Dutton.

Lord, C. 1976. Evidence for Syntactic Reanalysis: From Verb to Complementizer in Kwa. In *Papers from the Parasession on Diachronic Syntax*. Chicago: Chicago Linguistic Society.

Luria, A. 1975. Scientific Perspectives and Philosophical Dead Ends in Modern Linguistics. *Cognition* 3.377-86.

Maratsos, M. P. 1974. Preschool Children's Use of Definite and Indefinite Articles. *Child Development* 45.446-55.

———. 1976. *The Use of Definite and Indefinite Reference in Young Children*. Cambridge: Cambridge University Press.

———. 1979. How To Get From Words to Sentences. In Aaronson and Rieber 1979, 285-353.

Maratsos, M. P. and S. A. Kuczaj. 1978. Against the Transformationalist Account: A Simpler Analysis of Auxiliary Overmarkings. *Journal of Child Language* 5.337-45.

Markey, T. L. and P. Fodale. 1980. Lexical Diathesis, Focal Shifts and Passivization: The Creole Voice. Paper presented at the Third Biennial Conference, Society for Caribbean Linguistics, Aruba, September 1980.

Marler, P. 1977. Sensory Templates, Vocal Perception and Development: A Comparative View. In *Interaction, Conversation and the Development of Language*. Ed. by M. Lewis and L. A. Rosenblum, pp. 95-114. New York: Wiley.

———. 1980. Development of Auditory Perception in Relation to Vocal Behavior. In *Human Ethology*. Ed. by M. von Cranach et al., pp. 663-81. Cambridge: Cambridge University Press.

Marler, P. and S. Peters. 1979. Birdsong and Speech: Evidence for Special Processing. In *Perspectives on the Study of Speech*. Ed. by P. Eimas and J. Miller. Hillsdale, NJ: Erlbaum Associates.

Marshack, A. 1976. Some Implications of the Paleolithic Symbolic Evidence for the Origins of Language. *Current Anthropology* 17. 274-82.

Marshall, J. C. 1979. Language Acquisition in a Biological Frame of Reference. In Fletcher and Garman 1979, 437-53.

McDaniel, C. K. 1974. Basic Color Terms: Their Neurophysiological

Basis. Paper presented at the Annual Meeting of the American Anthropological Association, Mexico City, November 1974.

McNeill, D. A. 1966. Developmental Psycholinguistics. In *The Genesis of Language*. Ed. by F. Smith and G. A. Miller. Cambridge, MA: M.I.T. Press.

Miller, G. A. 1978. Pastness. In *Psychology and Biology of Thought and Language*. Ed. by G. A. Miller and E. Lenneberg, pp. 167-85. New York: Academic Press.

Moorghen, P.-M. 1975. Analyse des marqueurs pre-verbaux des créoles de l'océan Indien. Paper presented at the International Conference on Pidgins and Creoles, Honolulu, January 1975.

Mounin, G. 1976. Language, Communication, Chimpanzees. *Current Anthropology* 17.1-21.

Muysken, P. 1981a. Creole Tense/Mood/Aspect Systems: The Unmarked Case? In Muysken 1981b, 181-99.

———, ed. 1981b. *Generative Studies on Creole Languages*. Dordrecht: Foris.

Nagara, S. 1972. *Japanese Pidgin English in Hawaii*. Honolulu: University of Hawaii Press.

Papen, R. 1975. "Nana k nana, nana k napa," or the Strange Case of "*e*-deletion" Verbs in Indian Ocean Creole. Paper presented at the International Conference on Pidgins and Creoles, Honolulu, January 1975.

———. 1978. The French-Based Creoles of the Indian Ocean. Unpublished Ph.D. dissertation, University of California, San Diego.

Passingham, R. E. 1979. Specialization and the Language Areas. In Steklis and Raleigh 1979b, 221-56.

Perlman, A. M. 1973. Grammatical Structures and Style-Shift in Hawaiian Pidgin and Creole. Unpublished Ph.D. dissertation, University of Chicago.

Piaget, J. 1962. *Play, Dreams and Imitation in Childhood*. New York: Norton.

Polomé, E. 1980. Creolization Processes and Diachronic Linguistics. In Valdman and Highfield 1980, 185-202.

Quine, W. 1960. *Word and Object.* New York: Wiley.

Quow (M. McTurk, pseud.). 1877. *Essays and Fables.* Georgetown, Guyana: Argosy.

Reichenbach, H. 1947. *Elements of Symbolic Logic.* New York: Macmillan.

Reinecke, J. 1969. *Language and Dialect in Hawaii.* Honolulu: University of Hawaii Press.

———. 1977. Introduction. In *Pidgin and Creole Linguistics.* Ed. by A. Valdman. Bloomington: Indiana University Press.

Rens, L. L. E. 1953. *The Historical and Social Background of Surinam Negro English.* Amsterdam: North Holland.

Roberts, P. A. 1975. The Adequacy of Certain Linguistic Theories for Showing Important Relationships in a Creole Language. Paper presented at the International Conference on Pidgins and Creoles, Honolulu, January 1975.

Ross, J. R. 1967. Constraints on Variables in Syntax. Unpublished Ph.D. dissertation, Massachusetts Institute of Technology.

Rowlands, E. C. 1969. *Teach Yourself Yoruba.* London: English Universities Press.

Rumbaugh, D. and T. Gill. 1976. Language and the Acquisition of Language-Type Skills by a Chimpanzee. In Harnad et al. 1976, 90-123.

Sag, I. 1973. On the State of Progress in Progressives and Statives. In *New Ways of Analyzing Variation in English.* Ed. by C.-J. N. Bailey and R. Shuy. Washington, DC: Georgetown University Press.

Samarin, W. J. 1971. Salient and Substantive Pidginization. In Hymes 1971, 117-40.

Sankoff, G. 1979. The Genesis of a Language. In Hill 1979, 23-47.

Sankoff, G. and S. Laberge. 1974. On the Acquisition of Native Speakers by a Language. In *Pidgins and Creoles: Current Trends and Prospects.* Ed. by D. DeCamp and I. F. Hancock, pp. 73-84. Washington, DC: Georgetown University Press.

Schiefflin, B. S. 1979. How Kaluli Children Learn What To Say, What To Do, and How To Feel: An Ethnographic Study in the Development of Communicative Competence. Unpublished Ph.D. dissertation, Teachers College, Columbia University.

Seidenberg, M. S. and L. A. Petitto. 1979. Signing Behavior in Apes: A Critical Review. *Cognition* 7.177-215.

Seuren, P. A. M. 1980. The Auxiliary System in Sranan. MS.

Silverstein, M. 1972. Chinook Jargon: Language Contact and the Problem of Multilevel Generative Systems. *Language* 48.378-406, 596-625.

Slobin, D. 1977. Language Change in Childhood and History. In *Language Learning and Thought*. Ed. by J. Macnamara. New York: Academic Press.

———. 1978. Universal and Particular in the Acquisition of Language. In *Language Acquisition: The State of the Art*. Ed. by L. Gleitman and E. Wanner. New York: Academic Press.

Slobin, D. and A. A. Aksu. 1980. Acquisition of Turkish. MS.

Smith, M. E. 1939. Some Light on the Problem of Bilingualism as Found from a Study of the Progress in Mastery of English among Pre-School Children of Non-American Ancestry in Hawaii. *Genetic Psychology Monographs* 21.199-284.

Snow, C. 1979. Conversations with Children. In Fletcher and Garman 1979, 363-76.

Somers, F. 1959. The Ordinary Language Tree. *Mind* 68.160-85.

———. 1963. Types and Ontology. *Philosophical Review* 72.327-63.

Spuhler, J. N. 1977. Biology, Speech and Language. *Annual Review of Anthropology* 6.509-61.

Steklis, H. D. and M. J. Raleigh. 1979a. Requisites for Language: Interspecific and Evolutionary Aspects. In Steklis and Raleigh 1979b, 285-314.

———, eds. 1979b. *Neurobiology of Social Communication in Primates*. New York: Academic Press.

Stephenson, P. H. 1973. The Evolution of Color Vision in the Primates. *Journal of Human Evolution* 2.379-86.

———. 1979. A Note on the Dialectical Evolution of Human Communicative Systems. *Journal of Human Evolution* 8.581-83.

Taylor, D. 1960. Language Shift or Changing Relationship? *International Journal of American Linguistics* 26.144-61.

———. 1963. The Origin of West Indian Creole Languages: Evidence From Grammatical Categories. *American Anthropologist* 65.800-814.

———. 1971. Grammatical and Lexical Affinities of Creoles. In Hymes 1971, 293-96.

Thompson, R. W. 1961. A Note on Some Possible Affinities between the Creole Dialects of the Old World and Those of the New. In *Proceedings of the Conference on Creole Language Studies.* Ed. by R. B. Le Page. London: Macmillan.

Tsuzaki, S. M. 1971. Co-Existent Systems in Language Variation: The Case of Hawaiian English. In Hymes 1971, 327-40.

Valdman, A. 1973. Some Aspects of Decreolization in Creole French. In *Current Trends in Linguistics Vol. XI: Diachronic, Areal and Typological Linguistics.* Ed. by T. A. Sebeok, pp. 507-36. The Hague: Mouton.

———. 1980. Creolization and Second Language Acquisition. In Valdman and Highfield 1980, 297-312.

Valdman, A. and A. Highfield, eds. 1980. *Theoretical Orientations in Creole Studies.* New York: Academic Press.

Valkoff, M. F. 1966. *Studies in Portuguese and Creole.* Johannesburg: Witwatersrand University Press.

Voorhoeve, J. 1957. The Verbal System of Sranan. *Lingua* 6.374-96.

———. 1971. Church Creole and Pagan Cult Languages. In Hymes 1971, 305-15.

———. 1975. Serial Verbs in Creole. Paper presented at the International Conference on Pidgins and Creoles, Honolulu, January 1975.

Voorhoeve, J. and J. M. Lichtveld. 1976. *Creole Drum.* New Haven: Yale University Press.

Warden, D. 1976. The Influence of Context on Children's Use of Identifying Expressions and References. *British Journal of Psychology* 67.101-12.

Washabaugh, W. 1979. On the Sociality of Creole Languages. In Hill 1979, 125-40.

Weinreich, U., W. Labov and M. I. Herzog. 1968. Empirical Foundations for a Theory of Language Change. In *Directions for Historical Linguistics*. Ed. by W. P. Lehmann and Y. Malkiel, pp. 95-188. Austin: University of Texas Press.

Welmers, W. E. 1973. *African Language Structures*. Berkeley: University of California Press.

Whinnom, K. 1956. *Spanish Contact Vernaculars in the Philippine Islands*. Hong Kong: Hong Kong University Press.

———. 1965. The Origin of the European-Based Creoles and Pidgins. *Orbis* 14.509-27.

Williams, W. R. 1971. Serial Verb Constructions in Krio. *Studies in African Linguistics*, Supplement 2, 46-65.

———. 1975. Internal Mechanisms in the Creolization of Sierra Leone Krio. Paper presented at the International Conference on Pidgins and Creoles, Honolulu, January 1975.

Wilson, W. A. A. 1962. *The Crioulo of Guine*. Johannesburg: Witwatersrand University Press.

Woisetschlaeger, E. 1977. A Semantic Theory of the English Auxiliary. Unpublished Ph.D. dissertation, Massachusetts Institute of Technology.

Woolford, E. 1979. The Developing Complementizer System of Tok Pisin: Syntactic Change in Progress. In Hill 1979, 108-24.

Young, J. Z. 1978. *Programs of the Brain*. Oxford: Oxford University Press.

Name Index

Aaronson, D., 321
Adam (child subject), 154
Akbar the Great, 289
Aksu, A. A., 161, 332
Alleyne, M. C., 2, 43, 48, 78, 82, 211, 303-4, 321
Antinucci, F., 163, 172-74, 313, 321
Aristotle, 44
Arnott, D. W., 318, 321
Ascher, R., 219, 316, 327

Bailey, B., 47, 68, 321
Bailey, C.-J. N., 89, 105, 321
Baker, P., 60-61, 69, 89, 308, 310, 321
Bastide, R., 300
Bellugi, U., 187, 190-91, 328
Berlin, B., 229, 238-39, 241, 243, 322

Bever, T., 62, 273, 292, 322
Bickerton, D., 1, 7, 8, 12, 28, 34, 43, 47, 58, 59, 68, 73, 77, 79, 80, 85, 88, 89, 96-97, 105, 160, 164, 192, 193, 306-8, 310, 313-14, 318, 322
Blake, W., 227, 316, 322
Blakemore, C., 233, 323
Bollée, A., 69, 83-85, 89, 323
Bowerman, M., 137, 141, 181, 198, 201, 205-6, 323
Bradley, E. A., 223, 323
Bradshaw, J., 120, 292, 323
Bronckart, J., 163, 165-71, 173, 256, 311, 323
Brown, R., 137, 142, 147, 149, 154-61, 181-85, 311, 323
Bruner, J. S., 136, 138, 139, 323
Burton, R., 222, 323

Subject Index

A-over-A principle, 36-37, 41, 64-65
acquisition strategies, 140-41, 201-2, 204, 212
adjectives, 68-69
African languages, 48-50, 118-20, 122, 303-4, 307
agriculture, 287-88, 319
akualele, 19
analogy, 186-87, 189
Annobones, 63
anterior tense, 58, 77, 79, 81, 83, 85-88, 91-93, 284-86, 306, 309
Aplysia, 282
articles, 22-26, 39, 56-57, 247-48
    acquisition of, 147-54
Australian Aboriginal creoles, 4
Austronesian, 120, 292-93
Aux-hopping, 313

Babel, Tower of, 290
Bantu languages, 49, 131
behaviorism, 317